VANISHING
VANCOUVER

VANISHING

MICHAEL KLUCKNER

VANCOUVER

THE LAST 25 YEARS

whitecap

PUBLISHER: Michael Burch
EDITOR: Theresa Best
ARTWORK AND LAYOUT: Michael Kluckner
INTERIOR DESIGN: Mauve Pagé (Page & Design)

Printed in China

LIBRARY AND ARCHIVES CANADA CATALOGUING IN PUBLICATION
Kluckner, Michael

Vanishing Vancouver : the last 25 years / Michael Kluckner.

Includes bibliographical references and index.

ISBN 978-1-77050-067-9

1. Historic buildings—British Columbia—Vancouver.
2. Vancouver (B.C.)—Buildings, structures, etc. 3. Vancouver (B.C.)—History.
I. Title.

FC3847.7.K555 2012   971.1′33   C2011-908305-1

The publisher acknowledges the financial support of the Canada Council
for the Arts, the British Columbia Arts Council, and the Government of Canada
through the Canada Book Fund (CBF). Whitecap Books also acknowledges
the financial support of the Province of British Columbia through
the Book Publishing Tax Credit.

For more information about books on Vancouver and its history by the author,
please visit michaelkluckner.com.

12 13 14 15   5 4 3 2 1

FRONTISPIECE: A remnant of an earlier Vancouver, when houses were small and
yards were big, at 28th Avenue and Sophia Street. More detail about this house
appears on page 94.

You bring your own time to a book, it is not imposed as with film and television. With a book you can stop to think something through, or go back and look at something again if you need to.

—DAVID HOCKNEY,
Secret Knowledge

I regret very much that I have painted a picture that requires description.

—WINSLOW HOMER,
responding to a question
about the meaning
of one of his paintings

So long as I remain alive and well I shall continue . . . to love the surface of the earth, and to take pleasure in solid objects and scraps of useless information.

—GEORGE ORWELL,
Why I Write

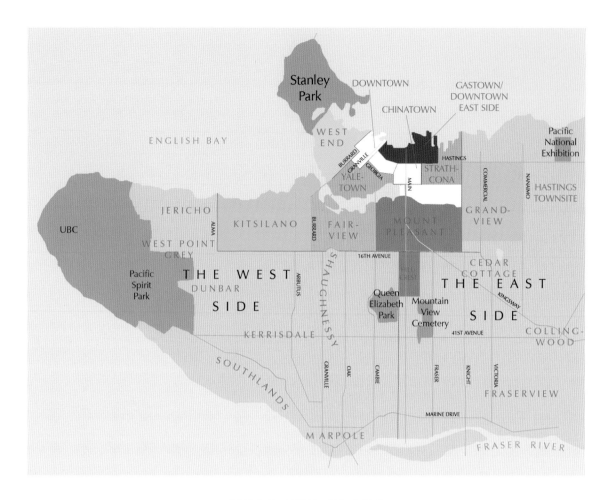

MAPS AND PLANS

CONTENTS

PREFACE

AT THE BEGINNING OF THE WINTER OLYMPICS MY WIFE, CHRISTINE, and I came back to live in Vancouver after more than three years overseas in Australia and a dozen years on a Fraser Valley farm. It was elating! The weather was crisp and bright, so different from sultry summertime Sydney, and all the traffic seemed miraculously to have vanished. Driving was like a trip back to the 1970s, yet unlike in that subdued decade, happy people thronged the streets day and night. From our temporary vantage point in Fairview Slopes, the new towers of the city shimmered in the winter sunshine.

My elation soon faded, however, as sweet February morphed into stormy March and reality resumed. On closer inspection the new Vancouver looked bland—seemingly endless ranks of high-rises downtown, relentless pale grey concrete and greygreen glass streaked with rain, squat towers with clipped little plazas occupying every block of the slopes above Granville Island. Most of the quirks and relics I remembered from earlier times had been erased—at 7th and Fir, a blue construction fence edged with wind-blown wrappers and paper cups surrounded the vacant site of an old corner store, a Québecois bistro when I left. Only the Wicked Café (two blocks away at Hemlock), once upon a time a corner store, too, remained.

A couple of days after I returned, still disoriented from jet lag, I walked through downtown, along Hastings and into Gastown. Woodward's was gone, or most of it at any rate. Where its modest W had once punctuated the modest skyline, an enormous tower, like something dropped from outer space, loomed over the century-old brick and stone buildings that citizen activism and small-business investment had saved 40 years earlier. It was *so* out of scale—how had that happened?

Buildings that were almost new when I left were shrouded by tarps, undergoing expensive repair for leaks and rot. It seemed incongruous—the leaky-condo crisis had been identified 20 years earlier, so why were buildings still so poorly constructed?

Yet there were many positive things, like the streetscapes in the old neighbourhoods that were a joy to behold. Bright paint, gardens running right out to the curbs, vintage homes reinvented by young families with their carefully marshalled renovation funds, farmers' markets, vegetables growing in allotments along old rail lines and on vacant lots—there was so much evidence of real conservation and sustainability, of a real environmentalism putting down roots, of a kind of urbanism as profound as the downtown lifestyle that dominated Vancouver's self-image. Perhaps my ennui was just culture shock, part of the long journey of making Vancouver home again.

Twenty-five years ago the quickening pace of change prompted me to begin the original *Vanishing Vancouver*, published in 1990 by Whitecap Books. In its preface I wrote:

One day in the summer of 1986—the Expo summer—I was walking through downtown on my way to the old James Inglis Reid shop, which I wanted to paint before it ceased business to make way for an expansion of the Pacific Centre shopping mall. I heard the bell in the clock tower of the old post office at Hastings and Granville sounding the hour, and the cry of seagulls disturbed by its tolling, and was suddenly struck by a wave of nostalgia for all the old times, and all the years that I had been in the city, and a recognition that many pieces of my past were slowly disappearing. For better or worse, I thought, the city is changing irrevocably, and some of the things that have been landmarks in my life will soon be gone.

As the eighties progressed, the city—especially its residential areas—endured a demolition spree. The theme of this earlier *Vanishing Vancouver* was my anger at the disposal of beautiful houses and gardens, cast away as if they didn't have any value at all. That their replacements appeared inferior to my eyes just compounded the outrage. There seemed to be so little appreciation by residents old and new of Vancouver's houses, no environmental or aesthetic mindset that would guide the builders even into preserving trees.

To me the case for keeping and reusing old houses was cut and dried, whereas the case for commercial buildings was more nuanced. Many of the commercial buildings that were up for replacement in Vancouver were almost laughably modest and undistinguished compared to the commercial buildings in other cities. Such was not the case with the fine Medical-Dental Building on Georgia Street, but it and a few other demolished buildings were anomalies, as many high-quality places were

Looking hairy and annoyed—my David Suzuki pose—on the 2000 block of West 36th in Kerrisdale, in front of a monster house recently added to a vintage streetscape, in 1989. (*HERITAGE CANADA MAGAZINE*)

TOP LEFT > The Crandall house at the northwest corner of Marguerite and 49th in Kerrisdale, built in 1914. Elmer Eugene Crandall was the agent for a line of enamel stoves from New Brunswick, and bought and built houses in his spare time. In the course of two marriages he had 14 children, the last of whom were born when he was in his 70s.

TOP RIGHT > The 1922 house of businessman David Christie at the northwest corner of 29th and Alexandra. It had four fireplaces, four bedrooms on the second floor and two more on the third.

LEFT > The block of Hastings between Richards and Seymour, as it was in 1989. I painted the century-old Innes-Thompson building (in the centre), which was doomed by a hotel development. Only the façade of the former Toronto-Dominion Bank building (on the right) was going to be saved but, following donations of the building itself and enough money to renovate, the building became the Morris Wosk Centre for Dialogue, a part of the SFU downtown campus, in the old Spencer's/Eaton's department store across the street.

adaptively reused. Sinclair Centre, The Electra, Birks, Simon Fraser University at Harbour Centre, CTV and HMV, the Morris Wosk Centre for Dialogue, the Segal Graduate School of Business, the Landing, Waterfront Station—these buildings are now so well established in their new names and roles it seems bizarre that anyone would have contemplated taking them down.*

Two houses I painted in 1989, shortly before their demolition, became emblematic to me of the waste in a culture "drunk on the now and the new," as architect Carl Elefante described our society. In Kerrisdale, on 49th Avenue at Marguerite, a fine large home with a wraparound porch and interior woodwork impossible to replicate, facing what was then still a gracious street, took a truck ride to the landfill and was replaced

---

*   These buildings were the combined post office, the Winch Building and customs warehouse, the BC Electric building, the Bank of Commerce, Spencer's/Eaton's department store, the main library, the Toronto-Dominion Bank, the Bank of Montreal, the Kelly-Douglas wholesale foods warehouse and the Canadian Pacific Railway station.

with a mean, stucco-and-brick-veneer monster that faced the side street. Another, 20 blocks north at Alexandra Street, was an elegant, spacious Tudor that appeared in a *Real Estate Weekly* advertisement in February 1989: "Builder is ready to plan new 8,300 square foot home. To customize to your specifications call now." Down came the old house but the lot sat vacant for more than a year. A bloated object of indistinguishable ancestry eventually replaced it.

The John Lennon song "In My Life," with its unforgettable opening line, "There are places I remember," became like a theme song for me and I shelled out 500 American dollars to a New York–based company controlled by Michael Jackson, of all people, for the rights to put the first stanza of the lyrics on the frontispiece. It was truly my period for the quixotic gesture.

By the time the book came out in 1990 it represented a kind of "instant history"— the physical change in the city had been so rapid that even recent arrivals could claim a kind of old-timer status. Vancouverites who usually found common cause only in the shared misery of November rainstorms grumbled about how they would walk through their old neighbourhoods and find it hard to identify where they had once lived. It touched a nerve.

The development frenzy has recently resumed. Although there was a hiatus in the '90s, when most houses with any character were priced so far above lot value that builders looked elsewhere, the recent wave of property purchasers from China want "new" and price is no object. Even substantial houses from the '20s and '30s are still being picked off, especially in Dunbar and West Point Grey, because the zoning allows a new house to be so much bigger. Yet apartments and condos keep getting smaller, while the prices for them get higher, too.

Bigger changes are happening on the commercial streets. For many years now, single-storey storefronts have been replaced with three- and four-storey wood-framed condominiums, most of them with shops on their main floor—a positive move. But recently the audacity of densification, with high-rise clusters touted for suburban parts of the city, has challenged the very nature of Vancouver—the yin and yang of dense core and human-scaled leafy "streetcar suburb." Affordability is the real casualty, of course, as existing buildings are replaced with more luxurious new ones. Sustainability—that wonderful lifestyle we are all to aspire to—is shouted at us over the roar of the bulldozers.

LIKE THE REST OF THE PLANET, THE VANCOUVER OF 2012 IS MUCH DIFferent from the 1986 version. That solitary man talking loudly on the street is not dangerous, he's just on the phone.

In a social sense it has really changed. People keep their lives private now in a way they didn't 20 years ago. But ironically, while some people have become more concerned with their personal security, others (whose identities are not linked to specific addresses the way they were a generation ago) flaunt private information and behaviour on the Internet.

In the past, most people had a "public face"—a landline listed in a telephone directory along with a street address. Establishment figures in the various *Who's Who*

Marooned in the middle of the concrete sea, the boarded-up 1907 house at 807 Drake had become, in 2010, like the billboard on the tiny parking lot next door— a surface for displaying advertising. The once-common scene of old buildings abandoned and awaiting demolition has become rare, as almost every lot in that part of downtown gets a new building, repeating the situation of a century ago when there were few vacant lots and well-maintained houses lined the streets.

WORLD TRAVELLERS BOARD CPA
JET FOR HONG KONG AT VANCOUVER
INTERNATIONAL AIRPORT, a circa
1965 photograph by Clyde
Herrington. Although the scene
looks almost quaint, the flying
part of air travel has changed little
in 50 years (except that in-flight
service now is much worse).
Compared to airport security
(and communications technology,
entertainment, coffee-drinking,
concepts of privacy and standards
of public dress), aviation has
evolved at a glacial pace, at least
from a passenger's point of view.

publications noted their mother's maiden name along with other personal information, sometimes even a date of birth, just the sort of thing a fraudster nowadays would use to steal an identity.

A Yellow Pages is still in print in Vancouver but the kind of criss-cross directory that once listed people's occupations and employers has gone the way of the dodo, the last edition coming out in 2000. According to my research the change began in the 1960s. "No return" became the listing beside numerous addresses when people couldn't be bothered filling out and submitting the address cards dropped off by canvassers. People were becoming rootless, mobile, indifferent to the sense of civic presence that a directory conveyed.

Many people now live in a virtual world, aided by the spatial anonymity of cellphones and the web. The online directories that have replaced the White Pages increasingly list people with just phone numbers, not addresses—if indeed they list them at all—and they are a fluid database, not archived the way print on paper was. Clearly, no future historian will be able to research the current Vancouver and its populace the way I and others have done with the earlier city, even if somebody—perhaps a reference librarian—downloads and preserves webpages in a database.

Twenty years ago most people were quite happy, even perhaps proud, to have their homes in a book, but they were not at all concerned. Family stories were, in a general way, sharable, as Vancouver was still, in a general way, a small town. That is less the case now.

It is true that many of the places in the original *Vanishing Vancouver* were already demolished by the time the book was published, so privacy was hardly an issue; regardless, I was on public property when I painted them and, just like a news crew, was free to record what I wanted.

Under new legislation, copyright has become cumbersome and expensive, ironically so in an age in which the Internet has created an expectation that information and images are free for the taking. (For example, on page 197, I wanted to use a splendid panorama of the China Creek cycle track, taken in 1954 by Ray Johnson for Caterpillar Tractor, but the city archives could not give me permission because the image is still technically under copyright, and will be for five more years. Johnson's whereabouts, after 57 years, are unknown.) Reproduction fees for publicly held photographs in archives and libraries take a major bite out of a book's small budget. Writers using information "owned" by others might win a moral battle while losing the war if they have to pay even a portion of their own legal fees. The "spectacularly ugly lawsuit," as Frances Bula described the action launched by the family of the late architect Arthur

Erickson against Cheryl Cooper of the Arthur Erickson Conservancy, is enough to put a chill into anybody contemplating writing a history book.[*]

Unlike the first *Vanishing Vancouver*, which was divided into neighbourhoods, this book is divided into themes: landmarks, the working harbour, the shop, the house, the apartment, gardens and agriculture, and a section on legacies and memories. My recent wandering lifestyle gave me the advantage of living in several furnished apartments, something I hadn't done since the 1970s, which triggered my interest in writing about multi-family buildings. The change in 4th Avenue in Kitsilano and its contrast with Commercial Drive prompted me to write the chapter on shops. Fewer grand places are featured than in my earlier books; readers of those books will perhaps notice my focus here on the modest, the shabby vernacular, the "organically evolved," as it were, in the middle of the gleaming modern city.

"Make no big plans" might be my motto, countering the axiom of 19th-century Chicagoan Daniel Burnham, who said that small plans "have no magic to stir men's blood." I am the antithesis of the Big Thinkers of the modernist era, the planners and architects who envisioned sweeping Radiant Cities and Grand Edifices.[†] Ever since I was young I've harboured a suspicion that we live in a fool's paradise, in an American-style house of cards (in a real-estate sense) that will collapse without warning. Although I've been wrong so far I'm still fascinated by the sort of people who eked out a living through the Depression and during wartime, wearing hand-knitted sweaters and tending gardens in the back yards of cottages, or who looked for "small solutions," in the '70s, like the ones presented at the 1976 Habitat Forum (see pages 202–5). In the midst of our glitter, I seek evidence that those sorts of places still exist.

I am a sort of architect *manqué*—I studied the history of architecture at the University of British Columbia but decided not to pursue its practice as a career. Rather like a crow following the plough, I have spent much of my time picking over the work of others and, as critical as I may have been from time to time, I respect the fact that planners, architects and politicians have to compromise a lot more in the pursuit of their projects than writers and artists do. Idealism rests comfortably on the pages of a book but is harder to achieve in reality.

---

[*] See "Battle Royal," *Vancouver* magazine, April 30, 2010.

[†] In this I find I have an ally in author and critic Witold Rybczynski. See *Makeshift Metropolis,* Scribner, 2010.

INTRODUCTION

The Save Our Birks campaign ended in 1974 when that splendid 1912 office building at Georgia and Granville was demolished for the Vancouver Centre mall. The button above shows the face of the Birks clock that stood for generations on the corner; the new owners of the jewellery company moved it back to its original (pre-1913) crossroads, at Hastings and Granville, when they relocated the jewellery store in the 1990s to more elegant surroundings in a former bank building there. (ARTIST UNKNOWN, COLLECTION OF KEN AND ANNE TERRISS)

ANCOUVER HAS ENDURED CRITICISM FOR THE QUALITY OF ITS HISTORIC architecture and urban spaces for generations, with most of the sneering coming from a city only about 50 years older—Toronto. It was a setting in search of a city, the pundits said, a marvellous stage set for a boring play. Our ears still ring from the axe blows to our helmet.

Given that Vancouver started out as a small port, strategic only as a transportation hub on the western edge of an underpopulated country, it's a wonder that the city managed to get rich enough to assemble so good a collection of downtown buildings. Railway freight rates ensured that western raw materials would be shipped to the east and manufactured goods would come west at tariff-protected prices.[*]

And where was the stability that might have created a magnificent downtown? Only a few years after the city was incorporated in 1886 it fell victim to a worldwide depression. The beginning of the Klondike gold rush in 1897, and the years that followed, until 1913, were generally prosperous, buoyed by migration, foreign investment and strong commodity prices. Depression and war ensued, however, and the good times returned only briefly in the late 1920s, then disappeared again until the 1950s, which was a period of fairly steady growth that lasted until the dead-dog 1970s.

After Expo '86, again buoyed by foreign investment and immigration, the city went on a demolition and building spree (the subject of the original *Vanishing Vancouver*). It paused to gather strength as the millennium approached and then went crazy again, until the first cracks appeared with the global financial crisis in 2008. The condominium boom of the past 20 years cleared off dozens of city blocks, a figure the Luftwaffe might once have been proud of.

"Rapid population growth stimulated widespread construction and caused the value of building permits from 1908 to 1912 to increase by 223 percent," wrote historian Robert A.J. McDonald, using words that could have applied to the first decade of this century. "Thousands of carpenters, bricklayers, stonemasons, electricians, plasterers, painters, plumbers and other craftsmen, along with their helpers and labourers, built houses, offices, shops, warehouses and factories across the city."[†] The value of building permits in the city peaked in 1912, then fell to one-tenth of that value by 1914; three-quarters of the financial institutions created during the boom years didn't survive the collapse.[‡]

---

[*] "Almost all capital goods for BC industries came from outside the region, with local machine shops limited mainly to supplying supplementary items and modifying imported machinery. Plants manufacturing consumer goods were of equally modest size." McDonald, p. 127.

[†] McDonald, p. 125.

[‡] MacDonald, p. 401. Building permits didn't climb back to the 1912 level until 1929, when they collapsed again. By 1933 they were one-tenth of the 1912 value.

Anyone studying Ireland's recent meltdown will hear in it a distant echo of Vancouver's.

This history has a neat symmetry to it—there is almost exactly a century between the greatest economic booms. The symbolic end to the earlier one was the sinking of the *Titanic* in April 1912, although the economy didn't really collapse for another year. In the modern city, the symbolic *Titanic* is the Olympic Village (now rebranded as The Village on False Creek), which hit the iceberg of buyer skepticism in the summer of 2010, a tentative signal that the party was over and the revellers were heading home. Only the influx of wealthy Chinese buyers kept the market on the boil on the city's West Side and in Richmond.

SAVING THE BEST

Forty-eight of the best historic city buildings, including financial and government edifices, churches, the Hudson's Bay Company store, the Hotel Vancouver and the Marine Building, were designated and protected by city council in 1974, using an amendment to the Vancouver Charter granted by the Barrett provincial government. The legislation was a response to the demolition of the Birks Building at Granville and Georgia and the SOB (Save Our Birks) campaign led by the Community Arts Council of Vancou-

ver. A generation earlier, in the polite 1940s, there had been a bat-squeak of protest from the Architectural Institute of British Columbia, the Vancouver Tourist Association and the Vancouver Board of Trade against the demolition of the magnificent "second" Hotel Vancouver at Georgia and Granville. By the 1970s, citizen activism had matured, having cut its teeth on the successful campaign to stop the downtown freeway and protect Chinatown and Gastown.[*]

Fighting the freeway and eight other events that "saved Vancouver" were the subject of a recent book by former mayor and premier Mike Harcourt, planner Ken Cameron and columnist Sean Rossiter.[†] Its chapters focus on public-policy decisions, the kind of big planning-levers beloved of social democrats, and include descriptions of the enactment of the Agricultural Land Reserve, regional growth strategies and

[*]   There is a chronology of those events in *Vancouver Remembered*, pp. 30–3.

[†]   Harcourt et al., *City Making in Paradise: Nine Decisions that Saved Vancouver.*

C.P.R. Hotel Vancouver, Vancouver, B.C. Canada.

Lies my postcards told me: four images of the second Hotel Vancouver at the corner of Granville and Georgia, occupied now by Pacific Centre and the TD Bank tower.

transportation planning. Surprisingly, at least from my point of view, the Heritage Management Plan of 1986, during the period when Harcourt was mayor, didn't make the list.

This city heritage plan came into effect under constraints that hadn't existed for the 1974 council of Mayor Art Phillips. In 1977, the Bennett provincial government had enacted new legislation that suggested owners of buildings might be entitled to compensation if heritage designation reduced the "economic value" of their properties. Accordingly, the city established a list of commercial and residential buildings and a set of incentives and procedures that would support and encourage owners. It was persuasive, not coercive; there were no big levers to pull.

The heritage planning department, during the tenure (1991–6) of planner and architect Robert Lemon, became very sophisticated at negotiating complex development proposals. Incentives were developed, including a density-transfer mechanism that had been pioneered in 1974 when little Christ Church Cathedral was allowed to sell its air space to the new office tower next door. The transfer system evolved into a density bank: for their heritage work, developers were rewarded with extra square-footage. This went into the bank, and other developers could buy it to add floors to their own towers in appropriate areas. There was strong support from the councils during the mayoralties of Gordon Campbell and Philip Owen, an era that ended in 2002.

Despite the number of buildings left unprotected and subsequently demolished, Vancouver would have been a much poorer city without this heritage policy. Western North American cities, with the exception of San Francisco, have all had to struggle to retain the layers of landscapes, the old amidst the new, that characterize mature cities elsewhere in the world. As one would gather from its full name, the heritage plan created a management process that gradually reduced the amount of 11th-hour confrontation seen in the Birks campaign of 1974 and the Medical-Dental Building campaign of 1989. By the early 1990s, when I was most active as an advocate, most projects were working their way through the system in a more-or-less satisfactory way. Neither people like me nor developers were getting everything they wanted, which probably indicated the system was working fairly well.

Some campaigns were more quixotic than others: an old fur-and-hide warehouse on West 2nd probably smelled too much to be turned into anything useful and was replaced by a much-needed lube-and-oil shop. The stylish Langara golf course clubhouse, a kind of overgrown house, couldn't be adapted to the needs of the modern

C.P.R. Hotel, Vancouver, B.C.

C.P.R. Hotel Vancouver, Vancouver, B.C.

Vancouver Hotel, Vancouver, B.C.

PREVIOUS PAGE > An unaltered image showing the hotel as it looked from 1916 until its demolition in 1949. The original hotel had opened in 1886 and was a gabled building on the corner. As the city grew, the hotel gained additions on its south and west sides (the small building on the right-hand side is one of those additions, retained as part of the 1916 hotel). Architect Francis Swales designed the 1916 building, one of the handful of Canadian railway hotels that didn't reflect the chateau style, first used at the CPR's Château Frontenac in Quebec City and continued in BC in Francis Rattenbury's design for the Empress Hotel in Victoria. This Hotel Vancouver was abandoned and demolished following a complex deal that allowed the CNR's hotel at Georgia and Burrard to take the Hotel Vancouver name. (JOHN VALENTINE & SONS POSTCARD)

TOP > An early version of Francis Swales's design, published as if the hotel had been actually built like this, and showing the retained wing from the earlier hotel on its right side. In his final design, the architect retained the *porte cochère* and the arrangement of wings around a central tower, but abandoned the fantastic flying walkways. Instead, the hotel's tower became a single slab with a roof garden, famous for its tea dances and panoramic views. (JOHN VALENTINE & SONS POSTCARD)

MIDDLE > The view from Granville Street, with a rather distorted perspective. The retouch artist added images of a hansom cab, a team of tiny prancing horses pulling a carriage, a motorcar and a chestnut vendor to spice up the immensely wide street in the foreground. (JOHN VALENTINE & SONS POSTCARD)

BOTTOM > The same image, closer in. Unfortunately, the hotel was too high to fit into the postcard format, so the artist removed the upper storeys and roof garden! Another bit of artistic license, visible on the right, is the white façade of the courthouse, now the Vancouver Art Gallery. Ironically, this image was "made expressly for the Canadian Pacific Railway News Service."

Until its demolition in 1989, the Medical-Dental Building on Georgia Street towered over little Christ Church Cathedral. The replacement tower referenced its predecessor in a distinctly postmodern fashion, with replicas of the Medical-Dental's nurse statues and art deco terracotta, plus a green metal turret that mimicked the Hotel Vancouver's copper crown on the other side of the street. The fledgling Vancouver Heritage Foundation sold off scraps of the old terracotta, many of which can be spotted in private gardens around the city, to raise funds for its projects.

golfer, and so on. But others eventually bore fruit: for example, the public awareness effort about the old, city-owned houses on Comox and Pendrell streets became the campaign to save "Mole Hill," as it was rebranded under the leadership of resident Blair Petrie and architect Sean McEwan. The area is now a 170-rental-unit village run by a community housing society.

The campaign for the Stanley Theatre on Granville was one of the few in that era that had a real clash of values. A victim of changing times—of television and multiplexes—the theatre was ripe for redevelopment in 1992. According to the heritage policy only its historic façade needed to be preserved. What went on behind it was up for grabs, at least as far as council was concerned, so the proposal from a developer to turn it into a shopping mall was warmly received. But the community felt differently. Heritage Vancouver and a coalition of theatre and film activists launched a major campaign that attracted political and business support—notably from MLA Dr. Tom Perry—and, eventually, led to the Stanley's preservation as a theatre. (A density transfer to new downtown buildings paid for a portion of its preservation.) Renamed the Stanley Industrial Alliance Stage, it quickly became a key venue in the city's dramatic landscape and, 20 years on, it's *the* cultural focus of the South Granville gallery and shopping district.

Another heritage challenge was the bequest in 1991 of the huge Glen Brae mansion in Shaughnessy Heights. Its owner, Elisabeth Wlosinski, had imagined a cultural, perhaps musical, centre, but the city felt it couldn't accept such a gift and, regardless, found it too hot to handle.

On the sunny morning that he arrived at the mansion to give a press conference about the donation, Mayor Gordon Campbell was greeted by a handful of happy heritage folk and a sign-waving horde of very well-heeled and angry protestors led by former provincial politician and commentator Gordon Gibson, who lived nearby. Fortunately for the neighbourhood's tranquility, the Canucks hockey team took it on as a children's hospice—hardly the single-family use of a building that is embedded in Shaughnessy's DNA but a cause too noble to be criticized. (Ronald McDonald House nearby is a similar anomaly.) In November 1995, Canuck Place opened as North America's first free-standing children's hospice.

Recognizing the need for an arms-length organization, the city proceeded to establish the Vancouver Heritage Foundation. After a false start in 1992, the foundation got seriously underway in 1998 with a board assembled by Lauren Wolf and chaired by architect Joost Bakker.* With seed money from the city, it began to raise funds and run programs, including an annual tour of heritage houses. It also provides grants and assistance for owners of old buildings, the most notable of which is the

* I was on the original board and chaired it in 2003. Earlier on, in 1991, I was the founding president of Heritage Vancouver.

Hycroft celebrated its centenary in the spring of 2011. The earliest of the grand Shaughnessy mansions, it has settled into its landscape of mature trees and gardens, planted by A.D. and Blanche McRae during their 25 years of occupancy. The mansion's layers of history reflect Canada's and Vancouver's own stories. Designed by Thomas Hooper, it was built on the edge of the Shaughnessy escarpment just east of Granville Street, with a fortune amassed from Prairie land, and West Coast lumber, milled by workers imported from Quebec (who created Maillardville in Coquitlam) to avoid a public backlash against "Oriental" labour. Its grand ballroom was the venue for an annual masked ball that was the highlight of the social season. McRae was quartermaster general for the Canadian army during the First World War and held the rank of Brigadier-General; he organized a provincial conservative "reform" movement in the 1920s, then became a senator for his work aiding the federal Conservatives. During the Second World War, shortly before his death, he donated the mansion to the government, which converted it into an annex to Shaughnessy Military Hospital. In 1962, when the hospital annex closed, the University Women's Club bought the building. Lectures and programs for club members now complement the mansion's public use as a venue for weddings and receptions.

True Colours program, developed in partnership with Benjamin Moore, which has painted dozens of houses and re-educated Vancouver's eye to the bold, bright historical palate of the old city.

The volunteer advocacy organization Heritage Vancouver has evolved into the conscience of the city's old buildings and historic spaces. Notably, during the presidency of architect Donald Luxton, which began in 2004, it used well-reasoned arguments couched in the language of planning and development rather than the more emotional, confrontational appeals of earlier times. Its "top ten endangered sites" list attracts a lot of attention from mainstream media.

THE HOME FRONT

By 1990 the desire to restore old houses had spread across the inner city, through Strathcona and Mount Pleasant, west into Kitsilano and east into Grandview (see the map on pages 90–91). Shaughnessy Heights already had design guidelines and a panel of citizens and experts to vet renovations and new projects (examined further on page 110). Douglas Park and Main Street were attracting families intent on putting down roots and renovating the old places. But in Kerrisdale and the relatively modest parts of Shaughnessy south of King Edward Avenue, residents' tempers reached the boiling point as the sound of the high-hoes drowned out the birdsong. The fight spread into Dunbar and West Point Grey in the early 1990s.

In fact, spot fires were springing up all over the city, some about heritage but many more about the loss of mature trees, affordable housing and, simply, too much change too fast. Under the zoning in effect at the time, most houses on 50-foot and wider lots were far smaller than what could be built, creating a development opportunity exploited by speculative builders who had their eyes on the wallets of the business-class immigrants flocking into the city in the wake of Expo '86. There was an equivalent opportunity on the 33-foot lots on the East Side, where the small bungalows from earlier eras of the city could be replaced by much larger houses (see page 121). On the West Side, "heritage" activity was typically focused on gardens and trees rather than reflecting any particular passion for the 1920s and 1930s Tudors and Georgians and Dutch colonials that lined the streets.

When Great Britain announced in 1984 that it would turn control of Hong Kong over to the People's Republic of China in 1997, Vancouver became one of the prime destinations for emigrants. Canada opened its doors, using an accelerated process for anyone able to invest in the country as part of the entrepreneur and business immigration programs, a distant echo of the head tax that all Chinese had to pay to enter the country between 1885 and 1923.

After 1987, Hong Kong became the top source of immigrants both to Canada and British Columbia. The numbers increased steadily from 1987, peaking in 1994, when BC (mainly the Lower Mainland) received 16,000 newcomers, one-third of total immigration.[*] That number declined as the '97 handover approached, indicating a comfort level with the new China of Deng Xiaoping, who declared, "It is glorious to be rich."

There was a spate of stories told and retold through West Side neighbourhoods, probably apocryphal, that became urban legend and were generally thought of as amusing rather than threatening. One concerned a Hong Kong businessman, picked up at the airport by a local realtor who drove him past houses for sale. After a couple of hours, during which the businessman had sat silently, the realtor turned around in his seat and said in frustration, "I've shown you twenty houses and you haven't said a thing! Do you want to continue or . . .?" The businessman replied, "I've already bought fifteen." In casual cocktail-party conversation you were never sure whether storytellers wanted their houses snapped up too or whether they realized that this kind of investment might eventually price them out of the city.

Some new residents petitioned the city to change their house addresses to numbers that had more number 8s in them (thought to be lucky) and no number 4s (thought to be unlucky). Most were turned down. Realtors put "Chinese prices" on houses: $388,888, for example.[†] A new meaning for an old word entered the language: an "astronaut" was an Asian-Canadian businessman, with his family residing in Vancouver, constantly criss-crossing the Pacific Ocean to tend to his transnational businesses. Stories made the rounds of wealthy teenagers left alone in big West Side houses with credit cards, fast cars and housekeepers to clean and cook. High schools like Point Grey in Kerrisdale became almost polarized, the Canadian children (of whatever race) not mixing with the wealthy new students.

On the West Side of the city—the desirable destination for the prosperous immigrants—both residents and newcomers experienced culture shock. There was an unease on both sides that sometimes bordered on racism, but probably had more to do with the perceived wealth of the new arrivals (on the Canadians' side) and the perceived "snoopy friendliness" of Canadians (on the side of these newcomers from the stratified environment of hyper-urban Hong Kong). Some new Chinese business people did believe there was a "bamboo ceiling"—that they were experiencing racist treatment in Vancouver—and many developed their businesses transnationally, as a consequence, it is said, of their perception that they were being blocked from entering the "non-ethnic open market." The alternative was the "ethnic consumer products market" in which Asian business people had always prospered.[‡]

In the neighbourhoods, the newcomers walked into a hornet's nest when they purchased the progeny of speculative builders who had knocked down old houses,

Like Hycroft a few blocks away, the 102-year-old mansion known as Glen Brae, at 1690 Matthews, has had a varied history. As had Hycroft's A.D. McRae, Glen Brae's William Lamont Tait made money from the West Coast's prodigious forests, processed at his Rat Portage shingle and sawmill near the south end of the Granville Street bridge. Following his death at 71 in 1921, the house languished for a few years until it was briefly, notoriously, rented by a branch of the Ku Klux Klan during an upswing in Canada's racist barometer. Thereafter, for decades, it operated as a private hospital for the elderly. In the 1990s it was again briefly controversial, as its owner hoped the city would turn it into a cultural facility in spite of its location in the midst of an exclusive residential area. Since 1995, Canuck Place Children's Hospice has managed it.

---

[*]   www.bcstats.gov.bc.ca/pubs/immig/imm971sf.pdf

[†]   A subject that returned to public discussion recently. See "Ethnic Chinese number superstition impacts housing prices," by Scott Simpson, *Vancouver Sun*, November 27, 2010.

[‡]   Lloyd L. Wong and Michele Ng, "Chinese Immigrant Entrepreneurs in Vancouver: A Case Study of Ethnic Business Development," by *Canadian Ethnic Studies Journal*, Spring, 1998.

clear-cut the lots (in an attempt to avoid any problems with feng shui) and built "to the max" structures that overshadowed and overlooked neighbours' back gardens. The new homes were "monster houses"—that term entered the language, too—and, according to the established residents, appealed only to the Chinese.

We had a neighbour from Hong Kong whose new house in 1988 swamped the footprint of an old two-bedroom cottage and extended into its back yard of fruit trees. The house was as large as could be and the garage, taking up much of the back yard, held three vehicles: a Volvo for shopping, a Ferrari with "Me First" ego-plates and a Rolls Royce. A man came every few weeks to detail the last two; the soapsuds and road grit ran into our vegetable garden. Evidently the neighbourhood was changing.

One advertisement I quoted 20 years ago from a 1989 *Real Estate Weekly* described a new house in a part of Kerrisdale where homes traditionally had been 2,000 or 2,500 square feet. As published, it said:

> *Archi. design. resid. sit. on 60×134' lot in one of Van.'s most prestig. neigh-bourhoods. Home offers 5000 sq.ft. of LUXURIOUS and UNCOMPROMIS-ING QUALITY. Total of 17 spac. rms, a warm fam rm, den, spac. kitch. sunken liv rm, grac. din rm. Up the elegant staircase to 5 BDRMS (2 enste) includ. beaut. MASTER SUITE W/GAS F/P & vaulted ceilings. This one of a kind resid. incl. nanny suite down, skylights, u/g sprinkler system & spec. lighting features. Offers to $1.148 million.*

Other advertisements mentioned features aimed at the target market, such as glass-enclosed "Chinese" kitchens.

The city responded to the neighbourhood outcry by revisiting its single-family zoning bylaw and holding public hearings that, I recall, continued to the point of exhaustion over five long nights. The community was so polarized, so suspicious, even as some speakers tried to reach across the cultural divide. Several new Canadi-ans spoke emotionally about their reception in Kerrisdale and South Shaughnessy. "People call our homes 'monster houses,'" a few said. "We are not monsters."

As the hearings continued, the reasons for the schism came into sharper focus. Most of the long-established residents arguing for go-slow, little-change "preserva-tion" zoning saw their homes as havens for their families, repositories of memories, places of gardens and tranquility. Yes, their homes were an investment, but by com-parison with many of the newcomers they didn't see the house and its property as a business opportunity. They liked, or at least tolerated, the aging peculiarities of their places, whereas the newcomers wanted "new."

There was that extraordinary gap—the business opportunity—in the zoning. As in the example cited above, a new house could be double the size and command more than double the price. Many newcomers from Hong Kong's free-enterprise hothouse thought that developing property was a logical thing to do—you developed it and made money. Why would anyone have been surprised? After all, they had come to Canada using business and entrepreneurial immigration programs.

As is usually the case, the sting of neighbourhood change eventually dulled.

Although the revised zoning bylaw had an impact, it was the market itself that improved the quality of new houses. There was an increased desire to replicate traditional house styles—the Tudors and Georgians and Dutch colonials of the interwar period (see page 113). The designs improved, with more new houses bearing the marks of architects' pens and fitting in much better than the first-generation monster houses. Affordability, which had been on life support, could not be resuscitated.

There were other neighbourhood changes, too. Flower gardening, that quintessential West Side activity, began to go out of fashion (see page 166) and the city enacted a tree-preservation bylaw that moderated the zeal of the high-hoe operators. For some, the lure of the condo lifestyle offered an alternative, a lock-it-and-leave *pied-à-terre* that was worth almost as much as a house, required less responsibility and left more time, perhaps, to spend at the Whistler chalet or the Gulf Islands weekender.

But regardless of architectural improvements, West Side neighbourhoods are still in flux. The last boom, the one ongoing in 2011, is dominated by buyers from Mainland China who were able to send prices further into the stratosphere. One open house in Kerrisdale in the spring of 2010 was typical: 84 groups of people came through, all but six of whom were from Mainland China. Six offers came in, all from Mainland Chinese buyers. Displaced or wannabe West Siders pushed into neighbourhoods to the east; in the Main Street area around King Edward—the old working-class district once called Hillcrest—even modest "fixer-uppers" and "old-timers" were bid up by competing buyers to a million or more. Who did the astonishing prices benefit, other than the realtors? Just people who wanted to move away—hardly a recipe for a successful city.

It is hard to know how many of these houses are occupied year round and how many are rented out, how many have just a granny parked in them, how many "residents" truly pay Canadian tax on their world income. But the same questions can be asked about Coal Harbour and Yaletown condos. The only conclusion one can draw is that there's an ever-widening gap between the people with lots of money and all the rest. Arguably that's the big change in Vancouver in the past 20 or 50 years. What once seemed to be a relatively egalitarian city doesn't exist anymore.

Small houses gradually infilled Kitsilano in the 1920s on the vacant lots left between larger homes, such as the one on the left, at 2704 West 12th, established in the prosperous years before the First World War. Burnt-out stumps from clearing fires, following the logging of the original forest, still dotted vacant blocks. The photograph shows the misalignment of 12th Avenue at Trafalgar Street due to the mismatch of the CPR's District Lot 526 survey on the near side with the one for District Lot 540 on the far side. An unknown city employee took the photograph during the process of 12th Avenue being upgraded to an arterial route, linking it with 10th Avenue at Macdonald Street to provide efficient automobile access to UBC. The arterial route was one of the recommendations of the 1928 plan for the City of Vancouver by Harland Bartholomew & Associates. (Bing Thom Architects sponsored the digitization of the plan, available through the CVA website, as a 125th birthday gift to the city in 2011.) The legacy of the jog is a very wide grassy boulevard on the north side of 12th Avenue.

THE BUSINESS OF HERITAGE

Since 2002, under mayors Larry Campbell, Sam Sullivan and Gregor Robertson, the heritage management system has begun to unravel. Staff haven't been replaced, council has become much more equivocal about heritage retention as competing interests for affordable housing and other social demands dominate their agenda, and they "blew" the density bank in 2006.

Rather like the city's long-term program to repopulate the downtown (see page 35), the heritage-building rehabilitation program introduced in 2003 became a victim of its own success. In return for property tax exemptions, some small grants for façade restorations and transferable bonuses that went into the "bank," developers invested more than $400 million in heritage-related projects in Chinatown, Gastown and the Downtown Eastside. Robert Fung's Salient Group ran the most significant projects, including the cornerstone Alhambra Hotel at Water and Carrall, where the Gastown revival had begun with Larry Killam's Town of Granville Investments company more than 40 years ago,* and the Paris and Flack blocks on embattled Hastings Street, bracketing the old Woodward's department store.

Too much density, more than could be absorbed in other projects, went into the bank. The Big Three projects that put the system over the top in 2006 were Woodward's (see page 46), where there was much more demolition than actual preservation; the Wing Sang building in Chinatown, where super-salesman Bob Rennie and partners received a bonus for creating what was essentially private space, including a personal art gallery; and the Evergreen Building at 1285 West Pender, a threatened piece of the late architect Arthur Erickson's oeuvre. Altogether, the three projects added over 500,000 square feet to the bank and, when the city suspended the program in 2007, Fung and others were left in the lurch.

The suspension coincided with the desire of some city councillors to start a parallel mechanism to finance community facilities in new neighbourhoods. Fung and Heritage Vancouver president Luxton cried foul and suggested that the city was about to go into competition against the people it had negotiated deals with years before. Councillor Suzanne Anton argued in 2008 that the heritage program had distorted development in the city; Luxton countered that heritage "does not have the luxury" of being funded through local capital plans or user fees. And Fung, as of 2011, was left holding about 400,000 square feet of unsold density. As in other schemes such as carbon trading, the value of a square-foot of a building can rise or fall. In 2003 a square foot of density in the bank was worth $25; it reached a high of $65 in 2008. "We negotiated in good faith years ago," Fung was quoted as saying in 2008. Any move by the city to alter the nature of the program "is really reneging on a good-faith arrangement."[†]

In this new reality, developers need to provide their own receiver sites for density. For example, Wall Financial bought and promised to renovate the old York Theatre near the north end of Commercial Drive, then sell it to the city for $10. That's right,

---

*   For a chronology of the Gastown revival, see *Vancouver Remembered,* pp. 45–9.

†   Information from interviews and articles in the *Globe and Mail,* July 3, 2008, and May 8, 2009.

$10. In return, it received, in 2011, 105,600 square feet of density that it can theoretically transfer to its other properties. However, with the existing permitted densities already so high, there appear to be few sites anywhere in the city where a larger building doesn't draw the ire of established residents.

The high finance of high-rise condominiums and commercial buildings seems a world away from the issues facing people who are trying to decide whether to fix up an old wooden house. But as the heritage program has faded to the point where it's "totally not a priority," as one insider described it, individuals continue to plunk down their money to buy old Vancouver houses, some as homes for their families, others to convert and densify. Building-code amendments allow owners of listed heritage buildings to obey different regulations—as a simple example, about the heights of railings—from those for a new home. Still, problems continue to arise.

Architect Robert Lemon, the former heritage planner, went public with his concerns in 2009, ironically during the receipt of a heritage award for converting 1356 West 13th Avenue from a rooming house into four strata-titled units. At that time, strata conversions of old buildings had to meet the requirements of the Homeowner Protection Act, passed in July 1998 to protect condo buyers from leaks. Insurance companies refused to warranty buildings with older windows and siding, "Even if," Lemon said, "they've performed for a century without a leak."

Building inspectors were demanding that original shingles and siding be removed and a plastic rainscreen then applied to the walls, and that old windows be replaced with double-glazed units, which typically have a life span of 12 to 15 years. "Historic buildings are inherently sustainable to begin with," Lemon told the *Vancouver Courier*. "You don't need to add an extra layer [and] put a rainscreen on it."* Anybody with a sharp eye viewing some renovated houses in Strathcona—the city's oldest neighbourhood—could see the impact of the policy: all the original fabric and patina, the essence of conservation, had been stripped and thrown away. Solid buildings were forced into the plastic-wrapped limbo that was an essential driver of the leaky condo crisis (see page 157).

After lengthy lobbying, the Homeowner Protection Act was changed to allow heritage buildings to retain their original siding when converted into suites, but anecdotal reports indicated that the building department was still demanding complete upgrades to fit the non-heritage code. One contractor described the city's attitude as "completely obsessed with liability issues."

Stories abounded of building *permits* costing $50,000 or more for a single-family house. Other stories told of the city reneging on promises, made a year or two earlier, to homeowners wanting to do permitted renovations because the city had changed its own rules. It's perhaps no surprise that so much work is completed without permits, the way basement suites—a major source of affordable rental housing—have been for generations. People doing such work are, one would think, careful to protect their investment, not wanting anything that might void their insurance or put them in the position of lying on a statutory declaration when they want to sell and move on.

---

*   Lisa Smedman, "Award-winning architect slams provincial, city regulation," *Vancouver Courier,*
     May 29, 2009.

A longer-term question is whether the level of city control is making everything look the same. Are all new townhouses and small apartments built in a kind of neo-Craftsman style? Are all the high-rises progeny of the same computerized design program, accepted on the downtown peninsula but sticking out like sore thumbs when developers try to put them into more suburban neighbourhoods along the various transit lines? Do all new West Side houses look like a hybrid Tudor and all new East Side ones look like a Vancouver Special on steroids?

This stylistic freeze-up may be due to the same convergence of design that makes someone else's Peugeot look like your BMW or perhaps to the city being as prescriptive now in its zoning policies as it was with the towers on podiums in Downtown South (page 40). There is also the sense that developers worry too much about resale to build anything innovative—as developer and pundit Michael Geller once

Developers hard at work providing housing for the city in the 21st century . . .

quipped, developers make sheep look like free thinkers. It is also possible that developers are all too willing to conform to planning department or design-panel dictates just to obtain the permit as soon as possible and get the shovel into the ground.[*]

As the years go by, it appears that the city's buildings *are* becoming far less diverse. If affordability were the raison d'être for conformity, because everything was built efficiently or used prefabrication (as some modernists dreamed a lifetime ago), perhaps all the sameness could be justified. However, prices skyrocketed and refused to fall in spite of the global financial downturn. Low interest rates and steady immigration have kept them up there.

[*]   Interview with architect Ken Terriss, 2010.

AFFORDABILITY

For most of the past 60 years, about half of Vancouver's lifespan, pundits have been wringing their hands over property prices and wondering how anybody can still afford to live here. The first 60 years were a rollercoaster ride due to a combination of world and local events repeatable enough to keep any heavily mortgaged homeowner staring at the ceiling all night.

From 1890 to 1900, prices rose steadily but modestly, about six percent per year, but for the next decade land values soared to the point where it was hard to find a lot anywhere in Vancouver for less than $600.* The frenzy continued until prices collapsed in 1913–4 and took down many of the early speculative fortunes in the city, such as those of the Miller brothers in Grandview (page 182). "Mortgage Heights" became a nickname for Shaughnessy, where the most prosperous beneficiaries of the boom had been flaunting their good luck.

Also affected was the wealthiest landowner of all, the Canadian Pacific Railway, which had received a huge piece of the future city in an 1885 deal with the provincial government. Vancouver archivist James S. Matthews added an interesting note to his files on February 4, 1949:

> *I said I was almost willing to wager [in a conversation with the CPR legal counsel] that it would be proven that when we gave the CPR their land grant, now Vancouver, we gave them "a lemon." I told him that Newton J. Kerr, last land agent, told me that there were 100 lots in 1939—vacant ones—at Kitsilano Beach, on which they had been paying taxes for thirty or forty or fifty years. That the original "Old Shaughnessy" was still vacant property, but that their real problem was out Oak Street way, where there were hundreds of lots on which they were paying taxes and which produced nothing save a crop of bushes.*
>
> *In 1909, lots at Kitsilano Beach were put on the market. Thirty years later about 100 of them were still vacant. During all those years the CPR were paying $30, $40 or $50 a year taxes. Some of those lots must have cost them $1,000 or $1,250 in taxes, without including compound interest, and they were offering them for sale for $600 or $800.*

In 1911, near the peak of the boom, a typical house (33-foot lot; living room, dining/kitchen, one bedroom on the main floor, two or three bedrooms upstairs and a bathroom) in Kitsilano went for about $5,000; a similar house in Grandview, also on a 33-foot lot, went for about $4,300. After the war, in 1921, when the economy was beginning to pick up, prices were still lower than a decade earlier: Kitsilano homes were about $4,500; one seven-room house on the water side of Point Grey Road went for $5,200. Over on the East Side, in Mount Pleasant and Grandview, single-storey, two-bedroom cottages were worth $3,500 or less.

---

*   MacDonald, p. 404.

The real collapse came during the Depression. Houses-for-sale advertisements almost disappeared because no one was buying and the few advertisements there were bore slogans such as "$200—balance like rent!" A bungalow on West 14th in Kitsilano was offered at $2,985; a "modern six-room house" near the beach was asking only $1,600. In Grandview the prices had collapsed further: a six-room house with furniture for $1,400, a house on East 2nd with seven rooms for $1,600, a five-room bungalow "facing park" for $1,350, a three-room cottage for $375 and a small house at 1430 Commercial Drive for $950.

It's hard to compare new apples with old ones, but the "median multiple" in Greater Vancouver in 2010 (median sale value of $540,900 divided by the median household income of $58,200) was 9.3, the most unaffordable of 272 metropolitan markets ranked in comparable countries.[*] A century earlier during the boom, when the average household income was about $850, the multiple was more like 6 for Kitsilano and 5 for Grandview. The fact that there was no income tax in Canada until late in the First World War makes comparing even harder.

In my family's collective memory, my grandparents bought their two-bedroom cottage at 2322 Cypress in the 1930s for $425, most of their life savings. They did, however, have my grandfather's $35 monthly pension from the Canada Vinegar Works, adequate until the company cut it back by $5 due to their own straitened financial situation (after my grandmother died in 1957, the house sold for about $6,000). The average annual wage in Vancouver (for people lucky enough to have jobs) in the mid-1930s was $950. Elsewhere in the city, hundreds of houses were given up because of unpaid taxes—some of which were returned through the "work for taxes" programs in the late 1930s.[†]

From the 1910s to the 1940s many people lived in better houses than they could have afforded to build themselves, confirming Cato's famous edict "to enjoy the fruits of another's folly." Although prices seem to have been incredibly cheap, few had any extra money to invest. Mechanic Erik Peterson (see page 92) recalled choosing to buy a car in the early 1950s with his savings from work in the Powell River mill, reckoning he needed it more than a lot on Oak Street he could have obtained with his $600.

"There was a stunning piece of news in this paper the other day," a *Province* editorial said on December 5, 1950. "It was to the effect that Vancouver is building up so fast that civic officials estimate that five years from now there will not be a vacant lot left in our city." The article went on to say that, according to city officials, "mammoth apartments" would be "one of the answers to our space shortage."

An article by Pat Carney, then a business reporter for the *Province* (a senator until her retirement in 2008), described land values in South Vancouver skyrocketing during the decade, going from $20 to $28 per front foot in 1950, to $90 to $100 in 1958. By 1961 people were "making a killing" in real estate: an eight-year-old house in Arbutus-Quilchena, 1,450 square feet with three bedrooms, sold for $23,500, $7,000 more than its cost in 1953. As always, most people were forced to buy high if they sold high

---

[*]   This is according to the *Demographia International Housing Affordability Survey*. "Vancouver's home prices rates 'most unaffordable,'" Brian Morton, *Vancouver Sun*, January 26, 2010.

[†]   Wade, pp. 54-5.

and, although they appeared almost wealthy on paper, they had little to show for it. There were few if any opportunities to downsize and still own without leaving the neighbourhood.

Prices climbed steadily in the 1960s. "Only 40 percent of our society can afford to buy a home today," realtor Henry Block told a newspaper reporter in 1967. According to Alderman Hugh Bird, that meant people who made $35 a day or less, at a time when conventional mortgages were between 8¼ and 9½ percent, were priced out of the market. Wage and cost inflation was a part of the problem: a typical house on the East Side cost about $14 a square foot to build, up from $11 a few years earlier; on the West Side, a brick-faced house cost about $20 a square foot.*

For several years there had been discussion about new types of housing and denser development: University of British Columbia planning professor Peter Oberlander argued in 1967 that apartments should be built on top of shopping centres and commercial developments; architect-planner Douglas Cowin was among the proponents of 20-foot-wide row houses. As a 50-foot lot could be had for $10,000, a two-bedroom townhouse on half that width could be offered for sale at about $11,000.

According to a 1973 news story, house prices "soared more than 50 percent between 1968 and 1972." The house on Kerrisdale's Wiltshire Street my parents bought in 1950 for $12,000—an amount my father recalled kept him awake at night—sold in the early 1970s for $44,000 (by 1975 it was probably worth $80,000, today more than $2 million). But there were still amazing bargains in transitional areas like Kitsilano, such as the large Peace House, as it was then called, a legendary hotbed of political activism at 3148 Point Grey Road. It was put on the market in the late 1960s for $17,000 but needed a huge amount of work, including a new furnace.†

Another example: a house on Kitsilano's Stephens Street in the block between 6th and 7th, divided as an up/down duplex, sold in 1974 for $42,500. There were so few potential buyers that the vendors offered a mortgage back at eight percent, a considerable discount on the bank rate. At that time, rents were much more in line with house prices—the two suites renting at $350 a month each would pretty well cover the mortgage payments. Other houses had assumable mortgages: I got into the market in my mid-twenties in Kitsilano in 1976, buying a duplex at 5th and Stephens with $5,000 savings and almost no credit rating or income. I recall the lawyer, in a posh office in one of the Bentall towers, eyeing my long hair and jeans when I dropped

My cartoon for a Mike Grenby article, "What to do with that cash?," in the *Vancouver Sun* in 1980. It suggests various strategies for renters and homeowners who had from $2,000 to $250,000 to invest, at a time when an average Vancouver house cost about $125,000. That high-interest period was the golden age for fixed-return investments like Canada Savings Bonds.

---

* Typical construction costs for a spec-quality duplex on the East Side in 2011 are about $145 a square foot, according to builder James Evans. Quotes from newspaper articles in August 1967.

† Jeannette Wall rented there at the time with her husband, Jeff, the artist. She described the house during an interview with me in 2010.

Affordability in the early 1970s: the house at 2232 Stephens in Kitsilano, bought for $42,500.

in to sign the paper to transfer the mortgage into my name, giving me a look that said, "I would never give you this mortgage if it were up to me." The interest rate was 11¼ percent, part of the reason why prices were so low.

The high inflation of the 1970s was crimped briefly by the wage and price controls that Pierre Trudeau had campaigned against and then imposed in October 1975. It soon resumed and house prices took off again, increasing about 35 percent at the dawn of the 1980s, when the Bank of Canada interest rate hit a record 16.2 percent. Mortgage rates reached a usurious level of nearly 20 percent and Kerrisdale, where a bungalow cost about $145,000, witnessed the largest price increases in Canada. In the ensuing crash, one of the few times that Vancouver house prices really declined, many people lost their savings and others, who had speculated on a second house, found themselves crippled by mortgage payments, just like their hapless ancestors in 1914.

Since 1982, the bottom of that recession, the housing market has been consistent. Consistently upward, that is. Low mortgage rates have allowed buyers to assume gigantic amounts of debt and created a "destructive real estate market," in the words of Andy Yan, a planner and researcher with Bing Thom Architects. Prices have become so high, he suggests, that the young and creative are leaving Vancouver for Toronto or Montreal where it is cheaper to live. "High housing costs have a great way of killing innovation and creativity. Can the next Facebook or the next Apple computer really come from Vancouver if you're too busy trying to pay the rent?"* Toronto has since regained the unaffordability title due to its high rents.

SUSTAINABILITY

"The greenest building is the one that is already built." That statement, by architect Carl Elefante, links the environmental movement with heritage preservation at a time when buildings have to do their part in reducing energy use. "A culture of reuse," part of the troika of reduce, reuse and recycle, ought to begin with the adaptation of existing buildings to future needs.†

The arguments for the economic value of heritage preservation have been well documented by economist Donovan Rypkema and others in the United States. Almost 30 years ago the Reagan administration allowed accelerated capital depreciation for

---

* Quoted in "There are two million reasons for high prices in Vancouver" by Don Cayo, *Vancouver Sun*, August 21, 2010.

† Most of this material is adapted from a lecture and symposium, on November 3 and 4, 2010, at SFU Harbour Centre campus. Elefante is a principal at Quinn Evans Architects, Washington, DC. Other corroborating material comes from the province of BC's heritage branch.

heritage work. Part of the argument for encouraging this kind of investment was jobs: in new construction, typically, half of the cost is materials, the other half jobs, whereas in rehabilitation only 30 percent of the budget is materials and 70 percent jobs. And, contrary to conventional wisdom, it's not necessarily more expensive to redo than build new.*

According to Elefante, the green buildings industry is "profoundly wrong" when it claims that existing buildings will have to be torn down and replaced by new, greener ones. Modern buildings are incredibly energy intensive to build—their steel, concrete and vinyl are created with copious amounts of polluting energy and when existing buildings are demolished all of their embodied energy goes into the landfill. All that new buildings can offer is a slowing of the rate of increase of energy use, whereas the greening of existing buildings offers a real opportunity to reduce the amount of energy our society uses.

The most energy-efficient commercial buildings were those built in the early part of the 20th century before modernist practices took hold. With opening windows and flexible spaces they are climate-responsive and can easily be modified. The most adaptable of all are the century-old Yaletown/Gastown-type of warehouses because they are generic. They are not individualistic and idiosyncratic, like many mid-century buildings that have to be torn down because they're unable to change. In Vancouver,

Not saved but at least recycled: two houses at 6th and Alberta were relics of Lower Mount Pleasant's working-class past. The blue one was apparently built in 1917 as an employee residence for the Standard Milk Company, whose plant was a few blocks away at 405 West 8th. BC Hydro obtained the land for a substation, essential due to the huge expansion in electrical demand on the nearby blocks, and made a sincere attempt to find a site where the houses could be moved (see the *Vancouver Sun*, November 8, 2008). When that proved unsuccessful, salvage stripped from them was donated to the Vancouver Heritage Foundation. Much of their mouldings and flooring ended up restoring an old house in Port Coquitlam.

---

* "It turns out it costs only two-thirds as much to gut a building and redo it than to rip it down and rebuild it. So for every three buildings we do, we get one free, in a sense." John Robinson, director of the UBC Sustainability Initiative, quoted in "UBC does more than study green initiatives—it's immersed in them," by Don Cayo, *Vancouver Sun*, July 9, 2011.

a leader in green architecture, Busby Perkins+Will, who also made their reputation for innovative modern design, adapted a Yaletown warehouse for their own offices.

Of the commercial buildings in a typical North American city, about half of the building stock—the towers of the mid- to late 20th century—are notable energy hogs. Modernist buildings erected between about 1940 and 1975 are the worst of all. From the energy-use point of view, their most valuable components are their concrete frames—everything else is stripped off and disposed of when the building gets an environmental upgrade. It's exactly the opposite with "historic" buildings, whose façades get kept because they represent materials and workmanship that can't be replicated.

Ironically, of all the types of walls in buildings, the traditional wooden one with wood siding, sheathing, lath and plaster—the traditional Vancouver house—is the most energy effective of all. Wood takes almost no energy to create compared to stucco, aluminum or vinyl, and is a natural insulator. The best way to make these kinds of houses more energy efficient is to replace the furnace. Adding wall insulation saves 5 percent, roof insulation 13 to 15 percent of an energy bill.

Replacing old single-glazed wooden windows only saves four percent of energy costs. New windows are not even recyclable, whereas wood windows are completely repairable and recyclable.* A reasonable estimate is that new double-glazed windows would have to last 30 years to pay back the energy that went into manufacturing them, but most last only 12 or 15 years before their seals fail and, typically, their panes begin to fog up. Some people with old houses use the traditional method of clipping single-glazed storm windows onto outside window frames for the cold season. In tests by City Green Solutions in southwestern BC, single-glazed windows with "storms" attached had the same energy performance as the adjoining wall.

The buzzword for commercial buildings is LEED (Leadership in Energy and Environmental Design): buildings are given LEED status in a rating system administered by the Canadian Green Building Council. For any building to perform at a low-energy level, users ought to adopt habits like wearing a sweater and turning the lights off when nobody's in the room—the sort of things everyone's grandmother tried to drum into them. The 21st century is a different era from the "one world, limitless energy" beliefs of the 1950s, when the province's biggest power utility, BC Electric, left the lights on 24 hours a day in its Vancouver head office.

"Going green" is one thing, but out in the neighbourhood lumberyards where homeowners go for solutions to draughty, chilly buildings, "green" is most likely marketed as "money-saving," especially on the East Side. Everything in Vancouver seems to come back to affordability.

---

* "You know why they call them replacement windows? Because you'll have to replace them," a state conservation officer told Elefante.

LANDMARK CITY

Twenty-five years ago the city was gearing up to try to repopulate the downtown peninsula, which had lots of daytime jobs but was dead after dark. Who then would have predicted that the 21st century's first challenge would be to preserve downtown office space?

In June 1987, city council agreed in principle to the rezoning of Downtown South—the three dozen blocks south of Smithe Street stretching from Burrard eastward as far as the Yaletown warehouses on Homer—to create a new high-density neighbourhood, and by doing so also to restore commercial vitality to Granville Street. As I wrote in 1990 in the original *Vanishing Vancouver*:

> *Although the rezoning proposal appeared to have a juggernaut's momentum, it suddenly stalled in October 1989, due to nagging concerns about the quality of life in a super-high-density area, unresolved questions about the fate of heritage buildings along Granville Street and the city's inability—without an enabling amendment by the provincial government to the City of Vancouver charter—to collect a fee from developers to pay for public amenities within the new area. But these are temporary setbacks and as certain as the rains of November, a rezoning and redevelopment of Downtown South will occur.*

The transformation has been stunning. The Downtown South area and its Yaletown neighbour, with its refurbished blocks of century-old warehouses, skillfully marketed the attractions of downtown living, walking to work, cycling on weekends, easy transit and car co-ops. Before the new towers existed, there really was no "downtown lifestyle" in Vancouver, except for the Beatty Street warehouse conversions of a decade earlier.* The West End of a generation earlier was densely populated, but it mixed grass, trees, beaches and buildings together in an almost suburban way. When you exited one of the new Downtown South condos you were on pavement, period.

THE ZONING POLICY THAT WORKED TOO WELL, a headline on a *New York Times* story in 2007, highlighted

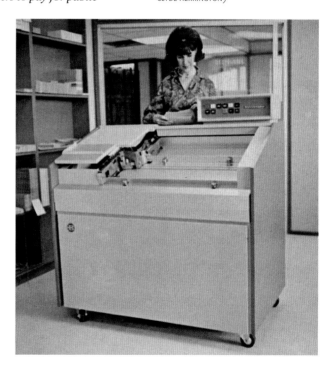

A 1960s-era office worker, the sort of young woman for whom the West End's small, affordable apartments were tailored. "At West Coast Electronic Data Processing Ltd., a Burroughs B200 Electronic Computer is utilized for the processing of data for all types of business records in BC. The operator is preparing to load the program into the Computer's memory by means of punch cards. Data is processed at the rate of 1,600 cards per minute and computed results are printed in excess of 700 lines per minute." (*INDUSTRIAL BRITISH COLUMBIA*, PHOTO BY CLYDE HERRINGTON)

---

* The thousand or so mainly poor people who lived in the area did not have a *lifestyle* in my use of the word.

Vancouver's dilemma. The story quoted newly arrived planning director Brent Toderian describing the "living first" policy of 20 years earlier as "genius," in that it doubled the downtown population to 80,000, yet conceded that the city had to shift gears to protect office capacity.

"In the grand scheme of dollars and cents," Toderian said, "residential is much more profitable." Unclear amidst the gushing prose about condo lifestyles and the double-page ads in the weekend paper from Rennie Marketing Systems is the number of condos snapped up by speculators, how many condos are vacant for much of the year because their owners have other residences elsewhere on the planet and how many of the new downtown residents use cars to travel to work outside their immediate environs.* As anybody knows who uses public transit in Vancouver and whose destination isn't accessible by a B-Line bus or SkyTrain, finding a bus and riding it from downtown only as far as, say, Kerrisdale can take the better part of an hour. Of course, getting downtown by bus is also a problem, which keeps downtown parking lots humming at even $30 a day.

A 2009 report authored by city planner Trish French suggested that nearly 6 million square feet of office and commercial space would be needed in the downtown area by 2030, 5 million of which could be found by changing zoning to disallow more residential in the core. However, as residential is eminently saleable it has driven up land prices, making straight commercial projects even harder to build in a city that attracts few head offices and where prospective tenants are likely to be relatively small businesses.

Mixed-use projects, with some office, some condo, some retail—such as proposals of the 1980s that were not then marketable—represent a compromise as developers try to make the numbers work in high-cost, rule-laden Vancouver. One recent building that is currently the third tallest in the city—the 41-storey Shaw Tower on the waterfront—is mixed use, with offices on the lower 16 floors and the upper 24 being home to 130 live/work condos. Jameson House at 838 West Hastings will also be mixed use, as will the new Telus headquarters at Georgia and Seymour.

The repopulation of downtown boosted Granville Street as an entertainment strip but hasn't seemed to reinforce downtown itself as a shopping destination. The downtown area seems curiously dead; the old retail heart around Georgia and Granville appears dispirited and downmarket compared with a generation ago. Much of the activity is out of sight, behind blank walls and underground in Pacific Centre Mall, the development that 40 years ago was going to compete with suburban malls by connecting the outskirts with the centre via a freeway.

Eaton's, the anchor tenant of the mall on the site of the old Hotel Vancouver (page 18), had panache but lost its way and disappeared in 1999. Sears, the current occupant of the store, is not the Simpsons-Sears of the 1950s Canadian past and will never shake its image as the place to go for a lawnmower or some really good car tools.

---

* In 2009, about 23,000 apartment condos (35% of the total number of them) were investor-owned; of these, about 17,000 were rented, which left about 6,000 that might be vacant for much of the year. See *Vancouver Condominium Rental Study*, by CitySpaces Consulting with Urban Futures Inc., December, 2009. Investors rented out 11% of houses.

Kitty-corner to it, the venerable Hudson's Bay Company store, which once sported its "Founded in 1670" coat of arms, is now part of the portfolio of an American private-equity firm.

Big-box chains such as London Drugs, Winners, Sleep Country Canada, Future Shop and Chapters have opened storefronts on or near Granville Street. Only a block or so away the tenants are mainly language schools, by-the-slice stand-up pizza vendors and the ubiquitous coffee shops with wi-fi. One "reason to go downtown" of the recent past, the venerable electronics and music retailer A&B Sound, disappeared from Seymour Street in 2008, a victim of its excessive expansion into the suburbs and the digital revolution. Replacing such destinations are the downtown campuses of UBC, SFU and BCIT, which bring in trainloads of budget-conscious students day and night and, not surprisingly, produce little retail buzz.

Those with money to spend still gravitate to Robson Street's boutiques, as they have for the past generation, but many shop uptown along Granville Street between the bridge and 16th and, increasingly, on 4th Avenue west of Burrard. Downtown shoppers seeking higher-end merchandise still have destinations like Leone, Birks, Cartier and Edward Chapman in the financial blocks along Pender and Hastings, an area that appeals to visitors from the chic hotels near the convention centre and to residents of the handful of deluxe new condo/office developments. A century ago the high-end retailers started migrating from Hastings to Granville; now they're back, although further to the west. Prestigious residences have returned to what was "Blueblood Alley" 120 years ago, although in a very different form.

Vancouver's downtown about 1960—graphic evidence of how much of the peninsula was vacant lots and surface parking, all land that at the time had commercial zoning. The bottom left of the picture captures the edge of the modern Downtown South neighbourhood. (PHOTOGRAPHER UNKNOWN; A PLASTICHROME POSTCARD BY NATURAL COLOR PRODUCTIONS LTD.)

ABOVE LEFT > The Beasley, under construction in 2010, incorporating most of The Homer.

ABOVE RIGHT > A 1989 watercolour of The Homer, at the northeast corner of Homer and Smithe, a classic small apartment building from a century ago, with a check in its façade to let light into the centre units. The coffee shop served good cheeseburgers and bottomless cups of coffee. Unlike today, at that time nothing tall intruded into the nearby sky.

One such is Jameson House, the most recent of Vancouver signature buildings to be designed by a "starchitect," in this case Sir Norman Foster. It incorporates two small heritage buildings, continuing "Foster and Partners' practice of designing contemporary interventions in historic structures that began with the New German Parliament at the Reichstag and the Great Court of the British Museum, and has recently been explored in a high-rise context with the Hearst Tower in New York."[*] As part of the development, the 1921 Ceperley Rounsfell building is being restored. In 2007, when the project's financing came unglued briefly, the building was suspended on a truss erected above the deep excavation for Jameson House's parking garage.[†]

In Gastown's ongoing evolution, furniture design outlets have returned to the prime retail space along Water Street, mixing with the restaurants and tourist shops and giving the area some of the flare it had 40 years ago. As the nearby blocks gentrify with Woodward's, the Flack Block and the Paris Block, Gastown will probably become more like Yaletown—home to people with cash flow. The jury will be out for some time on whether these heritage redevelopments will be as inclusive of the poor as their proponents claim them to be or whether the Downtown Eastside, "our outdoor mental asylum that it seems no one can do anything about,"[‡] will simply be pushed eastward, to wreck Strathcona.

[*]   Elif Sungur on www.dexigner.com.

[†]   "Vancouver building suspended after financing falls through" by Jessica Kerr, *Journal of Commerce*, March 16, 2009.

[‡]   "Larry Beasley's Simple Plan" by Frances Bula, *Vancouver Magazine*, December 1, 2008.

TOP > This photograph, taken circa 1970, with the then-new Canadian flag flying, looks northwest from Georgia and Granville at the first two towers of the Bentall Centre, crisp and sleek compared with the crested brick Marine Building in the centre distance. The jumbled buildings directly below the photographer, including the Hotel Angelus and Colonial Theatre, stood on the block bounded by Georgia, Dunsmuir, Granville and Howe; they were razed in the early 1970s for the IBM Tower, the Four Seasons Hotel and the first northward expansion of Pacific Centre. (PHOTO BY DAN PROPP)

BOTTOM > The opening of the second Bentall Tower, on Burrard at Dunsmuir, on June 11, 1969, with Clark Bentall at the microphone, Mayor Tom Campbell on the far right and white-haired Charles Bentall next to him. *The Fountain of the Pioneer* by George Tsutakawa, dedicated on opening day, is still there, one of a handful of plaza sculptures to endure in this restless city. Tsutakawa created and installed about 60 fountains on plazas and in parks in North America and Japan between 1960 and his retirement in 1976. Born in Seattle in 1910, he went to Japan as a child and became immersed in Japanese arts and cultural traditions before returning to Seattle in 1927 and reinventing himself as an American artist. He taught for many years at the University of Washington. (PHOTO BY RICHARD STACE-SMITH)

The Jaeger store on Granville in 1986; its upper-storey façade is now pasted onto the side of the Pacific Centre shopping mall. The building to the left of it is the old James Inglis Reid store (page 68).

TOWERS ON PODIUMS

One of the handful of Downtown South buildings to survive to celebrate its 100th birthday is The Homer, at the northeast corner of Homer and Smithe. It provides a corner of the podium for a condo tower called, astonishingly, The Beasley, after Vancouver's co-director of planning during the 1990s development boom.

The developer would hardly have named its new tower The Homer for fear of people identifying it with Mr. Simpson of the television series. (The street's namesake was actually a New Westminster merchant who was a member of parliament in the 1880s.) But at first blush the name Beasley sounds equally inappropriate—Miss Beazley is a character in Archie comics. Its naming is an indication of how respected Larry Beasley is in the development community.

Most recent projects have gleaned the zeitgeist, or anglo-history, to find just the right name. On West Georgia there is the Shangri-La Hotel, the city's tallest tower at 61 storeys. The name of The James, a condo project in southeast False Creek on the site of James Doherty's Progressive Engineering Works, "honour[s] the property's industrial heritage without going too deeply into the history." An admirable understatement.[*] Another condo development on Homer Street sought inspiration from the ancient Homer and became The Iliad.

Larry Beasley was "emblematic of Vancouver's new image as the 21st century's utopian city, an image that is now one of our prime exports," wrote Frances Bula in *Vancouver Magazine*.[†] As did former councillor Gordon Price, the most planning-literate politician of that era, Beasley travelled the world "spreading the Vancouver gospel" (Bula's words), trying to assist cities as diverse as Dubai and Beijing in planning comprehensively and humanistically. He became the super-salesman of a group of city planners, all of whom leaned heavily on the work of his predecessor Ray Spaxman and Spaxman's mentor, Walter Hardwick, who turned "new urbanism" into codes and rules, and empowered developers to give them form in concrete, glass and rusting rebar.

Like Jameson House in the financial district, The Beasley and the Canadian Linen building at Drake and Richards are the best examples in Downtown South of keeping a bit of the past alive and incorporating it into new developments. Another project, from the 1990s, incorporated the Henry Abbott house at Georgia and Jervis, the last of the Blueblood Alley mansions of the 19th century, although it was criticized for

---

* "Why a 'James' might be in your future" by Felicity Stone, *Vancouver Sun*, July 24, 2010.

† "Larry Beasley's Simple Plan" by Frances Bula, *Vancouver Magazine*, December 1, 2008.

Dunsmuir Hotel, Vancouver, B.C.

retaining little of the original house's materials. Nevertheless, they're not façades, unlike the missteps of a generation ago such as the old Jaeger store's art deco bits, emblazoned like a tattoo on Pacific Centre's beefy flank.

All these schemes have had to address the scale difference between the old and the new. The Canadian Linen building, for example, is only one storey—an art deco design from 1928 by City Hall architects Townley & Matheson—sitting next to a 29-storey condo tower, but it works very well as a supermarket in the ensemble by Stuart Howard Architects.

A few of us who attended the city-sponsored public meetings of 20 years ago about the future shape of the residential downtown tried to argue for low-rise types of building, more like Paris's six-storey, mansard-roofed apartments. There were precedents, notably the 1970s-era Anchor Point on Burrard Street at Pacific. Architectural historian Harold Kalman described its design in 1978 as part of "a democratic process. Public resistance to aloof, high-rise 'point towers' inspired civic officials to change the zoning bylaw, to encourage apartment buildings to be lower and stand closer to the sidewalk."[*]

How things changed in a decade, for point-tower models quickly won the day. They would be cheaper to build than five- or six-storey concrete buildings, one developer told city council, meaning they could be more affordable. People wanted views, said the marketers, and if the towers were widely enough separated everyone could share the water and the mountains. There was, of course, the West End, the successful example from a generation earlier, which had its share of tall towers.

The form of the new buildings was stringently prescribed, as Beasley explained in an article in 2000: "Design guidelines, enabled by the zoning, set the form. The guidelines emphasize thin towers with small floor-plates, and the base of the tower is hidden behind a nicely scaled minimum three-story street wall. At street level, these towers almost disappear from one's perception."[†] Ironically, as most people seem to be looking at their phones as they walk, the towers do indeed disappear along with everything else.

"The Beasley regime was so formulaic," reflected James Cheng, architect of the Shaw Tower and the Shangri-La Hotel.[‡] While this "single building typology" added thousands of living units to the downtown, architect Joey Giamio

The Dunsmuir Hotel, at the corner of Richards, is one of a handful of old hotels left in the central business district. It was designed by architects Parr & Fee for David Gibb & Sons in 1908, and was a Salvation Army hostel for many years; the provincial government recently purchased it along with 23 other SROS (single room occupancy hotels). (JOHN VALENTINE & SONS POSTCARD CIRCA 1912)

Drawing of the Canadian Linen Co. Ltd. building, in *Sun Directories*, 1936 edition, page 867, CVA. (UNKNOWN ARTIST)

*   Kalman (1978), p. 222.

†   American Planning Association's *Zoning News*, April 2000.

‡   Quoted by Lisa Rochon, *Globe and Mail*, January 11, 2007.

Dominion Construction Company dominated the city's building industry from the time of its founding in 1911. Charles Bentall joined Dominion in 1912 as assistant general manager, and became general manager in 1915 and principal owner and president in 1920. Born in England in 1882, he started work as a draftsman; his first job in Vancouver was as structural engineer for the False Creek works of J. Couglan & Sons in 1908. Dominion Construction pioneered "the package"—a building designed, engineered, built and financed to the requirements of a client—and the industrial estate concept. Charles lived out his long life in a suite on the main floor of Gabriola (page 143). Charles's son Clark took over the company in the 1950s and ran it for 40 years. Dominion Construction merged in 2010 with another long-established firm, Stuart Olson, to form Stuart Olson Dominion. Stuart Olson was a carpenter who emigrated from Sweden to Edmonton and founded his namesake firm in 1939.

wrote, "it has resulted in a product qualified only by its incessant sameness." Difference is represented "in tweaks and gimmicks," including the curious cantilevered structures that mimic the metal awnings on the loading docks of the original Yaletown warehouses.* They cover block after block, making the West End seem wonderfully diverse and interesting by comparison.

A less aesthetically driven criticism was that of writer and critic Helena Grdadolnik, who pointed out that these buildings would have to be demolished if the 500-square-foot condo were to become no longer marketable at some future date. Should that need for adaptive re-use seem unlikely, consider the fates of the old BC Electric building on Burrard at Nelson and the distinctive, cable-hung Westcoast Transmission building on Georgia at Broughton, both now converted into condos. "Because of how they were originally built, you were able to move walls within the space and change it for new use, for residential use, allowing them to change as the demographics of the city changed," Grdadolnik said.† In the new buildings, the walls are concrete and poured in place, the room configurations fixed for all time.

RESIDENTIAL TRIUMPHANT

The Hotel Georgia, the 1920s landmark at Howe Street facing onto Courthouse Square, exemplifies the victory of residential over commercial in the downtown. The hotel has been restored and a thin condo tower rises above the site of its parking garage. Although the debate during the past five years in the architecture community has focused on the city's failure to get architect Bing Thom's design for the garage site, an earlier plan by the Bentall Group would have demolished both hotel and garage and replaced them with a whopper of an office building.

In the early 1990s Bentall hired Skidmore, Owings and Merrill, the Chicago firm famous for its skyscrapers, to design a replacement building for the Hotel Georgia site. Smallish hotels like the Georgia had fallen on hard times in the climate of the day, and James Cheng Architects did an evaluation that effectively condemned the Georgia as too expensive to upgrade. Council seemed eager for a new building and to believe, collectively, that the arguments for retaining the hotel were mainly sentimental. Gordon Price, for one, saw an opportunity to get a real exclamation mark stamped on the city's increasingly flat-topped skyline.

The American firm delivered a design for a massive building. Decorating its top would be an abstract sculptural metal piece, perhaps a reference to the dramatic statement made by buildings of the 1920s, such as the Chrysler Building in New York City. Vancouver, it seemed, was about to enter the big leagues.

Advocates for the Hotel Georgia made their case to the developer and its patient architect, Adrian Smith, who became increasingly frustrated by our provincialism.

---

*   In Min, p. 163.

†   "The Best Argument for Demolition" by Bryan Lynch, *Georgia Straight*, September 22, 2005.

I recall him saying to me, "We've been tearing down buildings like this in Chicago and New York for 40 years. You have to move on." What about a small, thin tower on the parking lot site adjacent to the hotel? No, he told us firmly; tenants wanted large floor-plates—what we proposed wouldn't be rentable. What about a building that left most of the hotel intact but cantilevered the office building above it? Pastiche, we were told—good design meant looking unswervingly to the future. (Fifteen years later, Jameson House is cantilevered above a small heritage building; two other projects, announced in 2011, will incorporate the old University Club and The Old Stock Exchange Building in a similar manner.)[*]

The Hotel Georgia, dead centre, is the only building on its side of the block to have survived. The Devonshire Hotel beside it made way in 1981 for the HSBC building, the Medical-Dental building beyond it was demolished in 1989 for the Cathedral Place tower and the low buildings in the foreground came down in the early 1970s for the plaza of the Four Seasons Hotel and Pacific Centre mall. Directly below the photographer, cars still parked on the site of the second Hotel Vancouver, and continued to do so until Pacific Centre broke ground in 1968. The photograph dates from 1964, as the Bank of Canada building is under construction in the right distance and the Bentall Centre is not yet visible. (PHOTO BY GEORGE WEINHAUPL)

As has been so often the case in Vancouver, the lousy economy came to the rescue. By the time the Bentall group had its ducks in a row the market for office space had cooled. The nagging question about Vancouver—whether large companies wanted to locate here—was once again answered negatively. And, it appeared, fewer businesses required the large floor-plates of earlier eras due to advances in computer networks and myriad other organizational changes.

It took an immigrant to see the value of the Hotel Georgia. Peter Eng, who had trained as an historian in Hong Kong, went into real-estate development and co-founded the institution now known as the University of Macao. As chair of the Allied Holding Group of Companies, he donated the old Toronto-Dominion Bank building at Hastings and Seymour to SFU, since converted into the Morris Wosk Centre for Dialogue (page 11), and developed the commercial units of the Electra building. He also bought the Hotel Georgia, which now operates under the name Rosewood Hotel Georgia. He had seen the growth of boutique heritage hotels elsewhere in the world and determined that the same thing could happen in Vancouver.[†]

The thin tower that had been proposed for the hotel's parking lot site turned out to be viable after all, but for condominiums, not offices. Bing Thom's original concept, in 2001, for a crystal spire counterpoint to the Shangri-La Hotel didn't survive the 2006 change in ownership of the site. Instead, other architects designed a 48-storey tower. Under construction in 2011, the tower features fashionably distorted elevations yet is "squared up and dumbed down," as described unkindly by architecture critic Lisa Rochon.[‡]

---

[*] Now in partnership with Gordon Gill, Smith is truly a starchitect with a globe-spanning portfolio, including Dubai's Burj Kalifa, the tallest building in the world, and the Trump International Hotel and Tower in Chicago.

[†] Peter Eng received an honorary Doctor of Laws from SFU on June 4, 1999. He also served on the first board of the Vancouver Heritage Foundation.

[‡] Citylab blog, January 11, 2007.

MOVERS AND SHAKERS

These pages show architects, engineers, clients and builders from the 1958 edition of *Who's Who in Canada*, who helped Vancouver modernize after the Second World War. A few from that generation, including architects Arthur Erickson and Ron Thom and artist B.C. Binning, are absent from that volume but are much better known now, with their work widely celebrated. They, and other absentees who were very significant as designers and mentors, such as Ned Pratt and Bob Berwick, are mentioned elsewhere in this book.

1 > Harold Nelson Semmens, born in Saskatoon in 1914, was Douglas Simpson's partner in the most accomplished modernist architectural firm in Vancouver in the 1950s. He graduated from the University of Manitoba in 1936, worked in Winnipeg and eastern Canada until the war (retiring with the rank of major) and moved to Vancouver in 1946. He dissolved his partnership with Simpson in 1957 but remained in Vancouver in private practice until 1962, when he moved to Montreal. He died in 1965. Semmens Simpson's main library at Robson and Burrard, now altered for CTV and HMV, and the United Kingdom Building at Hastings and Granville are the survivors of their downtown work; Hycroft Towers at 16th and Granville is their most significant surviving apartment building.

2 > Douglas Colborne Simpson was a Winnipegger, two years younger than his partner Semmens and also a graduate of the University of Manitoba. After wartime service he began his career in 1946 in charge of a research project into prefabrication for the National Research Council. With Semmens he shared the Massey Gold Medal for Architecture in 1952 for the Marwell building on West Georgia Street (demolished). He left Vancouver in 1957 for Hawaii, working there and in Fiji and Australia until his death in Honolulu in 1967. His and Semmens's own modest homes from the late 1940s survive in "Little Australia," the set of streets with Antipodean names on the edge of the University Endowment Lands, at 4862 and 4872 Queensland Drive.

3 > Hugh Allan Martin was president of Marwell Construction Ltd., established in 1936, which built many of Semmens Simpson's modernist designs in the 1950s. Born in Los Angeles in 1914, he made an advantageous marriage to a daughter of Gordon Farrell, president of the BC Telephone Company.

4 > John Huntley Read was chief engineer for Marwell Construction in 1946-7 before becoming a partner in Read Jones Christofferson structural and civil engineers. His work in Vancouver included the Customs House (demolished), additions to the Woodward's store (demolished) and the Vancouver Public Library on Burrard Street.

Born in Antung, China, in 1916, he was educated in Shanghai and had his early career as a draftsman and technical assistant there, before leaving for Vancouver in 1939.

5 > Albert Edward Grauer, commonly known as Dal, was one of the brightest of the progressive young executives in British Columbia in the 1940s and 1950s. Born on a farm at Eburne on Sea Island in 1906, he became the province's Rhodes Scholar in 1927 and, in 1946, following a meteoric rise through the ranks, became president of BC Electric, the largest power utility in the province. Tax fights with the province, which believed it could save millions of dollars that were being paid to Ottawa if it nationalized the private company, and Grauer's resistance to Premier W.A.C. Bennett's dream of hydroelectric dams on the Columbia and Peace rivers, sealed his company's fate. Grauer died of leukemia in 1961, just as the government moved to take over BC Electric and create the BC Hydro & Power Authority.

6 > Tom Ingledow was vice-president and executive engineer of BC Electric during the era in which it erected its landmark modernist buildings on Burrard Street—the Dal Grauer Substation in 1953 and the head office building, now the Electra condo tower, in 1957. In the former, according to Heritage Vancouver, "architect Ned Pratt and artist B.C. Binning created, in essence, a three-dimensional 'canvas' which, when viewed through the exterior glass and steel grid, has been said to resemble a Mondrian/De Stijl painting." Ingledow developed the operational program that inspired architects Thompson Berwick & Pratt to create the "lozenge" open-floor plan for the head office. Born in England in 1900, he enlisted young and served both as a pilot and as the lieutenant of a machine-gun corps during the First World War. He died in Vancouver in 1972.

7 > John Young McCarter of McCarter, Nairne & Partners was born in Victoria in 1886. He articled there with the architect Thomas

10 > Gerald Hamilton, born in Hamburg in 1923 and educated in Leeds, joined Sharp & Thompson, Berwick & Pratt in 1950 before going out on his own in 1951, "specializing in commercial industrial work as well as large apartment projects," according to his biography. Like many architects of that generation, he listed a range of artistic hobbies, including "drama, piano, composing of music, painting," and also enjoyed mountaineering. The distinctive H.R. MacMillan Space Centre ("the planetarium") on Kitsilano Point, erected in the late 1960s, is his best-known work.

11 > Alvin Jackson Narod was a civil engineer, one of the sons of a Vancouver doctor and one of the few Jews listed in 1950s *Who's Who*s. He founded Narod Construction in 1948 and built numerous projects all over the province, including Kerrisdale Community Centre, part of the George Massey Tunnel and Langara Gardens. He retired in 1978 after suffering heart trouble but Premier Bill Bennett encouraged him to come out of retirement in 1980 to spearhead the construction of BC Place stadium. Following its successful, on-budget completion in March 1983, Narod had a heart attack two days before he was slated to take Queen Elizabeth II on a guided tour. Nevertheless, he got out of his hospital bed, put on a suit and attended the opening ceremony. He died several days later.

12 > William Wilding had a general architecture practice specializing in churches. Born in the Belgian Congo in 1927, he was educated in Glasgow and worked for a few years in the early 1950s with McCarter & Nairne before going out on his own. Denman Place, the 1968 hotel, cinema and mall complex on Comox Street, is his major local landmark (with Norman Jones).

13 > Robert Ross McKee, senior partner of McKee & Gray architects and engineers, was a Vancouver native—a rarity among the group of architects and engineers whose designs transformed the postwar city. Born in 1914, he received a Bachelor of Architecture from the University of Washington in 1938 with honours in design. He travelled extensively in Europe in 1953–4, doing work on prefabricated housing. He is remembered for the starkly modernist Granville Chapel on Granville Street at 43rd Avenue, built for the Plymouth Brethren in 1948–9. His firm also designed and engineered the distinctive SuperValu stores that were once quite common in the city, and technically advanced as their glue-laminated arches required no internal columns to assist in holding up the structure. One survivor is now a Value Village on Victoria Drive at 48th Avenue; a period interior photo of a SuperValu store is on page 75. He died in West Vancouver in 1986.

Hooper. In Vancouver his early work included the renowned Marine Building, the Medical-Dental Building (demolished) and the BC Telephone Company building. During the war he headed the Federal Housing Program in British Columbia and from 1951 until 1953 served as a director of Central Mortgage & Housing Corporation. His firm had the best connections to the conservative architectural taste of the Eastern banking establishment, yet it managed to construct modernist buildings on Granville Street in the late 1950s, for the Toronto Dominion Bank at Pender (now a Pharmasave) and the Canadian Imperial Bank of Commerce at Dunsmuir (now a Shoppers Drug Mart). The huge main post office on West Georgia Street is another of his firm's 1950s designs. He died in Victoria in 1981.

8 > C.B.K. Van Norman, born in 1907, was another architecture graduate from the University of Manitoba who moved west. He established his practice in Vancouver in 1933, specializing in fine residences that simplified traditional styles such as the Cape Cod, and obtained large commissions, including one for work on the Powell River townsite. He "developed a wide reputation for progressive architecture," according to his *Who's Who* entry, experimenting with modernism at an early period. His later work included a shopping centre (Park Royal), modernist office buildings (the Customs House and the Burrard Building) and Corbusian phalanxes of high-rises, such as Beach Towers on English Bay. He died in Vancouver in 1975.

9 > Ross Anthony Lort, born in Birmingham, England, in 1889, apprenticed with the architect Samuel Maclure. He worked in a variety of styles, including modernism, on the Vancouver International Airport (now the South Terminal) and the reworked facade of the original Vancouver Art Gallery on West Georgia (demolished). He died in Vancouver in 1968.

The operation was a success but the patient died. After $353 million of investment, the Woodward's department store that was "saved" is a relic "like a jewel box," as heritage commission chair Richard Keate described the only retained façades of the 1906 section at Hastings and Abbott. The city got so swept up in the rhetoric around the development project that it threw away its own rule book, demolishing most of a reusable building. All this happened in the era of sustainability, of reuse and recycle, of Vancouver's aspirations to green leadership.

From other points of view, Woodward's is probably more of a success story. A little social housing has been mixed into a flashy new market development; dramatic new architecture has been created; a much-needed contemporary arts school has been added to the desperately poor Downtown Eastside. As a cautionary tale, however, Woodward's shows what can happen when a developer tries to ride a number of horses at once.

For almost 20 years through every stripe of council, an informal policy kept the Victory Square buildings, especially the remarkable Dominion Building at Hastings and Cambie, pre-eminent in their little patch on the edge of downtown. New construction was to be comparatively low rise, subservient to fine historic edifices like the Carter-Cotton (Province) and the World (Sun Tower) buildings. Instead, a condominium tower now towers—there's no better word for it—over the historic neighbourhood.

In the 1980s Woodward's was the middle-class bulwark against the increasingly troubled Skid Row, then being renamed the Downtown Eastside. The firm had spread itself widely across BC and Alberta and, along the way, lost control of the land its stores sat on as it raised money for expansion. One shrewd real-estate hand, former mayor and developer Tom Campbell, predicted privately that it was a strategy for disaster.[*] When the chain went bankrupt in 1993 and was sold to The Bay, the Hastings Street store was closed for good rather than rebranded as a Bay (or Zellers) outlet.

There appeared to be little value in that kind of department-store retail in that part of town. A few blocks west, Sears had been unable to make its Harbour Centre makeover of the old Eaton's store work and gave it up to SFU in 1990. Into the Woodward's vacuum moved the increasingly radical homeless community, which began to see the building's shell as a social housing solution, an expectation that increased as the '90s progressed. The Fama proposal in 1995 for mixed housing came to grief because of neighbourhood opposition, at which time governments began to get involved, with the province eventually purchasing the site for $22 million in 2001. Shortly after the Liberal government took office, it put the project on hold. Then, in the summer of 2002, a private developer optioned the site with a proposal that it said would respect the heritage designation and provide 417 market rental units. The neighbourhood didn't agree, and people occupied the site with a tent city under the store's marquee, an action that became legendary as the "Woodward's Squat."

The following March, under its new, left-leaning council, the city bought the

The Woodward's "W-43" tower looms above Number 81—that is, the 81st building connected to the city water system, at 322 Cambie Street. Built in 1888, two years after the city's incorporation, its hexagonal corner turret is like a refugee from San Francisco. Its builder, James Ford Garden, a Dominion land surveyor, served as mayor from 1898 to 1900 and as an MLA from 1900 to 1909. He is the namesake of Garden Drive and Garden Park in East Vancouver.

---

[*]   Campbell, speaking in the 1980s with Gordon Wyness of the James Inglis Reid store (page 68), a neighbour of Campbell's head office building. Campbell repeated his opinion to me when I interviewed him in 2001.

A detail of a watercolour from 1989, looking past the Arco Hotel on Pender Street to the Woodward's store and its W tower on Hastings, back in the days when the W was the tallest object east of downtown. The Arco, like the Dunsmuir on page 41, is one of the 24 SROS (single room occupancy hotels) bought by the provincial government since 2007 to try to stabilize the supply of affordable housing. One recent high-quality renovation nearby was the turreted Pennsylvania Hotel at Carrall and Hastings, reopened with 44 small apartments in 2009. All the hotels are operated by non-profit societies.

Woodward's building from the province for about $5 million and began the process that ultimately led to redevelopment. The proposal by Westbank Projects/Peterson Investment Group and architect Gregory Henriquez won out over competing ones from Millennium and Concert/Holborn. Using his most enticing slogan to date, "condo king" Bob Rennie marketed the tower in the spring of 2006 with the headline "Be Bold or Move to the Suburbs." In the ensuing stampede, the building sold out in 24 hours. The demolition occurred on the last day of September.

The new 43-storey W tower, on Cordova near the Cambie end of the block, is a dramatic flatiron that references the Europe Hotel a few blocks to the east and, in its colour scheme, the 12-storey Dominion Building a block away. It is a beautiful building to those who like to look at architecture in isolation, but it blows the scale of Victory Square and Gastown to the wind. Its postmodernist mimicry is reminiscent of that *enfant terrible* of 20 years ago: Cathedral Place, on the site of the Medical-Dental Building on Georgia Street, a pastiche that included copies of the nurses from the old building's parapets and a deconstructed green-painted pyramid roof similar to the weathered copper one on the Hotel Vancouver across the street. But while Cathedral Place is only slightly taller than the buildings that surround it, "W-43" positively looms.

The south face of the W tower borders a pathway that narrows to a courtyard framed on the other side by SFU's new facilities. The ensemble accomplished what few city projects have managed since the heyday of malls like Pacific Centre: it created an internal street more attractive than the two streets that were supposed to be rejuvenated—Hastings to the south, Cordova to the north. The whole development turns inward.

As with the design for Pacific Centre/Eaton's, the Woodward's design reinforces its inward turn by presenting a doorless expanse of sidewalk. A wall runs about 175 feet along Hastings—seven times the 25-foot width of a typical storefront on a typically successful downtown street.* Glimpses through small windows at the shelves of London Drugs and a selection of posters that romanticize the old department store in its prime are all that is offered to the Hastings Street pedestrian.

Unlike Woodward's itself, which had two entrances on its Hastings frontage and constantly changing window displays, London Drugs has one entrance, accessible only from the courtyard, not from Hastings. Perhaps, at the moment, few mom-and-pop businesses would have taken up a boutique there and animated the street. Only a Subway takeout lights that long stretch of sidewalk. The doorway into SFU is locked, with a sign saying PLEASE USE CORDOVA STREET ENTRANCE—actually, the entrance is off the inner pathway. The entire development angles to the west, away from the mean streets. Gentrification never had such powerful symbolism.

---

*   Twenty years ago there was an uproar when the Bank of Montreal consolidated three storefronts in Chinatown at 164–70 East Pender Street. The bank was accused of deadening pedestrian activity.

EDUCATING THE SCHOOL BOARD

In feudal towns it was the baron's castle, in religious ones the church's spire or the mosque's dome, but in Vancouver neighbourhoods it's the public school that rises above the rooftops of the commoners—a fitting metaphor for a democratic society. A century ago dozens of new schools accommodated a huge influx of students, the result of migration to the city and the province's 1901 decision to make education compulsory for all children between 7 and 14.

In that long-ago time those brick school buildings were objects of pride, indicators of the city's progress and the values of its citizens. Today, things are different—every public expenditure is cheese-pared to find the most "fiscally responsible" outcome. But this parsimonious attitude is not recent—taxpayers resisted school improvements even during the prosperous 1920s, generously supporting schools again only during the baby-boom era.

The city's oldest school is Carleton Hall, the 1896 wooden building at Kingsway and Joyce, part of the three-school set that is the symbolic heart of Collingwood; in 2011, Green Thumb Theatre signed a 20-year lease with the school board and started a capital campaign to convert the school into its administrative building. The 1897 brick section of Strathcona elementary is a year newer; several blocks to the east is the first Admiral Seymour school, a fine wood-framed building from 1900.

In the boom a century ago, consulting school architect Norman Austin Leech designed nine large brick schools, using a plan he developed, with projecting end wings that could be added when extra classrooms were needed. Cecil Rhodes Elementary, now L'École Bilingue on 14th west of Oak, is a good example of this "barbell" plan.[*]

In hilly South Vancouver, a separate municipality where few grand trees were planted and the majority of houses were single storey, the schools really stood up above the landscape. Architect Joseph Henry Bowman designed a dozen of them, each with eight classrooms—four on each of the two floors—above a concrete basement, divided into girls' and boys' gyms, for use on rainy days. He had already demonstrated his ability to create standardized designs while working for the BC Mills, Timber & Trading Company from 1897 until 1908 using the firm's prefabricated wall system (page 99). Bowman's schools include Selkirk, Tecumseh, the third of the Carleton schools and the landmark Norquay Elementary, built by the McPhalen Brothers in 1912.[†]

Architects Perry & Fowler designed the city's Old People's Home on the remote eastern edge of the city, on Boundary Road, in 1915. It shared a tract of a government reserve with the Provincial Industrial School for Girls, now part of a condominium development at 868 Cassiar Street. No doubt its Tudor style would have evoked visions of the Old Country for many of its aged British-Canadian residents. It was renamed Taylor Manor in 1946 in honour of former mayor Louis D. Taylor, who served eight terms in office but died in poverty that year. Although it is a designated heritage building, with a bronze plaque near its front door, it has fallen into disrepair since 1998, when its residents were moved next door into the new Adanac Park Lodge.

---

[*]   The essay by Commonwealth Historic Resource Management Ltd., "Schools Heritage Value Final Report, March 2008," available online, is an excellent overview of school development in the city, including the shifting policies toward open, experimental, formal and traditional classroom environments.

[†]   "Joseph Henry Bowman" by Jim Wolf in Luxton, ed., *Building the West: The Early Architects of British Columbia*, p. 166, and Vancouver building permit registers. Bowman was also school architect for Burnaby.

At the site of Sexsmith Elementary School on Ontario at 59th, Bowman first designed a one-room wooden building in 1912, then a brick building a year later to accommodate the exploding population. A replacement school has recently been built on its playground and the old schools have been abandoned.

Townley & Matheson, architects of City Hall, designed the last school on the West Side before Point Grey amalgamated with Vancouver in 1929—Point Grey Junior High School in Kerrisdale. Its style is Collegiate Gothic and its corner towers were meant to evoke Oxford's "dreaming spires." To our fevered childhood imaginations—I was a student at the school—they were guard towers and proof the school had been designed by a prison architect. The fact that the school remained open despite the devastation of Typhoon Frieda in October 1962—the only school, we believed, where children didn't get an unscheduled holiday—just added to its legend.

Many of the Lower Mainland's schools, including 90 of the 109 in Vancouver, were built before 1967, when seismic requirements were first introduced into the building code. Now, the average age of Vancouver's schools is 67 years. The province conducted a seismic survey of all BC schools in 2004 and subsequently committed $1.5 billion over 15 years to make them earthquake safe.

According to the school board's website, "heritage value is one of several criteria that [it] considers when seismically upgrading or replacing school facilities. Other important criteria include consideration of life safety, building life-cycle costs, education program requirements, and overall project costs." On the surface a suitably responsible statement, it nevertheless is vague enough to allow the board to act in any way it sees fit. "Education program requirements" is one particular time bomb. How else to explain the construction of a new school in place of the fine, well-maintained 1924 Lord Kitchener at King Edward and Blenheim? The demolition of Charles Dickens Elementary followed a similarly fluid interpretation of "overall project costs." Another mystery for the newer schools is "building life-cycle costs"—little False Creek Elementary, for example, has needed to be renovated twice at a cost of $2 million since its construction in 1977.[*]

Between 1996 and 2011, with capital funding provided by the Ministry of Education, the Vancouver School Board completed 28 major capital projects, including 20 full seismic upgrades and three partial seismic upgrades to existing buildings, three replacement schools and two new schools. Cheaply assembled frame replacement schools are considered equal, by some in the public and in the school board, to the neighbourhood landmarks. This is a disposable society, not one where investments are protected by regular maintenance. Declining enrollment in East Side schools is another reason cited for non-investment, a problem exacerbated by parents moving their children into crowded West Side schools in the belief they'll get a better education there.

Kitsilano High School's fate may be similar to that of Magee, demolished nearly 20 years ago once a replacement school rose on its back field. A combination of community consultation and bean-counting appears to have led the school board to the

*   See "Is your old school about to be demolished? Lessons to be learned from Charles Dickens Elementary in Vancouver," by Noel Herron, *BCTF Newsmagazine*, April 2009.

conclusion that its "heritage revitalization," as consultants described it, could consist of the demolition of everything except its 1927 façade. As Humpty Dumpty said to Alice, "When I use a word it means just what I choose it to mean," which seems to work even for a school board.

FOR WHOM THE BRIDGE TOLLS

Greater Vancouver is one of the more bridge-dependent, geographically challenged regions in the world. A major river with islands, an expansive harbour and a "false creek" have combined to make bridge-building (and -bitching) a major local pastime.

The city's earliest bridges were trestles across False Creek connecting the Gastown area with roads to New Westminster and the farms of the Fraser River delta. Bridges from Yaletown across False Creek and across the north arm of the Fraser to Sea Island were completed in 1889 and a direct road, now Granville Street, was cleared through the forest to link them. A swingspan bridge, finished in 1909, replaced the first Granville Bridge and survived until the modern one was completed in 1954.

The Pattullo Bridge, built during the Depression by the provincial Liberal government and named for the premier in 1937, was the first bridge of the automobile age.

Public schools (in this case Seymour Elementary in the Kiwassa neighbourhood east of Strathcona) are the neighbourhood landmarks, standing high above both cottages and mansions and offering, in theory, a path to a successful future regardless of the circumstances of one's birth. Seymour Elementary, built in 1907, stands in front of an earlier 1900 wooden school; multiple school buildings on a single site are common in Vancouver, reflecting the rapid population growth of a century ago. The brick Seymour Elementary's twin is Lord Roberts school in the West End. Architect William T. Whiteway is best known in the city for designing Louis D. Taylor's World Building, a.k.a the Sun Tower.

A postcard photo from about 1954, taken from the southern end of the Kitsilano Trestle. The new Granville Bridge was in use but the old, 1909 one was not yet demolished. Twenty years later, in the 1970s, industrial Granville Island began its transition to a retail and entertainment zone (compare the middle photo on page 63). The low, green-roofed building, Wright's Ropes, became the public market; the buff-coloured building, Arrow Transfer, became Bridges Restaurant. (PHOTO BY J. C. WALKER)

It kick-started the sprawling development of North Delta and Surrey and gave New Westminster's shopkeepers a golden age that ended in the 1960s with the opening of the freeway. As the Pattullo is badly congested and its narrow lanes have been the scene of a number of deadly head-on crashes, TransLink announced in 2010 that it will be replaced by a six-lane bridge, possibly funded with tolls. At this writing in 2011, options for refurbishing the bridge are also under consideration.

A year after the Pattullo opened, a Guinness-financed company completed the Lions Gate Bridge to connect the city with its British Properties subdivision on the slopes of Hollyburn Mountain. The most elegant bridge north of San Francisco's Golden Gate, it only needed two lanes until automotive mobility really got going in the 1950s and a narrow third one was squeezed in.

The Social Credit government's first budget in February 1953 created a Crown corporation called the Toll Highways and Bridges Authority for capital projects in the province. The Socreds had been elected on a policy of "pay as you go" and a promise to reduce debt. Under the new minister of highways, flamboyant Kamloops Pentecostal minister Phil Gaglardi, 1955 became the "Year of Bridges" for the region. The province started work on the Second Narrows and Oak Street bridges plus Highway 99 and the south arm crossing that became George Massey Tunnel, and purchased the Lions Gate Bridge that year as well.

Motorists were as enthusiastic about tolls a half century ago as they are today. For example, in June 1957, following the decommissioning of the old Marpole Bridge, motorists attempting to dodge the 25-cent toll on the new Oak Street Bridge took the rickety crossing over Mitchell Island and jammed traffic on Fraser Street all the way north to 30th Avenue. Tolls were removed from Oak Street in 1959.

The bridge at Second Narrows replaced a road-rail toll crossing dating from 1925. The new bridge opened in 1960 and is notorious for its collapse during construction on June 17, 1958, when 18 workers were killed. Its recent name, Ironworkers Memorial Second Narrows Crossing, dates from 1994. Together with the 1954 Granville Bridge,

Two hand-tinted postcards from about 1938, when the Lions Gate Bridge opened, before any clearing had begun on the bridge's raison d'être: the British Properties subdivision on the slopes of Hollyburn Mountain above the old, ferry-dependent community of Ambleside. During the Great Depression, the bridge provided work for all manner of Vancouverites, including the impoverished sculptor Charles Marega, whose twin concrete lions turned out to be his last commission. He died the following spring.
(GOWEN, SUTTON CO. LTD. POSTCARD)

it is the only piece of infrastructure from that era in the Lower Mainland that hasn't become hopelessly choked with traffic.

The remaining tolls on the province's bridges disappeared just before the 1963 election. Thus unleashed, with no user-pay system to constrain them, commuters accelerated their march across the fields and farms of the Fraser delta, thwarted only by the creation of the Agricultural Land Reserve in the early 1970s. The symbol of that unconstrained time is the elegant Port Mann Bridge, opened in 1964 along with the freeway through Burnaby that connected Vancouver with new subdivisions in Guildford, Fleetwood, Langley and beyond. "Flying Phil" Gaglardi, renowned for his high-speed driving, thought the bridge so perfectly engineered that he briefly proposed an 80-mile-per-hour speed limit. So rapid was the urban sprawling, however, that the bridge and its various interchanges have been plugged solid for decades, with an average speed during rush hour of more like 20 miles per hour, in spite of lanes for high-occupancy vehicles added a dozen years ago.

"... A weekly pass would be a better buy ... in the event of mass evacuation due to nuclear attack it would help us to provide speedier passage ..."

THE VANCOUVER SUN

January 27, 1956

One of the myriad cartoons by Len Norris of the *Vancouver Sun* in the 1950s and 1960s about the Lions Gate Bridge, its congestion and its tolls. Norris, a West Vancouver resident, would have used the bridge every day to go to work. He retired in 1988 and died in 1997.

(USED WITH PERMISSION)

The Port Mann Bridge, like the Pattullo, is a tied arch—an inverted suspension bridge. The Knight Street Bridge of 1974 is a balanced cantilever.[*] All the new bridges on the Fraser, including the Golden Ears (tolled), the deftly named Alex Fraser, the SkyTrain bridges at New Westminster and Brighouse, the new Port Mann and the Pattullo replacement are cable-stayed.[†] While the Alex Fraser and the New Westminster SkyTrain are quite elegant in their way, none of the others will be finalists in a beauty contest. Perhaps form really does follow function in the brutal fiscal world of the 21st century. At least one bridge will be a record-holder: the new Port Mann Bridge, at 50 metres, will be the widest long-span bridge in the world, eclipsing the 80-year-old record holder, the Sydney Harbour Bridge.

By the 1990s the Lions Gate Bridge had been congested for nearly 40 years and seemed doomed. But just when the provincial government decided it had no money to put into a new crossing, Vancouver arrived at a consensus that there were too many cars going through the downtown anyway.

Visitors to the city still say, "Yes, the Lions Gate Bridge is beautiful, but what about the future?" Evidence of Vancouver's changing nature emerged in the Burrard Bridge bike lane trials of 1996 and 2009. During the first trial, abandoned after a week, traffic backed up into Kitsilano and sardined bus riders along with drivers. By the time of the second one, enough changes had been made to automobile and transit routes that there was little congestion. Traffic on the Burrard Bridge declined to levels of the placid '70s.

When tolls get established on the new bridges, and perhaps reinstated on the old ones, almost exactly a half century of free motoring in the Vancouver region will end. That's one of the few things where there's unanimity in BC politics: a return to the Socreds' "pay as you go," now expressed as "user pay."

---

[*]   Harris, "Bridges of Greater Vancouver" in Davis, ed., p. 212.

[†]   Technically, according to Wikipedia, the Golden Ears bridge and new Canada Line bridge to Richmond are extradosed bridges rather than cable-stayed ones.

TOP > The Pattullo Bridge's completion in 1937 ushered in a prosperous era for the shopkeepers along New Westminster's Columbia Street. Mobile suburbanites in the newly opened subdivisions of Surrey were able to travel quickly to the City Market and cinemas, which had opened in the 1920s. (FOLKARD COMPANY, MONTREAL, CIRCA 1950)

MIDDLE > The Ironworkers Memorial Second Narrows Crossing, as it is now called, just after its opening in 1960. Tolls remained on many Lower Mainland bridges until shortly before the 1963 election. The following year, the provincial government completed the Highway 1 freeway along Vancouver's eastern edge, through Burnaby and Coquitlam and across the Fraser River at Port Mann. Until 1992 and the completion of the Cassiar Connector tunnel, traffic from the freeway used Cassiar Street and crossed Hastings Street at a traffic light before continuing onto the bridge. (PHOTO BY ROLLY FORD)

BOTTOM > The unfettered route of the commuting suburbanite, as it was in the 1960s, shortly after the Port Mann Bridge and freeway linked Vancouver seamlessly with the Fraser Valley. Most of the foreground's sylvan scene is occupied today by the Cape Horn Interchange, a spaghetti tangle of roads and ramps connecting United Boulevard and Lougheed Highway with the new Port Mann Bridge, part of the provincial government's Gateway Project. The project will reintroduce tolls to the main highway system for the first time in a half century, and guarantee a car-captive future for the next half century. (PHOTO BY H.D. VON TIESENHAUSEN)

WORKING HARBOUR

V ANCOUVER BECAME A SIGNIFICANT CITY NOT BECAUSE OF ITS "WEST Coast lifestyle" or "Vancouverism"—both recent inventions—but because of its location. Pacific Ocean access, a spacious and ice-free harbour, enough serviceable land for industry and proximity to the international border—a commercially strategic counterbalance to Seattle—all helped make it grow. The Canadian Pacific Railway (CPR) used Vancouver as a hub of its globe-spanning transportation system, and even the American company that was the CPR's archrival, the Great Northern Railway, had no trouble finding Canadian partners who would run a spur line from the city to the international border.[*]

At the beginning of European settlement in the 1860s, proximity to raw materials made the Burrard Inlet shoreline profitable. Immensely valuable stands of Douglas fir and cedar were cut down, skidded to tidewater and floated to the sawmills, emerging as some of the best building timber the world has ever seen. In that respect, Burrard Inlet was little different from the myriad coves, fjords and river mouths between Oregon and Alaska. Ships loaded shingles, boards and Vancouver toothpicks, as the big beams were called, and delivered them to customers as far afield as Australia and China.

When the railway arrived in 1887 a real city quickly replaced the logging camps, fishing camps, saloons and shacks that had popped up and burnt down during the

A CPR liner, probably the *Empress of Asia*, returning from the Far East and steaming past Brockton Point, about 1920. Passengers would disembark and could easily remain in the CPR's system, either boarding a transcontinental train to connect with eastern Canada and Britain or staying at the Hotel Vancouver at Georgia and Granville. (GOWEN, SUTTON CO. LTD. POSTCARD)

---

[*]   See *Vancouver Remembered*, p. 61 and 104–5.

previous 20 years. The pace of logging accelerated to meet the huge demands of settlement all across the Canadian West, and one can imagine a tree on what was to become a Vancouver city lot being felled, skidded out, sawn up, loaded onto a wagon, hauled by horses back to exactly the same spot where it had been cut, then reassembled into a house. From the tree's point of view, should it have had one, the outcome might have been acceptable.

The other mills along the early waterfront were canneries, with salmon the other resource. The technique of vacuum-sealing food into tin cans was little more than a decade old when the first cannery opened at Annieville, near the south end of the Alex Fraser Bridge, in the 1870s.

In the years since, Vancouver has managed to develop an excellent separation between working harbour (Burrard Inlet east of Lions Gate Bridge) and pleasure harbour (English Bay, dotted with sailboats moving among the anchored freighters). The CPR's intention to build ocean docks on Kitsilano Point, and the Vancouver Harbour and Dock Extension Company's dream of industrializing the western ends of Sea and Lulu islands, came to naught a century ago. The recent expansion of Port Metro Vancouver, as it is now called, has occurred along the south arm of the Fraser River and at Deltaport near the Tsawwassen ferry terminal. Unfortunately, due to security issues in the wake of 9/11, there is now an almost complete separation between the port and the citizens as well.

Nevertheless, this working harbour and adjoining industrial lands, and the determination of all levels of government to keep them intact, make Vancouver a real city rather than a recreational one. Real cities create a wider range of occupations than cities that allow the real-estate market to determine "highest and best use." Left unanswered, however, is the question of whether many Vancouverites can find affordable

As if at a seance, Young Vancouver gazes into a crystal ball and contemplates . . . future port facilities! Artist "Bundy" illustrated the industrial complex promoted by Charles Fenn Pretty's Vancouver Harbour and Dock Extension Company, intended to occupy the western ends of Sea and Lulu islands a century ago, for the *Point Grey Gazette*. However, by the time the illustration was published, in the June 14, 1913, edition of the paper, the boom was over and the idea never resurfaced. Sea Island became Vancouver International Airport once commercial aviation was invented and the western end of Lulu Island became subdivisions, a golf course and parkland, separated by a dyke from the Fraser delta's environmentally sensitive wetlands.

homes near their work.* A newcomer could be excused for wondering, apropos of the condo and property boom of recent years, whether any Vancouverites have real jobs and instead just buy and sell real estate.

According to conventional wisdom, western Canadians export raw materials and import manufactured goods, a variation on the old adage of selling cheap and buying dear. Indeed, Vancouver has never been much of a manufacturing town. Bulk cargos of grain, woodchips, coal and sulphur leave the port, and containers full of consumer goods arrive from countries such as China and head eastbound on trains.

The opening of the Panama Canal in 1914 created a new route for prairie grain destined for Europe—now it could be moved westward and shipped from Vancouver. Member of Parliament Harry H. Stevens convinced his Conservative colleagues in the Borden government to build LaPointe Pier and the Dominion Number One grain elevator at the foot of Salsbury Drive. When, due to the war, it was briefly unused and unprofitable it was dubbed "Stevens' Folly." Now called the Pacific Elevators terminal, it is owned by Viterra (the new name for Saskatchewan Wheat Pool), as is the Cascadia Terminal near Second Narrows Bridge. A second grain elevator was built, by the National Harbours Board, on the east side of Ballantyne Pier near the foot of Heatley Street. Ballantyne Pier is now used for overflow cruise ships—the ones that won't fit at Canada Place.

Benjamin Tingley Rogers, clowning with two "savages," as his wife described them in a family photo album, during a sugar-buying trip to Fiji in 1895. (COLLECTION OF GUDEWILL FAMILY)

ONLY A FEW BUSINESSES IMPORTED RAW MATERIALS OTHER THAN logs for processing. One example that comes to mind is the BC Sugar Refinery, extant on the waterfront west of Clark Drive after 120 years. In 1890, Benjamin Tingley Rogers, who was only 25, negotiated tax concessions and a free supply of water for several years, as well as a bonus from the infant city in return for establishing the refinery. He also married Mary Isabella Angus, the niece of the president of the Bank of Montreal, who was also a director of the CPR.

A secure supply of cane was Rogers's major problem. Two of his sugar-carrying sailing ships were lost in 1893; another, the *Cambusdoon*, left Java bound for Vancouver in 1895 and spent 98 days becalmed on one tack in the Pacific, eventually arriving after 182 days. That year, following the "sugar war" with R.P. Rithet & Co. of Victoria, who were agents of Butterfield & Swire in Hong Kong, Rogers and his wife boarded an Empress liner headed for Asia and the South Pacific. He was 30, she 26.

---

* An interesting contrast is Sydney, Australia, about twice the size of Vancouver, where freighters have been banished from its famous harbour and relocated south to Botany Bay. Sydney Harbour is now pleasure boats from one end to the other, interspersed with passenger ferries and the occasional cruise ship. Most of its industrial heritage, including magnificent wool sheds and factories, has been replaced by tourist-oriented entertainment areas and condos.

After four months, and visits to Saigon, Singapore, Fiji and Australia, he ordered a supply of sugar and returned to Vancouver.

A similar trip in 1900 through the South Seas brought Rogers no closer to a stable source of sugar. In 1905, he travelled to Fiji with his assistant J.W. Fordham-Johnson, later the province's lieutenant governor, to acquire a plantation where he could grow his own cane. Run by the Vancouver-Fiji Sugar Company, the plantation became a little patch of colonialism he controlled from Vancouver, with indentured Indian labourers, dormitories, a hospital and a home for the resident manager. Although financially successful, it endured personnel problems reminiscent of those of the characters in Somerset Maugham short stories. In 1924, BC Sugar disposed of all its assets in the Fiji Islands, replacing them with sugar-beet farms in Alberta and, eventually, a plantation and mill in the Dominican Republic.* In 2008, Lantic Sugar Limited and Rogers Sugar Ltd. merged to form Lantic Inc., but sugar in British Columbia still bears the Rogers name.

The Rogers family *business* story alone would make a good TV miniseries or blockbuster novel. B.T.R., as he was known, lived his life at about twice the pace of an average man, amassing a great fortune but dying at age 53 in 1918 of a cerebral hemorrhage.† Taking over was his eldest son, Blythe, who himself soon died when his heart, weakened following a military accident, failed.‡ Second son Ernest ran the company brilliantly until he drowned while yachting near Pender Harbour in 1939. Third son Philip expanded the refinery to meet wartime demand but his control ended prematurely due to alcoholism. Only the fourth son, Forrest, ran the company through to

The harbour, photographed between 1938 (when Pier D at the foot of Granville Street burned) and 1954 (when the Customs House, one of the early modernist buildings in the city, rose on the corner of Burrard and Pender, just to the right of the Marine Building; bottom left in the photo). The balance visible between freight and passenger traffic in the harbour still exists today. Pier B-C, with the berthed liner, evolved into the Canada Place convention centre and, in season, the cruise ship terminal. Both freight and passengers—today, just on the West Coast Express commuter trains—use the CPR tracks to the east. In the distance, some of the finger piers still exist but, in recent years, two container terminals, Centerm and Vanterm, have reclaimed much of the shoreline between them; their giant orange gantries dwarf everything else in the contemporary port. Since this picture was taken, construction along the water's edge has left the Marine Building high and dry behind a new convention centre and high-rise buildings. (GOWEN SUTTON CO. LTD)

---

*   See Schreiner, pp. 38–43.

†   Rogers was the second-wealthiest BC businessman to die in the era before 1940, leaving net assets of $1.24 million. Only newspaper publisher Walter Nichol had more—nearly $2.8 million. See McDonald, *Making Vancouver*, p. 135.

‡   The Blythe Rogers inheritance, through his widow, Alix, ended up benefiting the musical community as the Alix Goolden Performance Hall in Victoria.

A VERITABLE SEA OF VOLKSWAGENS UNLOADS AT NATIONAL HARBOURS BOARD DOCK—a photograph by Clyde Herrington in *Industrial British Columbia*, published in 1965. Since then, the port has expanded vastly beyond its historic Burrard Inlet base. Wallenius Wilhemsen Logistics and Fraser Wharves, both on the south arm of the Fraser River, handle automobile shipments into the port today.

a normal retirement age before handing it over in 1973 to his nephew, Peter Cherniavsky, the last member of the family to assume the presidency.

B.T.R.'s widow, known even to her close friends as Mrs. Rogers, buried three of her four sons, served for generations on the refinery board and wrote a history of the company when she was in her late eighties. She was a noted patron of the arts in Vancouver, helping to found the art gallery and supporting the symphony until her death at the age of 96 in 1965. Two of the three homes they built, Gabriola on Davie Street and Shannon on Granville Street (page 170), survive.

Stories concocted about B.T.R. have a way of becoming urban legend. One recent one reported in the *Vancouver Sun* concerned an alleged tunnel between his Gabriola mansion and Maxine's, the little Spanish colonial nightclub at Bidwell and Davie that had been a "beauty school, boarding house, brothel, restaurant, cabaret and gangster hideout," to "allow him private access to his favorite girls."[*] The club dated from 1936, which was 18 years after Rogers's death and a decade after his widow moved to Shannon.

Another B.T.R. "sighting" came in an email to me in 2010:

> *My in-laws purchased a property several years ago [near] the Pacific Truck Border Crossing. According to a previous owner who lived in it for 30 years, the house was originally built by B.T. Rogers as a hunting and fishing lodge. The property backs onto the Little Campbell River and was built in 1914.*

[*]   Randy Shore, writing about Maxine's on December 7, 2009, quoted and refuted the story.

Apparently, during Prohibition, Rogers used this as a roadhouse to distribute liquor to the US.

In reality, Rogers died three years before Prohibition began in the United States and never had a lodge anywhere, preferring his yacht.

ANOTHER IMPORTER AND PROCESSOR OF THE 1940S AND 1950S WAS as equally colourful as Rogers. Australian Sir Walter Randolph Carpenter operated his company from a small peninsula the Aboriginals had called Kumkumalay, at the foot of Dunlevy Street. This was the city's first industrial site, where the lumber mill Hastings Mill operated from 1865 until its closure and demolition in 1928. Although a shacktown on the site housed some homeless men for a time during the Great Depression, nothing substantial happened there until Carpenter chose it for a copra mill. It had wharves for unloading and a rail spur, connected to the CPR mainline, for shipping to the North American market.

Born in Singapore in 1877, Carpenter had American parents who were trading in Australasia when their activities were constrained by the Civil War. According to the *Australian Dictionary of Biography*,

> *When World War I began Carpenter realized the importance of copra in making munitions and for food, and bought it wherever he could find it and raise credit, chartering "almost anything that would float," including an old sailing ship, to get it to England. He took enormous risks but made huge profits and was ideally placed to expand into New Guinea after the Australian government had expropriated German property.*

Carpenter's company came to control much of the copra trade in the South Seas. He was a tough competitor—it was said his initials stood for "Would Rob Christ"—yet he was knighted in 1936, during the Depression, for his philanthropic work.

However, he was by then becoming suspicious of Australia's "socialist trends" and worried about the country's ability to defend itself. By the time war broke out he had transferred most of his capital out of the country. When his ships and airplanes were

A section of a 1940s-era, accordion-style promotional handout by BC Packers, telling children a rather grisly tale of a family of friendly singing salmon who were chopped up and cooked in a can.

The Marine View Cafe at the Campbell Avenue fishermen's wharf was one of the handful of places on the waterfront where a "civilian" could sit and observe the working harbour. I spent a morning there painting in October 1989—dutifully including the top of the ketchup bottle and the ashtray—the month before the café moved to the refurbished American Can Company buildings on Alexander Street.

commandeered by the British and Australian governments he was able to continue business only once he bought two freighters in the US. He chose Vancouver for his new mill to process copra from Fiji, then a British colony not occupied by the Japanese army, and settled permanently in Vancouver in 1941. He briefly leased the Hollies on The Crescent before moving into the Banffshire Apartments on Jervis. In 1948 he and his wife took out Canadian citizenship.

His primary business was shipping; he purchased six naval supply ships in 1946 and began a passenger and cargo service connecting Vancouver with Hong Kong and Australasia. The *Lakemba*, *Rabaul* and *Suva* were three of his ships. He ran the copra plant through another company, BC Vegetable Oils Ltd., and for a time was a significant player on the city's waterfront. However, he died suddenly while on a visit to Sydney in 1954 and was buried there. Evidence of his activities here quickly disappeared.

The historic peninsula evolved into a container terminal, an evolution in goods handling that has transformed the look of the port. Today known as Centerm, the site covers 75 acres with two berths and six huge cranes. It is a near-twin in shape and capacity to its neighbour, TSI Vanterm, which stretches from Clark to Commercial. Terminal Systems Inc., a wholly owned subsidiary of the Ontario Teachers' Pension Plan, ships oils from the controversial West Coast Reduction plant that occupies a corner of its own site at the foot of Commercial—the plant is controversial because of the odour, best described as rotting flesh, which escapes that industrial enclave and wafts through neighbourhoods near and far on hot days.

There is still marginal housing between Hastings Street and the port—illegal rooming houses and derelict apartment buildings, the kind of places that catch fire with tragic consequences, as one did on Pandora Street in the winter of 2010. However, parts of Grandview and Hastings-Sunrise to the south and east have become quite upscale in the past couple of decades, with homeowners fixing up and painting

Salmon Fishing on the Fraser River, B.C.
"Gathering the Harvest from the Deep."

TOP > On the Fraser River a century ago, round-bottomed Columbia River boats were a safer and more popular design than flat-bottomed Fraser River boats. The fisherman and boat-puller (oarsman) started work at six on Sunday evening and usually spent the following six days on board, cooking and sleeping under a tarp. The boats were worth about $70 but could be rented from canneries for $15 to $20 a year; the most expensive item was the gillnet, worth $118 in the early 1900s. Over half the fishermen were Japanese—for the years 1903 to 1908 their average profit was $92 a season. (Yesaki, p. 15–6). (JOHN VALENTINE & SONS POSTCARD)

MIDDLE > False Creek in 1982, looking down from Burrard Bridge onto the fisherman's wharf established in the 1960s on the site of Sun'ahk, the Aboriginal village. On the left is the Kitsilano Trestle, used by the CPR and the BC Electric Railway Company's interurbans and streetcars for almost a century; it was removed in time for Expo '86 and the "yachtification" of False Creek. After 1913, when the Squamish people were expelled from their reserve, the shoreline became home to a disparate community of shack- and houseboat-dwellers. Another group occupied a piece of shoreline east of the Cambie bridge; a third used an inlet on False Creek's north shore, at Columbia Street. Some of the "shackers" were able to use taps on adjacent property and obtain electricity, which they often shared with their neighbours. Waste disposal, water pollution and fire were the biggest hazards. In 1937, on False Creek, there were 108 boats on the water and 18 shacks, home to 167 adults and 21 children. Nearly 550 people lived in 56 shacks and 93 houseboats on Burrard Inlet, including a community on Coal Harbour which was dubbed the "Shaughnessy of the shoreline." (Wade, p. 50)

BOTTOM > Coal Harbour, about 1965, was still home to a portion of the local fishing fleet. Just out of sight on the left is the Bayshore Inn, whose construction kick-started the transition from industrial to residential and the eviction of the houseboaters. I wrote about the history of Coal Harbour in *Vancouver Remembered*, p. 134–8. (PHOTO BY DAN PROPP)

The view from the pedestrian overpass at Keefer Street onto the CNR tracks—the connector between Burrard Inlet and False Creek—looking south toward the old frame houses that line East Georgia Street. Blackberry bushes swarm across every available patch of land. A perusal of city directories confirms the mix of ethnicities in the area—in the postwar years, for example, there were a lot of Eastern European and Chinese names. J. Ezak, a tapman at the Ambassador Hotel, lived in the tall weathered house with the brown roof in the 1950s; carpenter Joseph Dziuzynski and his wife, Annie, lived in the red-roofed one. The Canadian government removed citizenship and immigration restrictions from Chinese people in 1947, two years before the Communists won the civil war and refugees flooded into British-controlled Hong Kong. As it had been since the city's infancy, Strathcona was the first port of call for Vancouver's non-British immigrants.

the old houses. The port is a democratic institution, however, sharing its smells and noises equally among all income levels. There is always some intrusion—a siren, seaplanes turning to land near Canada Place, trains whistling and shunting in the middle of the night—to remind people that they live on the edge of the working harbour.

S EVERAL STRUCTURES ON VANCOUVER'S BURRARD INLET WATERFRONT have disappeared over the years. On the BC Sugar Refinery grounds, a small museum that B.T.R.'s grandson Martin Rogers put together became hard to visit due to port security and finally closed. Bud Kanke's Cannery Seafood Restaurant on Commissioner Street closed in 2010 after 39 years. Poor access—such as gates like a border crossing on the access roads—was cited as a reason.[*]

Another building that disappeared—a generation ago, long before terrorism threatened the port—was the Marine View Cafe at the Campbell Avenue fish docks. The café was on the upper floor of an ice-making building and attracted a diverse crowd for its simple, fresh seafood lunches. Back in the day, that is the 1960s, the Campbell Avenue docks were an ideal place for a student to look for a summer job, either as crew on the myriad fishing boats that loaded ice and landed their catches or in the packing plants themselves. The building was demolished in the spring of 1990. The only remnant of fishing industry left on the waterfront is the Canadian Fishing Company plant, now known as Canfisco, nestled into the cove created by the Centerm container terminal.

The Burrard Inlet part of Port Metro Vancouver was CPR land until a century ago, when a complex set of agreements allowed access to the railway rivals Canadian Northern Pacific (now CN) and Great Northern (now BNSF), whose yards and terminals used the False Creek flats and fronted onto Main Street at today's Pacific Central Station. As originally envisaged, ships were going to use a canal that followed the low-lying "canoe route" near Glen Drive (which sometimes flooded during very high tides) to get to Burrard Inlet, linking to a basin in the dredged-out False Creek flats east of Main Street. Instead, the False Creek flats were completely filled in, partly with soil from the Grandview Cut, where today's Millennium SkyTrain line travels.

The canal route instead became a rail line—the subject of the watercolour on the next page—winding picturesquely through the industrial and residential area west of Glen Drive and more or less bisecting the locus of artists' studios opened every November during the East Side Culture Crawl. Great Northern's warehouse used to stand on a dock just to the west of the Campbell Avenue fishermen's wharf; both sites are currently vacant. The Canadian Northern Pacific dock, from which its steamships served ports all the way up the coast, stood at the foot of Main Street. Today CN has waterfront yards occupying a swath of land bisected by the Heatley Street overpass west of the old BNSF dock. The CPR's N Yard occupies the land west of Columbia Street all the way to Waterfront Station.

---

[*]   See Alexandra Gill's restaurant review in the *Globe and Mail*, November 10, 2009.

THE VANCOUVER SHOP

The INDEPENDENT SHOPKEEPERS OF VANCOUVER ARE UNDER PRES-
sure as never before, struggling to survive against civic tax policy, competition from international-brand stores and suburban malls, Internet shopping and the inevitable upward pressure on real estate that threatens them every time a lease comes up for renewal. For the past couple of generations consumers have been unfettered, mobile and perhaps even disloyal, willing to spend $5 in gas to save $2 on a sticker price. Road congestion (and reduced car-ownership in some parts of town) might be forcing more people to shop locally but whether independents are benefitting is anybody's guess.

Almost forgotten in all the changes have been the individuals whose brands once inspired such loyalty: William Taylor Money and his mushrooms, Richard Carmon Purdy and his chocolates, John Murchie and his teas and coffees and the Spencers and the Woodwards and their department stores. A more recent retailer is John Hill, who moved west in the late 1940s and purchased Reid's Dry Goods at Hudson Street and Marine Drive in Marpole. In 1960, the family name went onto the former Osborne's Kerrisdale Dry Goods store on 41st Avenue, then moved across the street in 1973 to the former Woolworth's store, where it remains today. The family is more famous now for its control of two other brands: Aritzia and Blue Ruby.

One of the "character" owners from an earlier era was clothier William Dick, the fruits of whose labours appear in the chapter on gardens (see page 174). Born in Scotland in 1879, Dick arrived in Nanaimo at age nine and started in the clothing business there. In 1906 he went into business at 45 East Hastings, a strategic location a half block east of the BC Electric's interurban station, then a major crossroads for the city's commuters and shoppers. He prospered sufficiently to move west with the city's business district, buying the building on the northeast corner of Hastings and Homer.

Dick "wore a bowler, always smoked or chewed a cigar and got everything there was out of life," his long-time credit manager Jack Mowatt said.[*] "Portly, cocky and a good man to work for," he competed enthusiastically against all comers. "We specialized in an 18-ounce botany-wool navy blue serge suit that sold for 15 dollars," Mowatt recalled. "The colour was guaranteed for a year—if it faded we gave you a new suit." Men flocked to the shop for paper collars, detachable cuffs and dickies, and bought five pairs of socks for a dollar.

> [Isidore] Claman would cut the price on a line of goods and Billy would
> undercut him. Then Claman would cut again and Billy would go under

---

[*] Newspaper clippings in the Matthews collection, Vancouver Archives.

cost, just throw them away. Oh, he was a real businessman . . . we never had a barber like some of them did to give the men a haircut while the women shopped. At one point he gave away safety razors to his male customers and boxes of chocolates to the ladies.

Dick was also engaged politically, serving as Conservative Party treasurer and as an MLA in the Tolmie Conservative government that was sideswiped by the Great Depression. He was "perhaps the most liberal of his party, pressing always for social reform, larger pensions for the aged and widening the scope of the minimum wage act." Somehow he found time to wheel and deal in real estate under the name B.C. Estates Ltd. His Dick Building, an art deco gem designed by Townley & Matheson in 1928, is a landmark at the southeast corner of Broadway and Granville. But even he was bitten by the Depression, and appealed the assessments on his home at 2000 South West Marine Drive ($38,000 for the house, $24,920 for the land) and his downtown store to the court of revision in 1934.

The good life caught up with him and he died after a short illness in 1939, aged only 60. His brother Hugh took the retail business over and ran it until 1955, when huge closing-out advertisements in the papers brought mobs of customers in search of bargains. Tip Top Tailors bought the store and building and is still in business in the city, though elsewhere. The building still stands, on a part of Hastings that is beginning to reinvent itself and move upscale again.

Hastings Street about 1950, looking west toward the Dick's Men's Wear store at Homer. Isidore Claman's store, in the foreground, competed enthusiastically with Dick's and the myriad other menswear stores on the downtown streets. The streamlined tram is a PCC, named for the Presidents Conference Committee that initiated a redesign of traditional streetcars in the United States in the 1930s. (PHOTO BY J.C. WALKER)

The James Inglis Reid storefront and interior at 559 Granville in 1986, its final year of operation. The building was a four-storey, self-contained factory.

Another legendary proprietor was James Inglis Reid (no relation to the dry goods operator mentioned above). The site of his butcher shop, at 559 Granville, still evokes nostalgic smiles from carnivorous Vancouverites of a certain age. Like Dick, Reid was a Scot who came to Vancouver in 1906, becoming a general provisioner under his own name in 1908. He sold Scottish specialties in 1917 after the arrival of "Horatio" Nelson Menzies, whose sausages were soon appearing even on fine West End tables. Cured and smoked hams and bacons brought customers from all over town, as did delicacies such as head cheese, black pudding, jellied tongue and, of course, haggis for Robbie Burns Day.

Vancouver in the early years had many shops that produced what they sold, but by the mid-1980s, when I took the photographs on these pages, Reid's was a rarity. His 1902 building originally had a standard shopfront, with a separate doorway to a stairway that allowed access to two upstairs floors of offices; after he bought it in 1922 he removed the staircase, widened the retail floor and turned the building into a four-storey factory, with a curing cooler and smokehouse in the basement and a bakery and sausage kitchen on the top floor.

Gordon Wyness, married to Reid's daughter Alison, managed the business for its last four decades and, toward the end, saw how the change in shopping habits doomed his downtown location. Traditionally, on their way to the streetcar after

TOP > The retail area, with cured meat hanging from hooks along the side walls and sawdust on the floor.

MIDDLE > On the left, Bob McMillan and Gordon Wyness deboning hogs in the cutting room behind the retail area; on the right, the bakery on the third floor, the windows opening onto Granville Street.

BOTTOM > The cooler at the back of the retail area, containing the cured hams that made Reid's famous. "We have one store only," their slogan began.

work, men would pick up the meat order their wives had telephoned in, but by the 1950s people were doing less food shopping in the downtown area. The exception was visits to Woodward's, several blocks away on Hastings. Reid's didn't close in 1986 just because Pacific Centre shopping mall came knocking, consolidating property for northward expansion—its era had passed.

Alison Wyness, a nurse by training, endowed a graduate nursing scholarship at UBC in honour of her husband and her father; she died in 2000 at the age of 88. Gordon, born in Vancouver in 1912, raised in Plenty, Saskatchewan, and a mechanical engineer by training, lived on in Vancouver (across the street from the house where I grew up) until his death in 2004. I recall him saying he never liked eating chicken because it reminded him of his prairie youth.

VANCOUVER'S OLD CORNER STORES HAVE ALL BUT DISAPPEARED IN THE past 20 years. Part of their charm was the way many of them used a traditional pitched-roof house, which provided accommodation behind or upstairs with a ground-level entry like a shop on a commercial street. Others were a boxy addition occupying the front yard of an ordinary house, still others had a boomtown front. There were as many variations as there were stores.

One of the last of the city's operating corner stores, the BK Grocery, at 34th and Nanaimo, painted in 1989. As a building, it is very unusual in that it is made of structural brick (evidenced by the brick arches above the window openings) rather than brick veneer over a wooden frame. A bricklayer named Harry Bridge built it in 1917; after a period as a laundry, it became a grocery store in the late 1920s, operated by Charles Noel.

A neighbourhood icon until fire destroyed it in 1989, Kerrisdale Grocery stood at the corner of Maple and 49th across the street from Magee High School, itself demolished in the 1990s once a new school building opened on its back field. More than 20 years after the fire, the store site still sits empty, except for trees that have grown to a considerable height.

Another part of their enduring fascination was their signs: rusting marquees with movable metal letters bracketed with round Coca-Cola or Pepsi logos, cigarette and ice-cream ads, notices taped to windows offering a car or guitar for sale, with the telephone number written on vertical strips torn into the paper for easy removal (in the age before Craigslist and cellphones). The push bar on the door would be an advertisement for the *Sun* or the *Province*. A small bell would hang from a bracket on the inside door frame and ding when the opening door clipped it, calling the storekeeper from a lamplit back room and the sound of conversation or a television.

Stores well stocked with candy settled on the periphery of city school grounds and were magnets for children's milk money at recess and lunch, contributing to the historic prosperity of the dental profession. A traditional Vancouver childhood might have included the command "Go to the store and get your mother some cigarettes! There's money on the table!" Many stores offered credit, allowing children to sign for things they were picking up on the way home. A few became beloved local landmarks, such as the Kerrisdale Grocery at 49th and Maple. In its case, the Quality Meat Market adjoining it is well remembered too. The same basic story, in which a child goes in and asks for a bone for the family dog and the butcher responds with, "Okay, as long as you don't throw it in the ditch," has been told to me a dozen times.

Yet to come was the era of corporate standardization, of a 7-Eleven in a strip mall or a Handi-Mart in a gas bar, both looking the same in Vancouver as they do in Winnipeg. This new kind of convenience store is built around the car and an "on the go" lifestyle, and features in-and-out slots for quick parking. It's anybody's guess whether they will survive the congestion of the modern, dense city or evolve further into a pedestrian-friendly model, like the corner stores they replaced. Even gas stations are much less common than they once were, property values being the likely culprit.

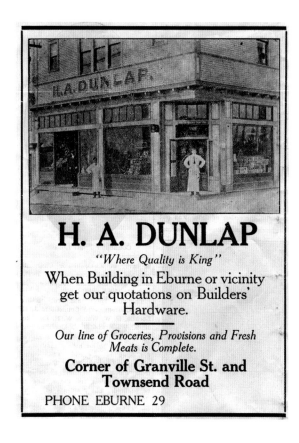

H. A. DUNLAP

"Where Quality is King"

When Building in Eburne or vicinity get our quotations on Builders' Hardware.

—

Our line of Groceries, Provisions and Fresh Meats is Complete.

Corner of Granville St. and Townsend Road

PHONE EBURNE 29

A grocery store a century ago, at 70th and Granville. It is a classic Vancouver shop design: a sheltered corner door and plate-glass display windows with transom windows above to bring extra light into the interior.

ABOVE RIGHT > A 1937 advertisement listing many of the Chinese-run grocery stores in the city, in an era of neighbourhood shopping.

NEXT PAGE > Scott's Grocery at Victoria Drive and Georgia Street is the last operating corner store in that part of East Vancouver. Like many corner stores, it has a main-floor shop with a suite above for the proprietor, contained within a typical hipped-roof house structure. Thomas Givens built it in 1920.

A century ago most grocery stores were family businesses unattached to any ethnicity (and running them was as respectable an occupation for a widow as managing a rooming house). By the 1930s, though, many of them had become "Chinese groceries," at least in the city's lexicon. From that decade through to the 1960s, for the majority in the city's better-off neighbourhoods, the stores provided a window onto a different class and race of people. Few Asian families lived outside of the Chinatown-East End district; of those that did, some used the "all-in-one" quality of a grocery store lease to house the family and earn a living, as witnessed by the advertisement on this page.

Everybody took turns: the Chinese or Japanese kid who was your schoolmate might be running the cash register when you stopped by the store before dinner to pick up something your mother needed. For example, the nephew in the family who ran the Granville Market grocery store on 41st Avenue near East Boulevard had a room at the back of the store overlooking the lane and was one of the handful of non-white children at Magee High School in the 1960s. In that age, buttoned-down and homogeneous for many of us, it was mind-expanding to know people like him.

Most of the stores were affiliated with large wholesalers, of which H.Y. Louie was one, supplying members of the Chinese Fruit & Vegetable Retail Merchants Association. Kelly-Douglas Ltd. and W.H. Malkin Company, both headquartered in "white" Gastown, had their own stables of corner stores. The move to self-service supermarkets began in Vancouver in the 1930s with Safeway and Piggly-Wiggly, more than a decade after the concept had taken hold in the US.

By the 1950s, most corner stores had retreated to the milk-pop-candy-cigarettes "convenience" role, surviving because unlike the supermarkets they stayed open evenings and Sundays. More recently some were able to specialize (Benny's Market at

ABOVE LEFT > The 1908 frame store and apartments at 1260 East 12th, just west of Clark Drive. Grocer T.W. Allen ran it until the 1950s; it continued in business until about 1970 as Tiege's Grocery. The other shops at the corner of 12th and Clark, built in the 1920s, have been either demolished or stuccoed and modernized.

ABOVE RIGHT > The BC Mills, Timber & Trading Company (page 99) manufactured prefabricated houses as well as bank buildings and a selection of modified houses for companies like BC Telephone. This was the Eburne exchange, on the south side of Marine Drive near Montcalm. One of its phone-company buildings survives today as the museum of the Aldergrove Heritage Society, at 3190 271st Street. (PHOTO FROM *POINT GREY GAZETTE*, JUNE 14, 1913)

Union and Princess in Strathcona offers Italian foodstuffs) or thrive because of loyal pedestrian customers in areas such as the West End, Kitsilano and Grandview. Danial Foods, the former Barclay Grocery, has made the transition into Persian specialties. The former grocery at Victoria and Grant is now a branch of the South China Seas Trading Company. The Arbutus Grocery at 6th and Arbutus evolved into an upscale coffee shop.

Other stores became even more specialized. The Venables Grocery at Lakewood Drive was just a block from Templeton High School and in a good location, as Venables Street was a busy commuter route before traffic-calming occurred. Carl Peterson was the confectioner in the '40s and '50s, Low Chum Chuck in the '60s and '70s. The store then became notorious in the neighbourhood for its operators, who were more intent on dealing drugs from it than selling the innocent confections of yore. At its worst, one neighbour recalled, customers looking for milk or butter were told to go elsewhere as everything was out-dated! The store was demolished a half-dozen years ago.

Today, even supermarkets are open from early in the morning until midnight or later, staffed by workers in shifts on a roster that is impossible for a family-run corner store to follow. The 7-Elevens and others of their ilk go round the clock. For the past 30 or so years, Sunday has been just another shopping day; it's amusing to recall that teenagers' driving lessons before the 1980s usually included a Sunday stint on an empty Safeway parking lot.

The traditional Vancouver storefront, like the ones on these pages, had an inset, sheltered entry—sometimes on the corner of the building—and was glazed between load-bearing posts with large plate-glass windows below and smaller windows forming a transom above, allowing the maximum amount of light into a high-ceilinged interior. Above the door there was typically a hinged window that could be opened for ventilation on hot days. Above the window tops there was space for an awning, often the striped-canvas type that could be pulled up whenever the weather seemed appropriate or left down to protect boxes of fruit and vegetables or sale items displayed on trestles outside.

Many of the shops were just single-storey strips along the commercial sidewalks, while others had a floor or two of apartments or offices above. Those kinds of designs survive today on East Hastings around Nanaimo, on Commercial Drive, on Victoria south of 33rd, on south Fraser and Main, on Granville Street in Marpole, on 4th near Alma, on Broadway west of Macdonald and along the older parts of Kingsway. Often the storefronts were modified many years ago (with glossy black-glass Vitrolite tile in the 1920s and 1930s, for example) and have been altered since with fluorescent signs or modern canvas awnings in quarter-barrel, dome, waterfall or corner-wrap styles.

A change to more mall-like storefronts with unsheltered doorways began on Robson Street in the 1980s and has spread as part of the high-end retail trend to South Granville and Kitsilano's 4th Avenue near Arbutus. Retailer Ross Hill, the son of James Hill, who founded Hill's of Kerrisdale (and grandson of John Hill, mentioned above), describes them as part of the inevitable evolution of street retail as businesses try to develop an "identifiable brand" and generate the sort of sales they can expect from a mall store. They are cheap buildings to erect, just one-storey tall with no need to provide expensive underground parking, yet their high ceilings and huge plate-glass fronts give them much more effective selling space.

A contrast is the new, generic Vancouver shop with two or three storeys of condos above—the kind that has been added to commercial streets especially around transit

By the 1960s—much later than in the United States—local people had turned their backs on the traditional greengrocer, butcher and baker, in favour of the modern convenience of a shopping cart. This photo by Clyde Herrington shows a Super-Valu on Davie Street in the West End. No scanners then! The Kelly-Douglas food wholesale-company set up Super-Valu in 1951 and, by the time this photo was taken, had more than 80 retail stores in BC. As of 1966, chains controlled 70 percent of the retail food business; in 2010, that number remained the same for BC but had dropped to 60 percent nationwide. (PHOTO, *INDUSTRIAL BRITISH COLUMBIA*, 1965)

ABOVE > In an era before sign bylaws, advertisers painted the sides of buildings with gay abandon. In 2011, a Shelly's 4x Bakery sign emerged from beneath a 50-year-old coat of stucco during the renovation of the former Victoria Drive Grocery, a 1922 building at the corner of Victoria and William in Grandview. Members of the community convinced the owners to retain the sign during the conversion of the old store into a pizza restaurant. The store's most recent use had been as an art gallery named Doctor Vigari (an anagram of the store's name made from the metal letters on its marquee, concocted by Simon Kendall of the band Doug and the Slugs); owner Bill Gotts relocated, under the same name, to Commercial Drive.

LEFT > Shelly's 4x Bakery, at 601 West 10th, was one of the business enterprises of William Curtis Shelly. In 1926, he organized Canadian Bakeries, which merged with McGavin's in 1961; he also owned an office building at 119 West Pender, invested in businesses, including Home Gas, and served as an alderman, park board member and minister of finance in the Tolmie provincial government that foundered on the shoals of economic collapse in 1933. He is credited with buying, in 1925 with his own money, the one piece of land in Stanley Park, near Brockton Point, for which legal title had been given to a "squatter," an Aboriginal woman who proved to the courts she had lived there for 60 years (the Aboriginal village in the park, Khwaykhway, at Lumberman's Arch, had been razed decades earlier with no compensation for its owners at all). Shelly had heard that a private firm was negotiating to buy the land and hoped to erect an apartment building. He was later reimbursed by the city which, he recalled, refused to pay him interest.

BELOW > Shelly's most dramatic investment, the Grouse Mountain Chalet, built in 1926 and destroyed by fire in 1962. Townley & Matheson designed and supervised construction of the superb rustic building, created from yellow cedar logs by Swedish and Finnish craftsmen.

crossroads. This design makes it difficult for a business to establish its own identity, according to Hill. Because the buildings have to meet an arbitrary height limit, the retail space is squeezed, with many of the shops operating in spaces with eight-foot ceilings. Display and lighting become more difficult. The strata ownership of the buildings complicates the situation for both the landlord and the retail tenant.

An example of the city's retail evolution was little MacKinnon's Bakery at 2715 Granville, which continued in business even as international brands like Restoration Hardware, Williams of Sonoma and Pottery Barn were moving onto the street. Until its closure a couple of years ago, the bakery was likely on a 10-year lease, negotiated before South Granville got so hot, paying about $20 to $25 per square foot annually, the kind of rent payable on The Drive or on Hastings around Nanaimo. Now, on South Granville, tenants might pay $50 to $60 and some tenants, moving into new premises, might pay even $80.

Laura's Coffee Shop, at 4th and Manitoba, a café since being converted from Filippo's grocery store in 1964, is the last of the traditional soup and burger lunch spots in the old industrial enclave of Lower Mount Pleasant. New cafés in the area invariably conform to the panini and cappuccino zeitgeist. Laura's adapted a traditional house-form to commercial use, as the city's corner stores had; Laura's is a 1904 house, converted to a shop and two suites in 1928.

In other areas, such as Main Street around King Edward, innovative retailers have moved in and created a neighbourhood brand, fixing up the buildings and then watching their rents creep up. Inevitably selling prices increase to the point that owners demolish the buildings. The street loses its diversity, the new storefronts rarely having the rich texture of the ones they replaced. By this time the innovative retailers have gone elsewhere to set up their edgy stores—for example, to the lower-priced strips along the old streetcar network, such as East Hastings near Nanaimo.

Taxes for city businesses are another issue, the rate being around five times what residences pay. "About 92 percent of assessed properties in Vancouver are residential, leaving just 8 percent commercial—a number that is steadily declining as the city increasingly becomes a place to live but not to work," wrote *Vancouver Sun* business columnist Don Cayo. "This relative handful of business properties pays half of the city's total property taxes. Yet the cost of services they use . . . adds up to only a quarter of City Hall spending."[*]

As the city rezones properties along commercial streets to encourage densification, businesses get whacked with ever-higher tax bills due to the increased assessments and the certainty that they will be driven away by the demolition of their buildings, by much higher lease rates, or both. The assessment spike in Richmond

---

*   *Vancouver Sun*, June 19, 2010.

along the Canada Line corridor, where densities will soar and the price of land was quickly bid up by speculators, prompted Richmond council to offer tax relief to merchants in 2011. Proposals to do the same for Vancouver's Cambie Street merchants fell on deaf ears.* In the end, only the big—those who can balance their books with revenues from profitable stores elsewhere on the planet—will survive.

Yoka's Coffee at 3171 West Broadway in Kitsilano was a remarkable retail survival story that ended in 2010, when the owners decamped for Victoria. Yoka Van Den Berg and her partner, Tristan (whose birth name is Larry Trotter), had served a loyal clientele for 27 years, roasting coffee in the shop and selling honey, chocolate and tea.

In the early 1980s Yoka was working for the apiary branch of the provincial agriculture department in the Okanagan, intent on a career in beekeeping. A traffic accident—she was hit by a car while crossing a street—changed her plans. No longer able to do strenuous physical work, she saw an opportunity when a Greek couple running a Kitsilano deli went looking for somebody to take over the coffee side of their business. She leased their roaster and started selling coffee in 1983, overcoming her resistance to naming the store after herself once an acquaintance in advertising—one of her photographer-partner's clients—had convinced her it was a good strategy.

Soon Yoka was able to buy her own 1930s-era, Royal coffee roaster, which she found in San Francisco, and establish her own shop, leasing a narrow storefront from a Chinese family who lived in the building. Although she could never get more than a two-year lease with a two-year option to renew, she and Tristan persevered and created a distinctive atmosphere. At the back of the shop she tended the roasting beans, their aroma infusing everything. Empty burlap coffee sacks with colourful logos were free for the taking. She and Tristan also sold coffee by the cup and provided newspapers and a stack of *BC Bookworld* magazines for reading at the counter or on a wooden bench on the sidewalk in the sun. A corkboard displayed posters for local cultural events and several of Tristan's photos hung on a wall.

When Yoka's started in 1983 there were about six coffee shops on Broadway west of Burrard. Today, with Starbucks, other chains and a few "early retirement dream" independents, there's hardly a commercial building on the street that doesn't have a place to drink coffee.

Although Yoka's rent per square foot quadrupled over the years, it was still affordable because

NEXT PAGE > From the fifth-floor balcony across the street, the boomtown front and pitched roof of the Nirvana restaurant at 2313 Main is clearly visible. Built in 1892, when Vancouver was only six years old, the building has been occupied by restaurants since the 1950s. A sign of the times on trendy Main Street in 2010, when I painted the watercolour, were the line-ups in front of the building on the right, a restaurant called Foundation, which serves vegetarian and vegan food and is "a little bit hippie, a little bit skater, and always crowded," according to an online review.

---

*   "Richmond property owners to get a tax break—Vancouver need not apply," by Francis Bula, *Globe and Mail*, May 27, 2011.

Buried houses (1): The view from Fraser Street into the lane south of Broadway. The 1897 house has been hidden behind a shopfront facing Broadway since 1932. These blocks of shops along Broadway have seen little change in the past 50 years.

the space was so small. But it allowed them just enough to make a living—and a diminishing one at that—with no hope of long-term survival, no equity and no retirement plan. "We [weren't] able to move elsewhere in Vancouver and start over," Yoka said. Their only option was to look for another city where they could buy a building and find some stability.

THE TREND TOWARD LARGER, GENERIC BUILDINGS AS THE CITY GROWS and owners maximize the value of their land is gradually eliminating the last of the boomtown fronts and buried houses from commercial streets. Also known as false fronts, boomtown fronts first appeared in great numbers in the aftermath of the California Gold Rush of 1849. They were the result of small frontier-town merchants attempting to make their simple shed and gable roof buildings appear larger and more important, like the flat-roof buildings of Eastern cities. The merchant wanted the casual shopper to see the shop sign (usually located on the false front), not the snow-capped mountains behind the building.[*] Gabled structures with false fronts were easy to build and their roofs shed the rain. They were the ideal first-generation buildings for a commercial street in an outlying suburb like Mount Pleasant in the city's early years.

The Nirvana restaurant building, illustrated on page 79, is an example of a boom-

---

[*]   Walker, p. 142.

town front: a rectangular false front, decorated with a bracketed wooden cornice, with a pitched-roof building behind. According to Heritage Vancouver researchers, the building was erected by J.W. Clark in 1892 and may be the oldest commercial building outside of downtown. It was the long-time location of A. Frith & Co., which sold "men's furnishings." Subsequent occupants included the Continental Cafe, Riviera Pizza and the Himalaya Restaurant.

The other illustrations on these pages show some of the last of the city's "buried houses," relics of the conversion of residential streets to commercial uses. The watercolour on page 80 shows the side of an 1897 house, visible from Fraser Street, with an addition facing Broadway that is home to Launderama and a tailor's shop. W.M. McKenzie added the shops to the front in 1932 and ran a grocery store there until the 1950s. It then became the office of John Grumey's Coast Electric Contractors. Grumey lived in the house. In 1960 he converted the shop to Grumey's Launderama, rented the house and moved away.

The watercolour on page 83 shows the back lane and house at 2052 West 4th Avenue, just east of Arbutus. Fourth Avenue was a commercial street from its inception

Buried houses (2): The house at the corner of Hastings and Dunlevy, built by future coroner and alderman Dr. Thomas Jeffs in 1901. The Sunkist Produce grocery store, added years later, has evolved into a florist's shop. Jeffs moved to Grandview in 1907 (page 103).

ABOVE > Buried houses (3): A set of three houses with shops occupying their front yards on Renfrew Street south of 1st Avenue. The houses were built, respectively, in 1937, 1921 and 1926, reflecting the slow settlement of Vancouver east of Nanaimo Street, which had many vacant lots and a semi-rural feeling until the population boom after the Second World War. This block developed commercially because the Burnaby Lake interurban stopped there.

RIGHT > The sheet-metal shop on the front of the Baptist church (built in 1903 by carpenter Roland Scarlett, who lived nearby at 6th and Arbutus) that became Bimini's pub, at 2010 West 4th, in 1975.

in about 1903, with shops clustered between Yew and Balsam in proximity to the West Fairview school, on the site of today's Safeway store. Streetcar service began in 1909, the same year that the second Granville Bridge opened, the trams turning from 4th directly onto it.

The shops built onto the front of this buried house in 1927 reflect the history of the community: Snowflake Cleaners and Dyers in the '30s; Dob-Sin Cleaners in the '40s; a manufacturer's agent in the '50s; Rendell-Paret, which offered build-it-yourself radio and electronics gear to "early nerds" in the '60s; and a poster shop that served the hippie community in the '70s. Other buildings on the block attested to the diversity of the community: 2068 was the office of the long-vanished *Kitsilano Times* newspaper; down the block, a Baptist church that had been converted into a sheet-metal shop was converted again in the 1970s into Bimini's, one of the city's first neighbourhood pubs.

The corner of 4th and Arbutus was ground zero for Kitsilano's hippie tribe of the late 1960s, with the Afterthought (the former Kitsilano Theatre) at 2114, the Phase

Four coffee house (later the Last Chance Saloon) at 2064, the Village Bistro nightclub and coffee house at 2081 and Doug Hawthorn's Blind Owl headshop next door to it.[*] The photograph on page 85 of the Kitsilano Theatre in the summer of 1930 hints at the number of houses on 4th Avenue at that time (as does the photo on page 82 from 1974, of Bimini's pub site).

P ART OF THE FAMOUS PLAYers chain, the Kitsilano Theatre served its corner of the community as did the Alma at 3711 West Broadway, which competed with the Hollywood near Balaclava. The Hollywood was the only one of the three to survive the television revolution of the 1950s.

A century ago, Hastings around Main was the centre of the city's entertainment district and the location of its early movie houses. It had begun to lose its status as the retail centre, which had shifted west toward Granville and south toward Georgia. Theatre mogul Alec Pantages was one who believed that Hastings was still the place to be and erected the

lavish Beacon Theatre in 1917 on Hastings just west of Carrall; it was demolished in the 1970s, long after audiences and almost everyone else had abandoned the area. Uptown movie houses opened, including the Strand at Georgia and Seymour in 1919 (demolished), the Capitol on Granville in 1921 and the Orpheum in 1927.

Odeon Theatres Canada Ltd., founded in 1941, provided the stiffest competition for the Famous Players houses. All through that wartime spring the new company made headlines—it was not affiliated with any other chain in Canada or the US and promised to show the best from both Hollywood and British studios. Its new Vogue on Granville Street, built by Reifel-family liquor interests, was, according to an

Buried houses (4): The house at 2052 West 4th Avenue, built by carpenter Alex Macdonald in 1905 for real estate agent Frederick Moore. Macdonald lived on the block, at 2078, as did his carpenter brother William, at 2006. The laying of tram tracks in 1909 confirmed the commercial use of the street.

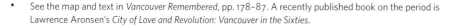

*   See the map and text in *Vancouver Remembered*, pp. 178–87. A recently published book on the period is Lawrence Aronsen's *City of Love and Revolution: Vancouver in the Sixties.*

advertisement published on opening day, "completely modern in design and will have a new type of projection machine which eliminates flickering and increases light by 20 percent."

Odeon started with the Vogue, the Paradise and the Plaza on Granville, the Beacon and the Lux on Hastings, and the Dunbar; all but the Hastings Street pair still operate today. In March 1941, Odeon announced it had acquired two sites for new cinemas and taken control of six more: the Rio on Broadway at Commercial (extant), the Kingsway on Kingsway at Joyce (now the Raja), the Fraser on Fraser at 47th (demolished), the Olympia on Hastings at Nanaimo (demolished), the Varsity on 10th at Trimble (demolished),[*] and the Nova in North Vancouver. The two new cinemas were the Park on Cambie at 18th and the Circle on Kingsway at Knight (demolished). The chain also added three theatres in New Westminster, one on Kingsway in Burnaby and two more in North Vancouver. In 1943 it added the Marpole at 1370 South West Marine Drive, now a live venue called Metro Theatre.

The Second World War is often remembered as a high point for the movie business, with people seeking escape from the reality of the daily news. In the summertime, however, according to Odeon district manager W.J. Long, business was bad due to daylight savings time and the wartime amusement tax. Nevertheless, as soon as the war ended, Odeon announced huge expansion plans, claiming to the newspapers that hundreds of new theatres would be added to the Canadian landscape.

Odeon's competitor, Famous Players, reached its zenith during the same period. In 1945 its Vancouver stable consisted of the Capitol, the Orpheum and the Dominion on Granville, the Strand on Georgia, the Alma, the Kitsilano and the Hollywood (listed in advertisements as part of the chain) in Kitsilano, the Broadway at 2530 Main

---

*   See "Martin family's theatre faces wrecking ball," by Charlie Smith, *Georgia Straight*, July 28, 2005.

TOP > On the site of a 1903 house at 2114 West 4th, R.E. Berry built the Kitsilano Theatre in 1927 as part of his movie and vaudeville circuit. It was soon absorbed into the growing Famous Players chain, performing its suburban movie-theatre role until 1955, when the immense popularity of television forced its closure. Three years later, a group of Russian immigrants led by E.A. Andreev formed a community association and bought the building, having signed an agreement that it would not be used again as a movie house. For a decade, it was a centre of the Russian community— of performances of a balalaika orchestra, choirs and dance groups, of lectures on history and culture, of bazaars and plays. By the late 1960s, however, the enthusiasm of the founders had waned and the association decided to rent the hall. It reopened as The Afterthought, a beatnik/hippie club. After a few years, the Russians took the building back and have run it as the Russian Community Centre ever since. (LEONARD FRANK PHOTO, VPL11044)

BOTTOM > The Alma Theatre at 3711 West Broadway, designed by William Dodd in 1925, was a purpose-built cinema, another part of the Famous Players chain. It closed in 1955. (LEONARD FRANK PHOTO, VPL11040)

(demolished), the Grandview at 1730 Commercial (demolished), the Kerrisdale at 2114 West 41st (altered), the Victoria at 5722 Victoria (demolished), the Windsor at 4092 Main (demolished) and the Stanley at 2750 Granville (now the Stanley Industrial Alliance Stage, see page 20).

However, the movie business was blindsided by television, which was introduced locally in 1948 to a handful of homes with tall antennae that could pick up the faint KING signal from Seattle. CBC began to broadcast in Vancouver in 1953, as did KVOS in Bellingham.[*] The end was swift. Famous Players commented that its attendance dropped by 50 percent in 1955 alone. "Five Vancouver theatres in the Famous Players and Odeon chains closed Saturday night," a news story on August 30, 1955, reported, bringing the total closures in the city to 12. The Beacon, Kerrisdale, Windsor, Alma and Kitsilano theatres were the victims that night. A year or so later, an undated news clipping in the city archives recorded neighbours' complaints about the abandoned Alma Theatre. The Kitsilano Theatre became the Russian Community Hall which, except for its brief period as a hippie coffee house and folk-music venue in the 1960s, it has remained since.

As if listening to "Pick Yourself Up," a classic song from the middle of the Great Depression, a few of the cinemas dusted themselves off and started all over again. The Hollywood celebrated its 75th anniversary in 2010, still owned and operated by the Fairleigh family who built it the year before "Pick Yourself Up" was performed by Fred Astaire and Ginger Rogers.[†] It was a retail survival miracle better even than Yoka's, but it was sold in 2011 and held its final screening on May 28 that year. The Dunbar is still showing first-run films, while the Rio presents a mixed bill of film and live shows to its edgy Drive clientele. A relative newcomer, the Ridge at Arbutus and 16th, is one

[*] See Bacchus, "Television," in Davis, ed., p. 427.

[†] See "Hooray for Hollywood" and "Survival of the Single Screen" by John Mackie, *Vancouver Sun*, October 23, 2010.

of Leonard Schein's stable, the others being the Park and the newish five-screen Fifth Avenue Cinemas. The Ridge has managed to survive the sea change of culture and technology, although rumours persist that the site will soon be redeveloped.

A further indication of the sea change in people's behaviour was the spate of closings and bankruptcies of video-rental shops in 2011. One, the venerable Videomatica at 1855 West 4th Avenue, had achieved iconic status when it announced it was giving up the fight after 28 years.[*]

PREVIOUS PAGE > The Ridge Theatre at 16th and Arbutus opened in 1950 to serve the Arbutus Ridge district. It survived the collapse of the neighbourhood Odeon and Famous Players chains and became a venue for quirky independent films such as *The Rocky Horror Picture Show* and cult classics such as *Casablanca* in the late 1970s. Its owner, Leonard Schein, founded the Vancouver International Film Festival in 1982.

THIS PAGE > Granville Street's Theatre Row in the late 1950s, the streetcar tracks removed but the granite sets that paved the edges along the rails still on the street. As a transit-only mall since the 1970s, it has weathered its share of problems with homelessness and crime, and has become a place for mass celebrations, as it was during the 2010 Olympics. (PHOTOGRAPHER UNKNOWN)

[*] "Videomatica to close doors this summer after three decades," by Martin Dunphy, *Georgia Straight*, May 2, 2011.

THE VANCOUVER HOUSE

To be a home, the house cannot be a machine. It must be passive, not active, bringing peace to the fluctuation of the human mind from generation to generation. For what charm can a house possess that can never bear a worn threshold, the charred hearth, and the rubbed corner?

—SIR EDWIN LUTYENS

THE NEIGHBOURHOODS OF VANCOUVER ARE VERY OLD-FASHIONED places, harkening back to the dream of home ownership, freehold land, stability and independence—the family in its modest castle—that sparked the huge migration from the old world to the new in the 19th century. They go right to the core values of North America and Australasia.

That Vancouver's old neighbourhoods actually work fairly well in an environmental sense is an argument for defending them and for resisting city hall and its persistent EcoDensity policy and infill tweaking of zoning that destabilizes homeowners and offers ever more possibilities for hungry builders to turn a house lot into a business opportunity. Stable, peaceful neighbourhoods are what's at stake: the vast majority of homeowners just want a nest and to be left alone in it.

A home is a family's savings plan, its bulwark against inflation and old age, a repository of memories and a sanctuary against the stresses of life. For developers, a home is a house, interesting to them if it can be expanded or replaced; if there's some profit margin in there based on the zoning or, say, a new "environmental" policy, they'll bid the price up, making it even less accessible to the average citizen. Or so it seems to me.

Even the expectation of revenue from a basement suite, legal or otherwise, helps to push house prices up. This may be good for the supply of affordable *rental* housing, but it's less so for the affordability of the house itself. "It's great," a realtor will say, "you get the revenue," which of course goes entirely to pay for the increase in the house price over 25 years of mortgage payments. Lane houses are adding a whole other dimension to the issue (see page 124).

"The suburbs" are often seen as the culprits for all cities' environmental ills because of the distances people travel to work and shop and the cost of providing transportation infrastructure, especially bridges in a topography like Vancouver's. But individual choice is a factor, too, combined with all the complexities of double-income families, children's needs and affordability. Those urban dwellers in the downtown condos might have jobs in Delta and need to drive there, but nobody says *their* neighbourhood isn't environmentally sustainable.

---

* In a review of Le Corbusier's 1928 *Towards a New Architecture*.

Those 'burbs in a Surrey or a Maple Ridge indeed force people into their cars—they were designed around an almost religious separation of residential from commercial and industrial. Retail became a pod—that is, a shopping mall—and once the traffic engineers got through with designing the arterials and the cul de sacs there was little pleasure for a pedestrian or cyclist. In those suburbs, walking is a recreation, not the kind of transportation it can easily be in an old Vancouver neighbourhood where many people are no further than a five- or ten-minute walk from one of the strips of shops along transit routes dating back to streetcar days.

This suburban environmental problem will be "solved" when road tolls become so onerous and the roads so congested that people will reduce the radius of their lives down to a few kilometres—a bike ride or short trip by car or bus or short walk to a train— staying local in order to preserve their sanity. But the huge question remains: why can't the Clearbrooks, the Langley Townships and the Coquitlams design new neighbourhoods that work as well as old Langley City, which has made the transition into the 21st century with a walkable and medium-density mix of housing and shops? (Hint: Ask the traffic engineers, the land-use planners and the big developers who want to master-plan new subdivisions.)

In the midst of all this, the challenge for Vancouver is to preserve its old neighbourhoods and houses. *They are not part of the regional problem.* They should be left alone!

The Beeman Cottage at 42nd and Macdonald in Kerrisdale, torn down in 2008, was one of the handful of remaining pioneer houses in the city—that is, places built on the ground, without proper foundations (the Beakes house, p. 209, is another). Bill Nesbitt, who owned it for many years, intended in the 1960s to replace it with a house he could move from the nearby apartment area, but when that deal fell through he upgraded the cottage enough to rent it to "honeymoon couples," as he described the type of tenants he was looking for. Email from Joe Clarke, Saltspring Island: "It seems we have a somewhat serendipitous connection to your subject matter as we owned the silver grey Datsun station wagon depicted in the image of the house at Macdonald and 43rd Ave . . . we were visiting our friend who was living in the house."

R ESIDENTIAL VANCOUVER IS A RELENTLESS GRID CRISS-CROSSED BY bus lines, a layout that was finalized more than a century ago. Front yards are shallow, back yards deep; almost all blocks are bisected by lanes lined with garages. Some large lots on the West Side have front driveways and side garages. As most garages appear to be full of the junk that overflows from houses, streets are lined with parked cars, leaving a single lane down the middle for traffic. Some garages have been converted into workshops, a few to illegal granny cottages, whose tenants add their cars to the street.

There are only a few "pioneer" dwellings left in the city—that is, wooden houses built on footings without proper strip foundations, basements or crawl spaces. Some may predate the arrival of electricity and city water or perhaps were erected by people too poor to afford such mod-cons. One such is the cottage at 145 West 11th, sitting at the back of its lot; an illiterate man named C. Stapleton had it connected to the water system in 1904 but it could be a dozen years older than that. What's believed to be the oldest house in the neighbourhood, that of teamster Robert Moore, was *moved* in

COMMON VANCOUVER HOUSE STYLES

Dates indicate the approximate period from first settlement until build-out.
The Vancouver Special and the Contemporary Builder were almost always
built to replace earlier houses.

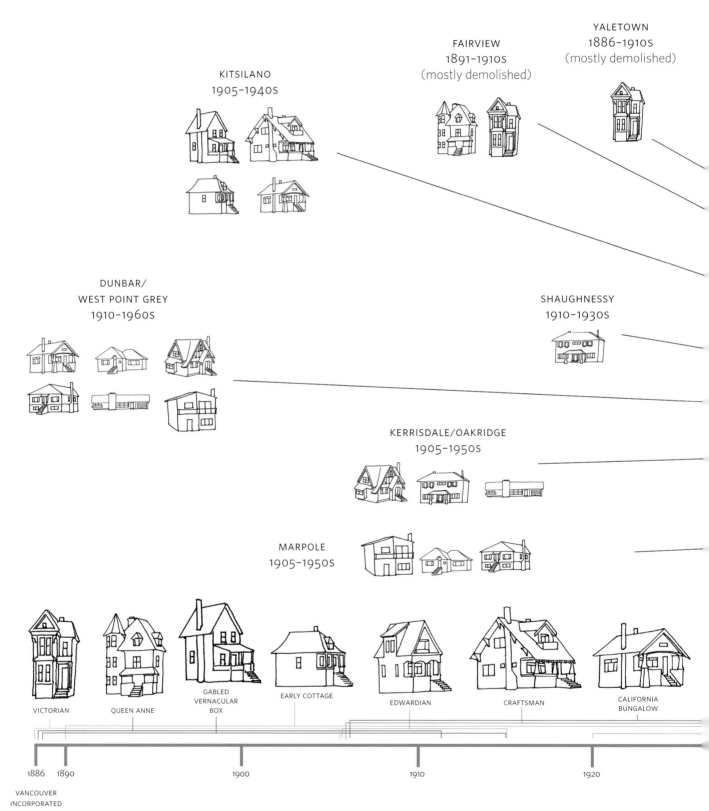

YALETOWN
1886–1910s
(mostly demolished)

FAIRVIEW
1891–1910s
(mostly demolished)

KITSILANO
1905–1940s

**DUNBAR/
WEST POINT GREY**
1910–1960s

SHAUGHNESSY
1910–1930s

KERRISDALE/OAKRIDGE
1905–1950s

MARPOLE
1905–1950s

VICTORIAN

QUEEN ANNE

GABLED
VERNACULAR
BOX

EARLY COTTAGE

EDWARDIAN

CRAFTSMAN

CALIFORNIA
BUNGALOW

1886   1890   1900   1910   1920

VANCOUVER
INCORPORATED

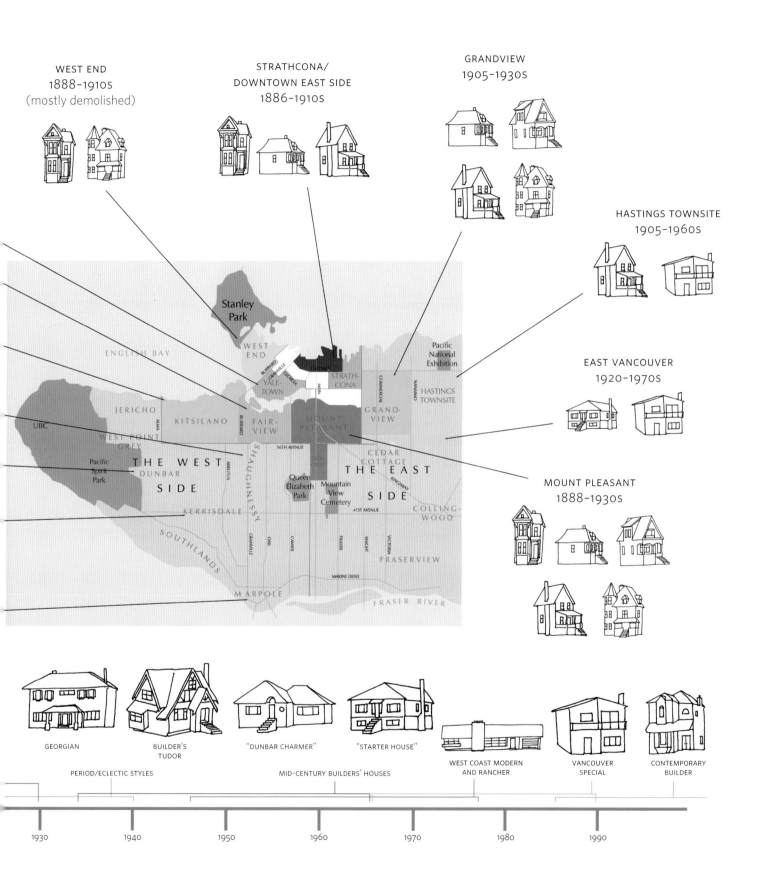

WEST END
1888–1910S
(mostly demolished)

STRATHCONA/
DOWNTOWN EAST SIDE
1886–1910S

GRANDVIEW
1905–1930S

HASTINGS TOWNSITE
1905–1960S

EAST VANCOUVER
1920–1970S

MOUNT PLEASANT
1888–1930S

Stanley
Park

ENGLISH BAY

WEST
END

Pacific
National
Exhibition

JERICHO

UBC

WEST POINT
GREY

Pacific
Spirit
Park

THE WEST
SIDE

DUNBAR

KITSILANO

FAIR-
VIEW

STRATH-
CONA

GRAND-
VIEW

HASTINGS
TOWNSITE

MOUNT
PLEASANT

16TH AVENUE

CEDAR
COTTAGE

THE EAST
SIDE

COLLING-
WOOD

KERRISDALE

SHAUGHNESSY

Queen
Elizabeth
Park

Mountain
View
Cemetery

41ST AVENUE

SOUTHLANDS

FRASERVIEW

MARINE DRIVE

MARPOLE

FRASER RIVER

YALE-
TOWN

COMMERCIAL

NANAIMO

ALMA

BURRARD

ARBUTUS

GRANVILLE

OAK

CAMBIE

FRASER

KNIGHT

VICTORIA

KINGSWAY

BURRARD
GRANVILLE
GEORGIA

MAIN

GEORGIAN

BUILDER'S
TUDOR

"DUNBAR CHARMER"

"STARTER HOUSE"

WEST COAST MODERN
AND RANCHER

VANCOUVER
SPECIAL

CONTEMPORARY
BUILDER

PERIOD/ECLECTIC STYLES

MID-CENTURY BUILDERS' HOUSES

1930   1940   1950   1960   1970   1980   1990

1891 from a few doors away at the corner of 11th and Columbia to its lot at 166 West 10th.

One pioneer dwelling that disappeared in the past decade was the Beeman Cottage at 42nd and Macdonald in Kerrisdale. Probably built as a guest house about 1911 for the Beemans' main home that faced 41st and was demolished many years ago, it later became a kindergarten run by Elsie Beeman and her sister.

Another pioneer place was Eric Peterson's cottage in Mount Pleasant near China Creek Park. A simple structure, it had charming fretwork on its porch posts and a narrow dormer set into the tiny upstairs roof, giving it more style than most of the shacks and cabins that appear in photos of the early city. A carpenter for P. Burns & Co. named William Bates built it for himself and his wife, Margaret, in 1907 at the lonely end of 7th Avenue where, at high tide, False Creek's shoreline came just about to the front gate. The 1908 directory shows just one neighbour on the block, a plasterer, but a painter and a bookkeeper shared the block to the west, higher up the hill, with the long-established Maddams family (page 196). The Bateses soon moved on, disappearing from city directories in 1910, and the house had a wide range of occupants for the next 40 years: tailors, dockworkers, people in various kinds of trade.

Erik Peterson and his cottage at 1016 East 7th, in 2010. Once a common type of pioneer dwelling, almost all of which have side gables and a long porch facing the street, these buildings have all but disappeared from Vancouver and its suburbs, except for those in rare stump farms in isolated parts of Surrey, Langley, Maple Ridge and other valley regions.

For the past 50 years the house has belonged to Erik Peterson, who came to Canada from Copenhagen in 1951. He was a skilled machinist but couldn't speak English when he arrived so his first job was with the Powell River Company as a labourer. After 11 months he had had enough of the sulphite smell and moved to Vancouver, where he worked the rest of his career as a mechanic for Dietrich-Collins. He was often outdoors in sunny weather chatting to passersby.

"In those days if you had a hammer and saw you called yourself a carpenter," he told me, referring to the quality of his house. He bought it in 1960 for $6,000, putting $3,000 down; with fees and interest it cost him $7,000. It had no heating system other than the wood stove in the kitchen, which he fed with mill ends and other offcuts of lumber he picked up from local construction sites, like the one for the small apartment building that went up next door to his house. The cottage was boarded up in the fall of 2011.

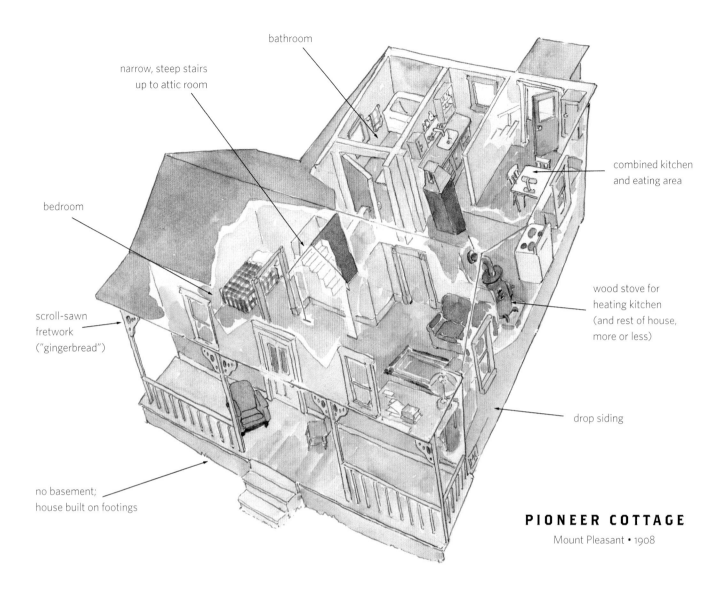

bathroom

narrow, steep stairs
up to attic room

combined kitchen
and eating area

bedroom

wood stove for
heating kitchen
(and rest of house,
more or less)

scroll-sawn
fretwork
("gingerbread")

drop siding

no basement;
house built on footings

PIONEER COTTAGE
Mount Pleasant • 1908

T HE CITY OF VANCOUVER PUT THE SURVEYOR'S STANDARD 66-FOOT
chain to good use when laying out its streets and lots.* Much of the city was initially subdivided into 660-foot-square blocks. There would be a roadway (one chain),
then a lot (two chains deep), then another lot (two chains deep), then another roadway
(one chain), then two more lots (each two chains deep)—altogether, 660 feet. A lane
took off 10 or 12 feet from each lot, leaving an average depth of about 120 feet. Going
the other way, a half chain—33 feet—was a convenient lot width, giving 18 lots to a
block plus 66 feet for a crossing roadway. The 33-foot lot gave builders the opportunity
to create comfortable detached homes for the "common man."†

---

* The 66-foot measurement evolved from field-ploughing in medieval Europe. A chain is 66 feet
(22 yards—just over 20 metres). There are 10 chains in a furlong, the distance an ox could pull a plough
without stopping to rest. Ten of those "furrows long" was a day's work, and was called an acre. There are
about 11 standard 33-foot city lots in an acre.

† Unpublished paper by Ken Terriss, "The Vancouver Special: an elegant solution to housing on 33-foot
wide lots." An abridged version appeared in Min, *Vancouver Matters*.

These 33-footers are the standard lot for much of Vancouver. Wider 50- and 66-footers are typical of Kerrisdale, postwar Cambie, Oakridge and parts of Dunbar and West Point Grey. With its curving streets, Shaughnessy has 100s and other lots best measured in acres.

"The basic planning of a small house on a narrow lot leads to a building two rooms wide, i.e. 12- to 14-foot rooms which, with walls, result in a 25- to 26-foot wide building," wrote architect Ken Terriss in 1996. "Another basic arrangement is to have a circulation and stair strip of seven or eight feet and a pleasant main room of 14 feet which, with walls, results in a building about 24-feet wide. If we want to walk all around the house, a must for a single-family residence, then we need a minimum of three or four feet on each side. That leads to a minimum lot width of 31 or 32 feet. Some houses have been built on 25-foot wide lots . . . but the resulting rooms are too narrow to be workable."

Space is wasted, of course, because the houses are detached. Like other cities of western North America settled toward the end of the 19th century, Vancouver never cottoned on to the row house. Row or terrace houses in older cities such as London, Toronto or Sydney are often as little as 10-feet wide, depending on the social class of the neighbourhood.

Even in the late 1920s, when apartments had become fairly common, nearly three-quarters of Vancouver's buildings were single dwellings. In working-class South Vancouver (that is, the district south of 16th and east of Cambie that was absorbed into Vancouver in 1929), more than four out of five houses were owner-occupied.[*] Between the late 1880s and the end of the boom in 1913, city water service had expanded outward trying to keep ahead of the demand for building sites; electricity was available to almost everyone by that time, the AC household current pushed into developing areas by the BC Electric Railway Company at the same time as the DC for its streetcars. Many householders could cook with the coal gas that was piped under the streets, also manufactured and distributed by BC Electric. Like today, property development was all about servicing land.

ONE ASPECT OF VANCOUVER'S OLDER HOUSES STRIKES NEWCOMERS AS passing strange: the long flight of stairs, sometimes 10 or a dozen steps, that leads up from the sidewalk to the front door. When you look at similar houses from the same period in warmer locales like Los Angeles or in colder ones like Winnipeg, they're built much closer to the ground. Are Vancouver's houses an ark set above the biblical winter floods?

Yet, cabins and pioneer homes, like the house on the next page and the tall Victorian houses (overleaf), were built closer to the ground. The change to the long flight of stairs coincided with the advent of central heating late in the 19th century. Homeowners who could afford a furnace had to allow a fairly standard basement height of six feet or so to accommodate the gently curved "octopus" ducts that distributed the heat; forced-air electric fans and ducting fitted between the floor joists came later.

Main Street, south of the city boundary at 16th Avenue, developed just after 1900 with a hodgepodge of discontinuous streets, where one speculator's subdivision plan didn't quite line up with the next one's. BC Electric laid streetcar tracks up Main in 1904 (destination: the principal gate for Mountain View Cemetery, at that time at the corner of 33rd and Fraser), spurring development of the area. At some point in that decade, probably in 1907 when subdivision plans were filed, the house at 304 East 28th made its appearance, facing north down Sophia Street but standing sideways at the back of a long garden plot carved out of the forest (see the frontispiece). At that time, Sophia Street there was called Welton and 28th was called Horne, after the area's owner, James Welton Horne, the pioneer Vancouver realtor who features in the classic, staged, 1886 photograph of the real estate office at the end of an enormous log on the site of the Hudson's Bay Company building. (CVA 1477-418)

*   Wade, p. 8.

Victorian houses typically have two-storey bay windows and brackets flaring from an off-centre gable.

ABOVE LEFT > The Big House at Coqualeetza in Sardis, a Thomas Hooper design from 1893 that I hastily added to my sketchbook on a grey winter day in 2004. It was demolished in 2010 by the Stó:lō First Nation board; some argued that it provoked bad memories due to its association, as the principal's house, with the Coqualeetza residential school, attended by First Nations people from all over BC between 1886 and 1939. Attempts to find it a new home away from the reserve could not be concluded in time. (See "House no longer a home," by Paul J. Henderson, *Chilliwack Times*, April 27, 2010.)

ABOVE RIGHT > Houses at 449 and 451 East Pender, painted in 1989 when they were more than a century old, the last survivors of a block of houses from the city's infancy. That August, transient campers burned the green house down and badly damaged the blue one, which was nevertheless rebuilt.

Basements also needed a substantial area for storing fuel (usually sawdust, sometimes coal) and a chute or doorway accessible from the outside. But this is no different from houses in colder climates like Toronto, where just a few front steps are typical.

The reason for the raised main floors, in Ken Terriss's reckoning, is Vancouver's mild climate. Foundations only have to go down about a foot and a half to get below frost depth. Basically the builder only has to remove the organic material before being at a good bearing for a foundation. This shallow excavation is in stark contrast to the situation in the rest of Canada, where it's not uncommon to have to dig five feet to get below frost depth. "Since excavation and concrete work are two of the most expensive and difficult aspects of wood-frame construction, especially so before they were mechanized, the builder will almost always keep them to a minimum."

Excavation was hard work. A bucket pulled by a horse could only scoop out a dent that then had to be deepened and squared off by hand. Steam shovels used for big excavations were expensive and unwieldy. And, as it turned out, most people liked living up above the sidewalk and yard on their "piano nobile" (in design consultant Richard Keate's words): Vancouverites "floating above the mud and rain in their high-basement houses." The added elevation is also good for "snoopervizing" the neighbours.

According to the zoning of a century ago, any area that was a foot or more below grade wasn't counted into the floor space. Thus, many basements were barely subterranean, although they were certainly dim due to the small windows that were usually installed just on the sides and under the stoop at the back. A furnace, fuel bins, winter laundry lines, work benches and storage shelves with a liberal scattering of mousetraps on the floor occupied the space; a major beam running from front to back interrupted the open-joist ceiling and reduced the headroom to below six feet. Dirt floors were quite common; in old basements, it's not unusual to see a patch of newer concrete covering the spot where an early furnace was cemented in generations ago.

When the economy went on the skids in the Dirty Thirties, the basements converted easily into accommodation, that "rite of passage" type of bolt-hole that ought to be part of the experience of anyone claiming to be a true Vancouverite.* Like the mantra "we don't mind the rain because you don't have to shovel it," the basement suite is an essential part of local culture.

Another feature of early Vancouver houses, especially of the tall, boxy, gabled vernacular ones (such as page 95), was the positioning of the front door to one side of the porch. This allowed for a wide, comfortable living room, usually with the dining room behind it. A staircase ran up from the vestibule along the outside wall, then turned inward onto the upstairs landing and hallway. It was easy to add an extra front doorway and split the vestibule in two, creating discrete access to a separate upstairs suite. And because half the porches were north-facing and therefore usable only about three months a year, one side of the porch would often be filled in, creating another room. By such strategies, Vancouver's houses adapted themselves to the changing needs of the population, staying alive until—with the gentrification of areas like Kitsilano and Grandview—new people came in and turned them back into "heritage houses," sometimes even removing the suites and returning them to single-family use.

VICTORIAN-ERA HOUSE ARE CARPENTERS' DREAMS, PATTERNED IN horizontal and diagonal siding and decorative shingles (especially fishscale) with elaborate fretwork on porch posts and gables. They're few and far between in Vancouver outside of Strathcona. Victoria and New Westminster still have a lot of them, but they are older cities, less altered by redevelopment.

An interesting example of the Victorian style, designed in 1893 by legendary architect Thomas Hooper, was the Big House at Coqualeetza on Vedder Road in Sardis on the southern edge of the Chilliwack sprawl. It was a significant part of the troubled history of the region's Aboriginal community. The Coqualeetza Industrial Institute was the second-largest Indian residential school in Canada and used the Big House for its principal's home. Run by the Methodist church, the school was phased out during the Second World War and converted into a tuberculosis hospital, which stayed open until 1968. Shortly thereafter, Skowkale First Nation, part of the Stó:lō Nation, occupied the property and used it as the seat of Stó:lō governance. The Big House was demolished in 2010.

Tastes had simplified somewhat from the Victorian style by about 1905, when the real housing boom began. Houses were less fussy in their detailing with simpler, stronger forms—a good thing given how many of them had to be built to meet the demand before the boom ended in 1913. Even though much of the woodwork was created off-site at the numerous sash and door factories, you have to marvel at the skill of the carpenters, working just with hand tools, and what they were able to accomplish.

Another Victorian: The Lindsay house, built in 1888 at 144 East 6th and possibly the oldest house outside of the Downtown Eastside, according to Heritage Vancouver researchers.

---

* My own subterranean life lasted just two years in the early '70s.

ABOVE > Carpenter P.D. Falco chiselled his initials into the siding of the house he built on Venables in 1912.

NEXT PAGE > A prefab by the BC Mills, Timber & Trading Company, recognizable by its distinctive pattern of wall panels and battens, assembled at the corner of Adanac and MacLean in 1906. BCMT&T's line of small, affordable homes found many buyers in that district in the first decade of the 20th century. In 2005, the pending demolition of two of the prefabs, which shared a double lot with a communally used space of century-old trees, known as Salsbury Garden, at Salsbury and Napier in Grandview, became a *cause célèbre* when a group led by neighbour Penny Street tried to stop it. Having won at the Board of Variance, the Friends of Salsbury Garden then lost at the BC Supreme Court when the judge ruled that third-party appeals (such as opposition by neighbours to a development) had no legal validity.

Nothing came in sheets, as plywood and drywall do today. Houses were framed with two-by-fours and two-by-sixes, sheathed with one-by-ten tongue-and-groove boards nailed diagonally onto the frame to increase its strength, clad in shingles or narrow board siding, rabbeted so that each board would overlap the one below. Floors were tongue-and-groove fir boards for the common people, oak with inlaid strips of eucalyptus for the few, with decorative linoleum "carpets" or tiles added to high-traffic and wet areas like bathrooms and kitchens. Wall studs were first covered in rough lath, the successor to the medieval wattle, held on by a million little nails hammered one at a time, then covered in plaster, the successor to the dung-and-lime daub. Plaster and lath houses have a solidity to them, their own sonic quality different from the reverberant "boom" of all but the most expensive modern drywalled homes. Many Vancouver houses are now more than a century old; the ones that have had a little maintenance over the decades are as solid as the day they were built.

The fact that so many houses were built so quickly during the first dozen years of the 20th century, and during the prosperous years late in the 1920s, is a tribute to the energy and productivity of the thousands of tradespeople of the day. Who were they? Research has tied some of the builder/developer groups of carpenters to sets of Vancouver houses. Bentley & Wear built the eight houses numbered from 2722 to 2758 West 7th in 1911 and another eight, 2203 to 2245 Stephens, the following year. A similar partnership, Archibald McLellan and Sinclair MacLellan, neighbours at 2049 and 2134 Semlin, built the six houses on the west side of Lily Street in Grandview in 1909 and 1910. Other names—the Pettigrews, Chin Wing, John J. Keenlyside, Fred Melton, the Harrison Brothers, J.A. Chisholm, Joseph Rainey, George Tyson—appear on permits for houses in old neighbourhoods like Kitsilano and Grandview. In the 1920s, contractor Charles Woodburn built houses in South Shaughnessy and Kerrisdale, including 5515, 5516, 5550 and 5584 Churchill, wood-burning a beam in the basements with his last name.[*]

Of the trades, electricians made the most—about $1,000 a year in 1911. Plumbers, bricklayers and masons made slightly less. Carpenters earned about $900 a year, painters and decorators about 10 percent less than them.[†]

As construction was so labour intensive—remaining so today, although with power tools, manufactured trusses and the rest of the industry's cornucopia it ought at least to be quicker—it's a wonder that prefabrication never produced a significant share of the city's housing stock. Whether called prefab or modular, it keeps resurfac-

[*]   For more than a decade, volunteer Heritage Vancouver researchers have been creating a database using the city's building permit registers, which were filed by date and had no cross-referencing. The 1901-21 section was launched on the Heritage Vancouver website in 2011.

[†]   See table, in McDonald, p. 102.

ing with each generation, most significantly during the Second World War. Modest wartime workers' houses still exist in North Vancouver and Burkeville on Sea Island. In eastern Canada, houses were designed for disassembly, parts of them prefabricated in factories so they could be erected in about 36 hours, a response to the limited resources and conservation ethic of wartime for people of low to moderate incomes.[*]

Many of the modernist architects whose careers started during the Second World War were interested in prefabrication as part of the social mission they adopted. The post-and-beam Ritchie House at 1032 Ridgewood Drive in North Vancouver, designed in 1950 by architect Ned Pratt, who worked with MacMillan Bloedel on the project, used prefabricated plywood wall panels as cladding.[†]

More recently, companies like Pan-Abode (established in 1948) have thrived, but for reasons that are unclear, few of its prefabricated houses have made it into Vancouver;

---

[*]   Lecture by Lorraine Gauthier, "Work Worth Doing," Morris Wosk Centre for Dialogue, November 5, 2010.

[†]   District of North Vancouver walking tour of Edgemont.

A row of typical old houses on 6th Avenue west of Ontario Street in Mount Pleasant, extraordinary now because it is the last one left north of Broadway. The unusual house of the four is the low bungalow, built in 1904, like a British colonial cottage, with wide eaves and a bell-cast roofline. A man named A. Colarch ran an automotive repair garage in the back yard for many years.

there are some in Deep Cove, Richmond and Delta. Mac-Blo returned to the field in the 1980s, spinning off a company called Nascor, which manufactured floor joists and pre-fabricated R-2000-standard wall units that could be customized to any arrangement of windows and doors.* Architect-developer Michael Geller has made modular and moveable housing a personal crusade, but so far has been shouting in the wilderness.

Over a century ago the BC Mills Timber & Trading Company (owner of Hastings Mill, on the waterfront, page 61) offered an extensive range of prefabricated homes. Many were erected in Vancouver but, alas, only a few remain. One example (see the watercolour on the previous page) stands at the corner of Adanac and Woodland near Commercial Drive. It was assembled there in 1906 and converted into three suites in 1960. Its entrance hallway is on one side, its bay-windowed parlour on the other. I know of two other B C M T & T houses that feature the gambrel roof style of the house at Adanac, at 1735 East 1st Avenue and 6051 Victoria Drive. The distinctive modular wall units of both have been covered with new siding and the original windows replaced with aluminum ones.

*   The farmhouse my wife and I built in Langley in 1994 was a "custom prefab" using the Nascor system.

Many old Vancouver houses are called "kits" by their owners. Most were not pre-fabricated but from pattern books—collections of floor plans from which builders could obtain drawings and lists of the necessary materials.[*] In reality, probably, most of the simple older houses in Vancouver came out of the heads of their experienced builders, whether in 1910, 1930 or 1950. The simplest of all were the tall gabled vernacular houses alluded to above, for their ease of modification into suites. They are easily recognized with their gabled façade and front porch, a separate structure attached to the boxy main house, and are as common in Winnipeg or Minneapolis as they are in Vancouver.

A very common style, now to be found most often in East Van, is the Early Cottage, illustrations of which appear on pages 104–5. With its hipped roof extending over a full-width front porch and single dormers on the front and back, it is the most

The two houses on the right, built in 1905 and 1910, anticipate the formal Edwardian style described on p. 102; the front porch is inset below an upper-storey gable, but the dormers have peaked roofs. The house on the left, built in 1909, is unusual only for having a hipped roof rather than the gabled one normal for that period. Its jerry-rigged fire escape, with a two-by-four as a handhold, would be every rooming-house tenant's nightmare.

---

[*] See Luxton, pp. 334–40, for an overview of ready-cut houses including the BCMT&T system and bungalow pattern books. According to historian Jim Wolf, the Homebuilders Lumber Company used plans by the architect Edwardes Sproat in the 1920s and created true kits with numbered pieces of lumber; one California Bungalow, at 1823 Venables, has been identified as its progeny. Future archivist J.S. Matthews contracted Prudential Builders to prefabricate, at their factory, his $3,500 house at 1343 Maple in 1911.

The Queen Anne style, unmistakable due to the corner turret.

BELOW > Architect Thomas Fee's 1903 home at Broughton and Pendrell, as it looked in 1989 as a rooming house called Holly Manor. That year, city council approved a heritage redevelopment that tidied it up and moved it closer to the corner, adding a bridging building to connect it to the vintage brick apartment house next door.

NEXT PAGE > The Jeffs Residence at Salsbury and Charles in Grandview, built in 1907 for Dr. Thomas Jeffs, a city coroner and alderman until his death in 1923. After nearly 90 years as a rooming house, it will be restored as part of a townhouse redevelopment.

modest example of the neoclassical revival of the late 19th century and thus can claim distant kinship with Shaughnessy mansions such as Hycroft (page 21) and The Hollies! Most of these cottages are single storey with four to six rooms, divided by a narrow central hallway; almost all have a bay window on the parlour side. The dormers are decorative; they dimly illuminate an almost useless attic—only a trap door off the hallway or kitchen provides access to it.

One of the popular BCMT&T prefabs was an Early Cottage—the Model J. A survivor is the house at 2165 West 13th Avenue.

The Queen Anne Revival is another style of early house still common in Grandview, with a few examples in Kitsilano and Mount Pleasant. The turret and the asymmetrical façade grant them a romantic air even on a cramped city lot. In the United States, the style evolved in the 1870s into spindled, patterned exuberance—like grand wedding cakes—but in Vancouver the detailing was usually more restrained, befitting the sober Canadian clientele.

The other definable style of early Vancouver house is the Edwardian, named for the brief reign of Edward VII during the first decade of the 20th century, a period that was also the start of Vancouver's biggest property boom. Edwardian-style houses, very common in Mount Pleasant and Grandview but rarely seen on the West Side, are a more stylish and formal version of the tall, boxy, vernacular house noted above. Unlike the latter, where the porch is a separate structure projecting from the main house, the Edwardian's porch is indented into the front façade, its posts holding up the upper storey and front end of the roof.

Edwardian houses are easily recognized by their very prominent triangular closed gable and—in most examples—large shed-roofed dormers on both sides, which appear to buttress the steeply pitched main roof. Their antecedents include American Shingle-style houses, echoes of which can be seen in the curving walls of the indented sleeping porches that are a feature of many Vancouver examples. The sleeping porch shows kinship with the Craftsman style, both reflecting the open-air movement of a century ago that saw people sleeping on porches year round and children swaddled in coats and mitts doing their school work outside.[*]

---

[*]   Intended to combat tuberculosis, the movement began in Germany in 1904 and rapidly spread to the rest of Europe and North America.

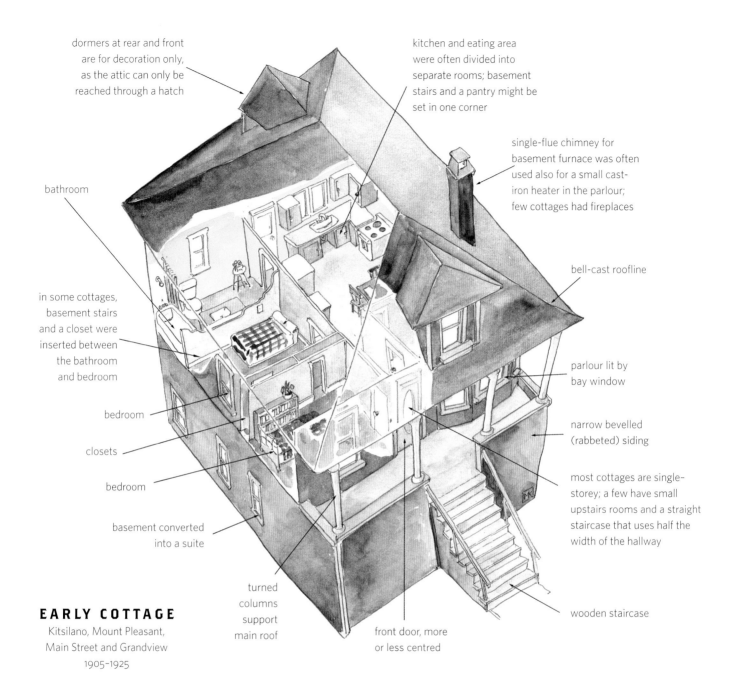

dormers at rear and front are for decoration only, as the attic can only be reached through a hatch

kitchen and eating area were often divided into separate rooms; basement stairs and a pantry might be set in one corner

single-flue chimney for basement furnace was often used also for a small cast-iron heater in the parlour; few cottages had fireplaces

bathroom

bell-cast roofline

in some cottages, basement stairs and a closet were inserted between the bathroom and bedroom

parlour lit by bay window

bedroom

narrow bevelled (rabbeted) siding

closets

most cottages are single-storey; a few have small upstairs rooms and a straight staircase that uses half the width of the hallway

bedroom

basement converted into a suite

turned columns support main roof

wooden staircase

front door, more or less centred

EARLY COTTAGE

Kitsilano, Mount Pleasant,
Main Street and Grandview
1905–1925

The Early Cottage was a simple bungalow for the worker and his family a century ago, costing perhaps $1,000 to build. Two bedrooms, an indoor bathroom and a modest parlour, dining area and kitchen—usually about 800 square feet of living area—fitted neatly onto a $300, 33-foot lot, leaving plenty of back yard space for some fruit trees and a garden.

The watercolour on the previous page shows a variant of the style with a half-width porch and cutaway bay window, at the back of the lot at the northeast corner of Broadway and St. Catherine's in Mount Pleasant. Built in 1905, it was buried for many years, like the houses on p. 80-3, by a double shopfront (now demolished) on the corner, the Homeway Confectionery, next

to the Maple Leaf (later K's) Barber Shop. A renovation in 2011, shortly after I painted the watercolour, closed in the porch and stripped the tired old house of its remaining character. I left out the blue security fence that has surrounded the property recently, presumably to deter homeless campers.

THE CRAFTSMAN STYLE OF HOUSE DISTINGUISHES WEST SIDE KITSI-lano from East Side neighbourhoods like Mount Pleasant and Grandview, where Queen Anne and Edwardian houses are the norm. Kitsilano is *the* Craftsman suburb, with blocks of bungalows that might have migrated intact from Los Angeles. The most lavish is the enclave north of 4th Avenue between Blenheim and Alma. More modest examples of the style are common on streets such as Macdonald and Stephens between 4th and Broadway. Smaller examples of the style, California Bungalows (single-storey houses with a gabled main roof extending over the front porch), are dotted throughout the area but can best be seen in the memorable row on 5th Avenue west of Bayswater.

In architectural history, the Craftsman style emerged from the American Arts and Crafts movement. (British Arts and Crafts houses, popularly called Tudors, have the dark and light vertical stripes of half-timbering and were the style of choice in Shaughnessy Heights, see page 110.) Charles and Henry Greene, brothers who practised architecture in Pasadena from 1893 to 1914, inspired and popularized the style.[*] Their best works are extraordinary examples of craftsmanship—wooden detailing, mixtures of textures, a love of wood for wood's sake—and style, often with a hint of Japan in the profiles and rooflines. The small California Bungalow became hugely popular all over North America, tapping into a dream of homeownership (and of southern California) as potent as the condomania that recently swept across Vancouver. Verse and song celebrated the new suburbia—modern yet rustic, easy maintenance—*My darling in a little patch of garden, tra la la.* The Bob Rennies of a century ago rhapsodized about bungalows.

BELOW > Two Craftsman houses I painted in 1989 shortly before their demolition. On the right, the long-time residence of city prosecutor Gordon Wood Scott, built in 1912 on a triple lot at 2880 West 28th Avenue in Mackenzie Heights. Its granite foundations and large, exposed wooden brackets are typical of the style. On the left, a California Bungalow—the modest variant of the style—has a similar love for the "real" surfaces of wood and, in its case, brick. It stood at the corner of 36th and Yew and was advertised as "What A Lot!"—meaning the lot was the only thing of value, according to the realtor and, as it turned out, the buyer.

* McAlester, p. 454.

CRAFTSMAN HOUSE

Kitsilano • 1910–1914

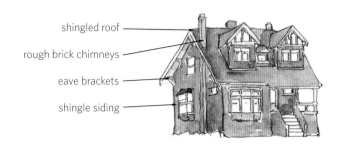

shingled roof

rough brick chimneys

eave brackets

shingle siding

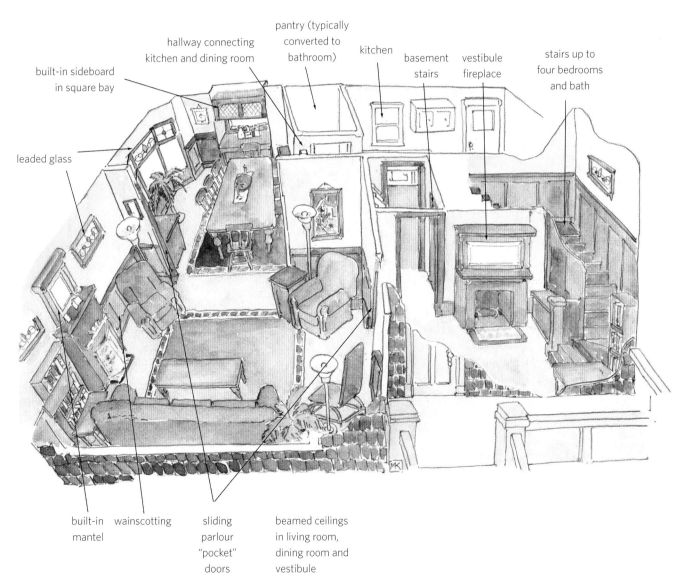

hallway connecting
kitchen and dining room

pantry (typically
converted to
bathroom)

kitchen

basement
stairs

vestibule
fireplace

stairs up to
four bedrooms
and bath

built-in sideboard
in square bay

leaded glass

built-in
mantel

wainscotting

sliding
parlour
"pocket"
doors

beamed ceilings
in living room,
dining room and
vestibule

The house at 1720 Waterloo in Kitsilano, built in 1925, is a relatively rare Vancouver example of the British Arts and Crafts style. With its sheltering, hipped roof and faux half-timbering, it harkens back to the English cottages of popular imagery, such as the much-reproduced watercolours of Victorian artist Helen Allingham. Offered for sale in 2010 as a property with development potential, the house looked like a goner, but as of this writing it has avoided a date with the bulldozer. The small white house nearby, facing Point Grey Road, designed by Ian Davidson with assistance from Dan White, did not. It was a rare example of a modern house built on a tight lot conforming to setbacks and the other constraints of urban living.

Compared to most early houses in Vancouver, the Craftsman exudes a rich warmth. Chimneys and porch posts contain clinkers, the rough, vitrified purple-tinged bricks from the hottest part of the kiln that were useless in buildings seeking a sleek look. Rafter-ends were exposed, eaves bracketed, walls shingled. Many had beautiful built-in cabinetry with bevelled glass insets, window seats, bookcases and colonnades that glowed under yellow lamplight, wainscots, leaded glass in floral designs, deep porches. They are cozy, almost cave-like with a "hobbit-house quality," in architect Robert Lemon's words, that make them an ideal nest. In Los Angeles, their prominent overhanging eaves offer protection from the hot sun; in Seattle and Vancouver they appear hunkered down and sheltering against the rain. They have a real separation between inside and out that appeals to many people, different from the seamless house-to-garden transition sought by fans of modernism.

The success of Craftsman houses in northern cities like Vancouver a century ago is an early example of technology triumphing over climate. Electric lighting made their dark interiors comfortable in the long winter. Earlier houses—the Victorians on page 96, for example, had narrow eaves and bay windows, both of which were ways of allowing the maximum amount of light into a house; the cutaway bay on the cottage on page 105 is another way of accomplishing this. The turret on the Queen Anne on page 103 is an even more dramatic method of allowing every available photon indoors. Many early houses were divided into small rooms that could be closed off with doors

and heated; Craftsman houses, on the other hand, were open plan, breezy and easy in *caliente* California yet possible to heat with a furnace in 1910-era Vancouver.

Craftsman—what's in a name? No wonder the houses are so popular among old-home buyers, as the name implies "quality." They are very stylish, yet their interiors absorb the clutter of a typical family. Just about any decorating style seems to work as long as it doesn't include really large pieces of artwork that need floor-to-ceiling wall space. There are purists who furnish them to period with Gustav Stickley sofas and chairs, more frequently perhaps in the heritage enclaves of Victoria and New Westminster than in straightforward, practical Vancouver. You get the sense that people like such old houses because they can make them their own—put their own stamp on them—in contrast to modernist houses, which don't really adapt. Rather, the owners and their stuff have to adapt to that style. Perhaps the difference in taste comes down to the clutterers versus the neatniks?

Why has neo-Craftsman become the default look for new houses, townhouses and even small apartment buildings in the Vancouver area a century after the arrival of the style? One reason could be that the articulated façades and woodsy details look homey, compared to the sleek stucco-and-steel of urban condominiums, and hold up well against moss and rain streaks. Architect Allen Price has a more cynical opinion: unlike modernism, in which edges and finishes have to be precise, Craftsman styles still turn out all right even when builders make all kinds of mistakes.

S HAUGHNESSY HEIGHTS WAS THE FIRST VANCOUVER NEIGHBOURHOOD to get a customized zoning schedule and design review process, intended to help its fine homes and estate gardens adapt to late-20th-century reality. Some homeowners had been unable to keep their houses up in the face of the same problems with mortgages and maintenance that average people experienced. Other homes had been roughly made over as fraternity or rooming houses in the decades from the Great Depression through the 1960s. Accordingly, in 1982, 369 homes built in the gilded years of the 1910s and 1920s, representing a kind of wealthy display maintained by squads of servants and gardeners, were identified as having design and craftsmanship that made them worthy of some kind of preservation.

Allowing conversions of some houses into suites and additions of coach houses to properties over half an acre appeared timely. There was no coercion, as none of the influential owners would allow the imposition of a restrictive heritage designation onto their house. The option of demolishing and building new was always on the table but seemed inconceivable—at least to people like me—as the old houses were so grand, so beautifully built.

However, the kind of wealth that had built the core of Shaughnessy Heights emerged again in the 1990s, following the immigration and real-estate boom of the post–Expo '86 years. Like the original residents—who had moved before 1900 from Blueblood Alley (West Hastings) to the Sunset Beach and Stanley Park edges of the West End, and again around 1910 to virgin Shaughnessy—these new buyers wanted new homes. But, unlike the originals, they lacked fresh fields to plough. Something would have to be flattened if their dream home was to have a Vancouver address.

The big Arts and Crafts (Tudor-style) homes, such as the Maclure & Fox-designed Nichol residence on The Crescent at McRae Street, seemed to capture the essence of

Opulent interiors characterized the homes of Shaughnessy Heights. The photo shows the foyer of Glen Brae, now Canuck place, as it was in 1940. (LEONARD FRANK PHOTO, VPL 16100A)

the neighbourhood and were in less danger than the supporting cast of lesser houses. The Craftsman style seemed especially vulnerable. In the summer of 1990 a stockbroker named Tony Nabata tried to get a permit to knock down an 8,300-square-foot Craftsman at 1037 Matthews; he wanted to build an 11,300-square-foot Tudor and stated publicly that his potential victim was not a mansion of Shaughnessy calibre (and not as good as the houses he had owned in Ottawa before moving to Vancouver). But a year later the city reached an agreement to rezone the property, exchanging the designation of the existing house for the construction of an infill dwelling.

Other houses of the Craftsman style, especially more modest examples like the one on this page, have either disappeared or are unlikely to survive. Their replacements are, in the main, muddled, fake-heritage "McMansions," meeting the period design guidelines and squeaking through the design review process but not preserving anything at all. According to its legal department, the city lacks the power to stop an owner who wants to build a new house; probably a majority in the neighbourhood believes that its true heritage is property rights.

The volunteers, both residents and experts, on the design review panel have had to contend with and try to improve some extraordinarily dodgy proposals. To my eye, the vast majority of the new houses look graceless and bloated, with roofs like little toupées atop bland walls and oversize double-height entranceways with double

The Craftsman houses of Shaughnessy Heights are a kind of supporting cast for the grand mansions but are, themselves, elegant and substantial buildings. They lack the ostentatious display of the new faux-heritage styles popular with many recent buyers and have been picked off one by one in recent years. This house, at 3738 Hudson, probably built around 1914 for G.W. Hobson, had been vacant for a year when I painted it in 2010 and was still vacant a year later.

front doors. It was easy to become annoyed just by the overdone, decorative, "heritage" cosmetics, but it was in the proportions of windows to doors, of roofs to walls, of chimneys to façades, that an educated eye could see the paucity of talent of many of the builders. There were few half storeys—the pitched roofs pierced by dormers that look so picturesque from the street—in the new designs. Clients wanted all the rooms to have full-height walls and none of the sloped ceilings of traditional homes.

Osler Street between The Crescent and King Edward was the site of the most relentless demolition and new construction. There and elsewhere in Shaughnessy Heights about 50 character houses have been lost since the design guidelines were adopted 30 years ago. However, two proposals to *retain* very significant homes attracted major opposition from neighbours because they involved both added density and strata-titling of the properties.

The first was Greencroft, the unusual turreted mansion of industrialist and lieutenant governor Eric Hamber at Cypress and Matthews. Hamber, whose change of wedding plans with tycoon John Hendry's daughter caused him to miss the maiden voyage of the *Titanic*, had a distinguished career. At the turn of this century his 1913 house was restored and its large property discreetly infilled with two smaller residences by architect Robert Lemon, landscaping by Eckford & Associates.

A more recent project, ongoing in 2011, involved the restoration of the mansion and garden, on The Crescent, of *Province* publisher Walter C. Nichol. The restoration preserved the immaculate period streetscape but added controversial townhouses to the bottom of the property, which curves down to the southeast corner of 16th and Granville. As one city staffer quipped, "it was a new type of public consultation process. People sent their lawyers rather than coming themselves."

As far back as anyone could remember, the corner at Granville had been a woodlot of mature trees. In early 2010, all the trees came down for the construction of the townhouses, exposing the side of the splendid old John West mansion higher up on the slope. For anyone familiar with photographs of Shaughnessy from a century ago when it was treeless, the sight was almost like travelling in time. And for anyone familiar with Shaughnessy's history, the townhouses are an evolution of the ones that were tucked behind Hycroft (page 21) in 1963, albeit on a much more prominent site.

What will become of the huge new Shaughnessy mansions? If there were another depression-war cycle like the 1930s and 1940s, with fewer wealthy people and a shortage of rental housing, they would certainly convert easily into rooming houses because, unlike the century-old mansions, every bedroom has an ensuite!

"Residence of Mr. J. West, a typical Shaughnessy Heights Home," from the *Point Grey Gazette*, Edition of Progress, 1913. It was the first home converted into suites following the adoption, in 1982, of a new zoning schedule for Shaughnessy Heights. Its next-door neighbour, the Chinese consulate, incorporates the Tudor house of physician and coroner William Brydone-Jack at 3338 Granville.

WHILE MODERNISM WAS GETTING GOING IN EUROPE AFTER THE First World War, North America continued its drift into architectural nostalgia. People had begun building Eclectic houses—as historians Virginia and Lee McAlester described them*—in the United States in the 1880s, for example, half-timbered Tudors, white stucco Spanish colonials with red tile roofs and symmetrical Georgians with shutters. Dutch colonials with gambrel roofs and Cape Cods had shutters, too.

Wealthy people in Vancouver built a few such houses before the First World War—the Mission-style John West house (see previous page) being a good example—but the period styles really got going in the 1920s. Some were very elegant products of the pens of architects such as Sharp & Thompson or Townley & Matheson; the latter pair built themselves houses in south Shaughnessy in picturesque English and French Norman styles respectively.†

In some of the "English" houses of that period, one side of the front gable extended downward in a graceful curve, like a buttress, across an arched gateway into a back garden, giving the house a cute asymmetry. That steep curve is sometimes called a cat-slide roof; it lent those houses a storybook, sometimes romantic quality, like that

Certain of a pending demolition, I spent an afternoon in the summer of 2010 putting the gloomy, deteriorated house at 4785 West 2nd Avenue into my sketchbook. Tucked into a forest glade surrounded by towering trees, it presented a stark contrast with the manicured, grand homes elsewhere on that exclusive block. Its rehabilitation by new owners is the exception rather than the rule in that part of West Point Grey; new mansions, especially on the nearby blocks of Drummond and Belmont, rank as the most expensive in western Canada.

---

* McAlester & McAlester, *A Field Guide to American Houses*.

† Fred Townley's home at 1636 Avondale was recently demolished. See its photo in *Vancouver Remembered*, p. 198.

Tranquil Wiltshire Street in Kerrisdale in 1970, 20 years before most of the homes on the block were replaced with monster houses. Just a couple of front gardens interrupted the expanse of lawn on the long block between 52nd and 54th. (PHOTOS BY RUBY KLUCKNER)

A typical leaded-glass pattern for 1920s houses, a design that I, as a child, always took to be either an angel or a football player.

of a Hansel and Gretel cottage. This was, after all, the era of Disney's *Snow White and the Seven Dwarfs*. Other houses looked a bit militaristic with crenellations and pixie-sized turrets over tiny front vestibules—it was also the era of Mussolini and Hitler.

The house on the previous page, in the mansion belt of "Extreme" Point Grey, is a wonderful example of that picturesque English style. Built in 1925 for John and Hattie Leek, whose Leek & Co. was a heating and ventilation supplier, it was the long-time home of the Sinclair family. In recent years it has become incredibly dilapidated, a mossy mausoleum on nearly an acre of forest trees, the kind of lot where, as one neighbour quipped, you have to check your watch to know whether it's night or day. It was occupied for many years by three aging sisters, whose sedans were left abandoned in the driveway when their owners could no longer drive. The house went on the market in the autumn of 2010—"a rare estate lot located in an exclusive and quiet neighbourhood just north of 4th and west of Blanca. Attention all developers and investors! Here is your opportunity to build a dream home," said the advertisement— and sold quickly for $300,000 more than its $4.8 million asking price.

The new owners, Arran and Ratana Stephens, attracted attention only when they removed nearly two dozen trees, in violation of the city's one-size-fits-all tree-preservation bylaw. As reported in the news soon after they bought the house, they intended to restore the house and add a greenhouse, a vegetable garden, arbours, a pond and an orchard of 30 trees.* Unlike what so many owners wanted to do in Shaughnessy Heights, the couple sought to use their considerable assets to add to a place rather than wipe the slate clean and start over. One could jump for joy over such a turn of events.

Once prosperity became widespread in the mid-1920s, builders got up to speed with the period styles, especially those working on the West Side. On the East Side, simple gabled cottages were the norm and affordability the touchstone, a pattern that continued until building ground to a halt again in the 1930s depression.

The house on this page is in Kerrisdale, built in 1929 by carpenter Alex Cochrane, who lived at 6976 Angus. A modest, middle-class, few-frills, solid family home, it is

---

* "Owner says he wanted to improve neglected garden" by Naoibh O'Connor, *Vancouver Courier*, December 8, 2010.

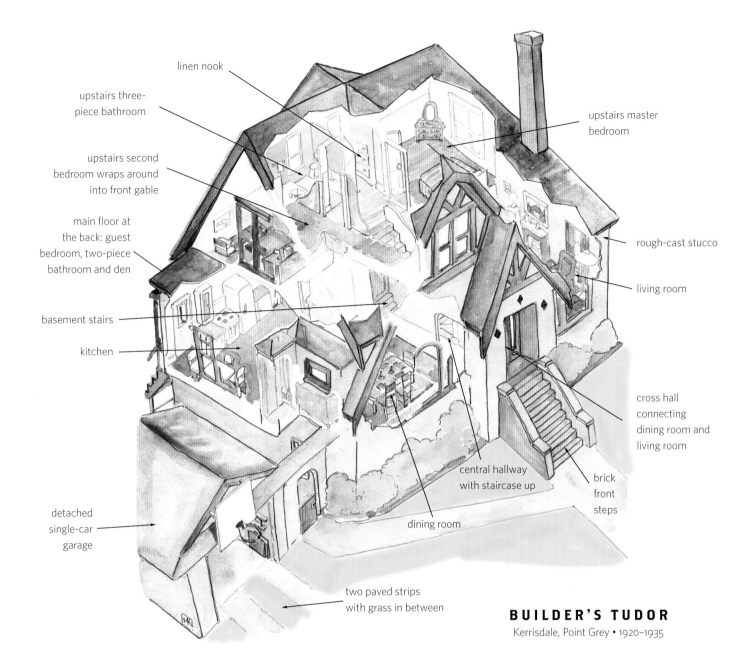

linen nook

upstairs three-
piece bathroom

upstairs second
bedroom wraps around
into front gable

main floor at
the back: guest
bedroom, two-piece
bathroom and den

basement stairs

kitchen

detached
single-car
garage

upstairs master
bedroom

rough-cast stucco

living room

cross hall
connecting
dining room and
living room

brick
front
steps

central hallway
with staircase up

dining room

two paved strips
with grass in between

BUILDER'S TUDOR
Kerrisdale, Point Grey • 1920–1935

part of the last generation of "average" places built with old-growth lumber. I spent the first 18 or so years of my life in it and can confirm that it was typical of its neighbourhood south of 49th Avenue and less posh than the homes north of 49th. It was a builder's Tudor, no more, no less. Some of my childhood friends lived in Georgian houses, one in a Spanish-style one, but all were basically the same. The house is one of a few left in a neighbourhood almost completely redeveloped with monster houses in the past 20 years.

The house was a classic cross-gabled design for a wide (66 foot) lot, a Tudor because the builder had added a little fake half-timbering to the nested front gables. Its walls were dressed with rough-cast stucco. The front door opened onto a central hallway with stairs dog-legging up from it. The living room and dining room had fine hardwood floors with dark eucalyptus piping around the edges (covered in wall-to-wall shag in the 1960s, of course); the former was used for Christmas and parties as the den, with its small couches and hi-fi, was a more comfortable and intimate family space. The arrival of television in the late 1950s precipitated a change—Dad building a rec room in the basement—because TV was a weekend thing, too intrusive on family life for the balance of the week.

In the small kitchen, the counters were originally tiled, then modernized with Arborite clamped along the edge by a grooved chrome strip. There was room for a table with an Arborite top and chrome-tube legs set against a double window that looked onto the garage roof. Through a spring-loaded door was the formal dining room. All-purpose "family rooms" didn't yet exist and no one could imagine wanting to watch somebody cook.

The upstairs bedrooms were quite cramped with sloping ceilings, and the upstairs bathroom was shared and small, the floor tiled with small black and white hexagons. A toilet and a tub with a shower curtain sliding along a chrome rod occupied one wall, a small vanity and towel rails the other. It would be another generation before ensuites became a required part of a Vancouver house. The downstairs bathroom was a "powder room" with just a toilet and a vanity.

It wasn't a lot of house for the size of the property but it was lavish compared with the kind of places built in those days on the East Side. Regardless of locale, in the baby-boom years most houses were chockablock with children, doubling up in bedrooms and lining up for bathrooms and the phone. Kids were kicked outside to play, and made good use of the big back yards as impromptu baseball diamonds and football fields. Many of the hut-like garages had basketball hoops mounted on their gables and some basements stored a net for the road-hockey games that occupied dry winter days. Children "made their own fun," as old people are constantly telling younger ones.

Beginning in the late 1930s and continuing for a couple of decades until ranchers and Vancouver Specials began to replace them, modest "starter" houses like the one on the next page lined block after block of East Vancouver, Burnaby and North Van. They were a mid-century vernacular, springing fully formed from the minds of experienced builders. Typically hip-roofed and at least partially stuccoed, they were a classic hard-times family bungalow.

"They were smaller and to use the space better the through-hall was eliminated," Ken Terriss wrote. "The tiny front entrance and vestibule were only for formal arrivals and salesmen; family and friends came

For New Homes See . . .

Lulu Island Lumber Co.

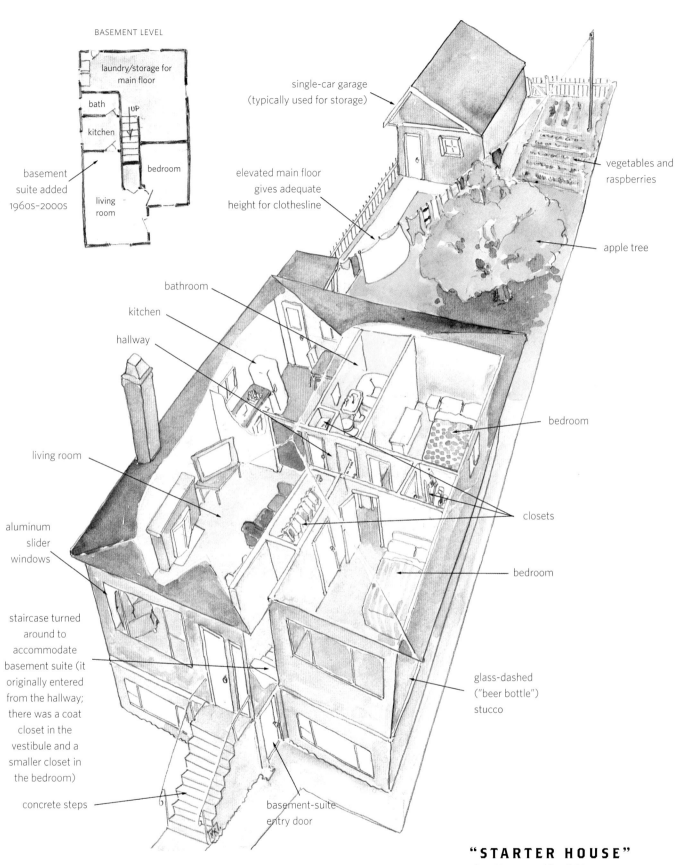

BASEMENT LEVEL

laundry/storage for main floor

bath

UP

kitchen

basement suite added 1960s–2000s

bedroom

living room

single-car garage (typically used for storage)

elevated main floor gives adequate height for clothesline

vegetables and raspberries

apple tree

bathroom

kitchen

hallway

bedroom

living room

closets

aluminum slider windows

bedroom

staircase turned around to accommodate basement suite (it originally entered from the hallway; there was a coat closet in the vestibule and a smaller closet in the bedroom)

glass-dashed ("beer bottle") stucco

concrete steps

basement-suite entry door

"STARTER HOUSE"
East Vancouver, South Vancouver,
Dunbar, Marpole, Kitsilano
1940s–1950s

in by the kitchen door. It was usually possible to get to the bedrooms and bathroom without passing through the living room. Economics seemed to have eliminated the front porch; we now had the most minimal set of steps and a tiny landing, sometimes without cover and often quite high above the ground as the basement was still kept as shallow as possible. One technical advance was the use of concrete steps that were more durable than wooden ones."*

Many have large windows installed at ground level facing the street. They are the first Vancouver house style that actively anticipated the conversion of the basement into usable space, probably as a suite. Because there was no porch, the principal rooms actually received adequate light.

M EANWHILE, FAR AWAY IN ANOTHER PART OF TOWN, AND THE OTHER side of the harbour, radical new post-and-beam modernist houses and split-levels were being fitted by young architects into less regimented plots of the West Coast landscape.

The West Vancouver home of artist and teacher Bertram Charles Binning, today sporting a plaque as a National Historic Site, heralded the new age when it was built in 1941 by architects Ned Pratt and Bob Berwick. It reflected Binning's romantic outlook: "His house opened most of its garden front—mediated by a trellised paved patio—to a landscaped lot that sloped down to Burrard Inlet and the maritime life Binning loved to celebrate in his drawings and paintings."† Binning's house has always reminded me of the psychiatrist Axel Münthe's reflection on his Villa San Michele house and garden on Capri half a world away: "I built it small because the soul needs more room than the body."

The many houses that followed in the 1940s and 1950s by architects such as Ron Thom, Arthur Erickson, Geoffrey Massey, Fred Hollingsworth, John Porter, Douglas Shadbolt, Barry Downs, Harold Semmens and Douglas Simpson dotted the pictur-esque edges of the city—West Vancouver, North Vancouver's Capilano Highlands, view lots in West Point Grey and the University Endowment Lands and wooded hide-aways in Southlands.

It was a magical time when people of modest incomes (including the young archi-tects themselves who built their own homes) could get hold of a piece of the West Coast dream. The young modernists of that era espoused a philosophy of improving society through good architecture, which worked well for their homes but less so during their forays into public housing (page 152). Their houses were *so* different from the builders' efforts of the 1920s on Vancouver's view streets in areas like Mackenzie Heights (similar to pages 114–5), where stock plans took no notice of the panorama and renovators later took houses' fronts or backs off to try to capture it.

The West Coast Modern style drew from European modernism, Frank Lloyd Wright's Prairie houses and the Japanese influences that were never out of fash-ion in Vancouver. "Nature looks at its best in juxtaposition to a geometric shape or

---

*   Unpublished paper by Ken Terriss, "The Vancouver Special: an elegant solution to housing on 33-foot wide lots."

†   Windsor-Liscombe, p. 43.

"... there's a lot to be said for this modern west coast trend to outdoor living ... but this year George has managed to condense it to a p'thy, concise, succinct phrase ... "

July 2, 1954

THE VANCOUVER SUN

Two versions of the West Coast lifestyle of the 1950s and 1960s. Ironically, Len Norris commissioned a modernist house for his West Vancouver lot not long after he drew the cartoon. (USED WITH PERMISSION; PHOTOGRAPH BY HERBERT L. MCDONALD, CIRCA 1965)

pattern such as, for example, pergolas or trellises ... the extension of the exterior into the interior produces a very successful blending of nature with man-made architecture," wrote Fred Lasserre, the founding director of the UBC School of Architecture about 1947.[*] Their most radical elements were the grade-level entries—such a difference from the long flights of stairs on older houses—and their roofs, sometimes low pitched but, in the most representative examples, flat.

"The significance of the flat roof lies in the potential liberation of the plan form, which provides great freedom to adapt a house to sloping and unusual sites, and allows the admission of light between roof planes via clerestory windows which reflect light deep into interior spaces," Douglas Shadbolt wrote. "In his house, Binning also demonstrated the potential relationship of abstract art to the new architectural forms, both by providing an interior gallery for his own works and by painting a mural on the exterior entrance wall of the house."[†]

Modernism—what's in a name? Like *craftsman*, the word *modern* releases its own kind of endorphins. If you're not a modernist you must be old-fashioned. Modernist style emerged from the same reduction to principles as the primal shapes—circles, squares and triangles—that underpinned Cézanne's painting at the dawn of modern

---

[*]   Quoted in Windsor-Liscombe, p. 43.

[†]   Shadbolt, p. 108.

art 120 years ago. The elimination of all detail, seen most extremely in commercial architecture of the time, such as the noble tedium of Pacific Centre's white walls and black towers, is another feature of the style. Buildings of this style are much harder to get right compared to the decorated buildings of earlier eras.

Essentially, these were houses to be seen in splendid isolation, and were almost anti-urban in their conception. In the architecture courses I took at UBC about 1970, I was one of the few students whose heart didn't beat faster at the sight of a flat roof. I just didn't get it, at least not for a rainy place like Vancouver. To me they lacked the sense of shelter, the cave-like quality, I thought appropriate to life north of the 49th parallel. But the style was still fashionable then and continues to be so today, 70 years after it arrived, with architects young and old.

A recent master of the modernist style was Dan White, whose austere, strongly angular buildings are much admired on the best of their picturesque West Coast sites but can be controversial as well. Some believed the house he designed at 57th Avenue and West Boulevard, now cowering behind a very tall hedge, clashed with its period neighbours. Fellow architect Ian Davidson described his work as "doing palaces for the rich," a statement that was intended to be complimentary.[*]

This view was always a problem for modernist architecture, as "The houses were supposed to be affordable for a broad spectrum of Vancouverites. But in fact they were within the reach of only the professional classes."[†] Some young architects and design-oriented people in the city today are looking to the Vancouver Special as a kind of hard-times modernism that can be stripped and altered to capture features of the style.

In the late 1950s and 1960s, the radicalism of modernist houses was tempered into a more traditional form with pitched cedar-shake roofs and stone chimneys while retaining open, rambling floor plans and easy access to patios and landscaped yards. Some were real ranchers on a single level, others split-levels, and were very common on the big lots of Oakridge, south Kerrisdale and Southlands at the time. Bob Berwick and C.B.K. Van Norman were the main progenitors of this "eminently practical" style that was taking the western United States by storm. "They became the prototypes for the intensive suburban development across the whole region and were probably the most influential houses in this period."[‡] Many have been demolished as new owners seek an even greater indoors.

As for Binning, he lived in his house until his death in 1976; his widow, Jessie, stayed on until her death in 2007. The Land Conservancy of B.C. now has title to the house and is raising an endowment of $300,000 to maintain it. Binning's most public and enduring piece of art is the colourful tile motifs on the BC Electric building at Burrard and Nelson, now known as The Electra.

The 1939 art moderne house at 3908 West Broadway sold in 2011 for $2.36 million, $400,000 above the asking price.

*   "The Many Mansions of Dan White" by Philip Marchand, *Western Living* magazine, May 1985.

†   Windsor-Liscombe, p. 131.

‡   Shadbolt, p. 112.

L OVE THEM OR HATE THEM, VANCOUVER SPECIALS ARE THE BIGGEST affordable housing resource in the city, as flexible and adaptable (and attractive, perhaps) as a shopping mall. Recent renovations of them, publicized in tours organized by the Vancouver Heritage Foundation, have drawn positive attention from the punditry.

It's obvious but worth stating regardless that beauty is in the eye of the beholder and that most people who live in Specials think they're just fine and don't have to be improved at all. If they hadn't worked so well and been so affordable they wouldn't have proliferated, expanding from their narrow-lot East Side origins across the city and morphing into larger and newer forms as the years went by. Builders easily found sites, picking up houses straddling double lots dating from the years when land was cheap and people wanted extra space for gardens. The 1903 Kerrysdale House at 2941 West 42nd Avenue—the namesake of the district—was one such victim in the 1960s; two Specials now occupy its property. Later, builders scooped up postwar starter houses and were able to double the square footage on the lot.

The original Special was the result of a relentless drive to reduce costs and find the cheapest way to enclose the maximum amount of space. Under zoning that was still in effect in the 1960s—which, at the beginning of the century, effectively created the long flight of stairs to a house's front porch—builders reckoned it made more sense to enter a house by going *down* a couple of steps. They eliminated the expensive front stairs (which no longer went to a porch anyway), putting a staircase inside the house rising to the main living rooms on the upper floor. Going higher with another floor would have been possible under the zoning but was too expensive.

A modernist house by architect Bob Berwick, at 1519 West 33rd. Built in 1937, it has an unusual "pinwheel" floor plan, in design consultant Richard Keate's words. Berwick's mother was the client; as Keate says, "Modern architecture has a well-established history of indulgent mothers-of-architects." The prominent chimneys and inset pyramidal roof with no eaves recall some of Frank Lloyd Wright's house designs. The house looked abandoned and derelict in 2011, but work commenced at the end of the year on infill buildings using the award-winning plans of architect Peter Cardew.

Pushing the site coverage to its limit, builders stretched the house into the back yard and created a main floor of about 1,500 square feet on a standard 33-foot lot—one on which 1,800 square feet ought to have been the maximum living area. But because the "basement" wasn't counted in the square footage, a Special could contain about 3,000 square feet of living area—much larger than what the city had intended. "In my renovation designs I almost never came across houses from the '20s to the '50s which had used their available area," wrote Ken Terriss in 1996. "However, now the builders, presumably pushed by the market, began to stretch the buildings to the limit."[*]

The typical house comprised, on the second floor, a kitchen, three bedrooms, two bathrooms and a living and dining area. The first floor contained the furnace and water heater, a washer and dryer and the roughed-in plumbing for an additional bathroom.

To reduce the amount of lumber and roofing material, the builders flattened the roof as far as they could, the low pitch adding to the boxcar façade so different from the up-down rhythmic triangles of a traditional mixed Vancouver block. Tar and gravel was the preferred roofing system, like that used for the flat roofs of commercial and apartment buildings, but, because of the slight slope, "tar creep" could be a problem. Asphalt shingles could also be made to work as long as the lapped edges were glued down.

Stucco was the cheapest possible finish and was practical for the long, narrow side yards because non-combustible siding had been mandated by building-code changes. Frameless, sliding, aluminum windows were the cheapest choice, removing the final element of articulation from the house's walls. The front elevation usually received a little decoration, however, with brick veneer applied to its lower portion and an aluminum railing attached to the very shallow second-storey balcony, providing a sort of security bar when the living room's sliding glass doors were opened.

Who's to blame . . . uh, who came up with the idea? There's a consensus that "plan services" (that is, drafting) firms formalized the evolving Special, turning it into a kind of semi-prefab for which permits could be obtained almost instantly. According to one story, a builder named Crawchuck had the original concept, which was then drawn up by a draftsman named Larry Cudney, who was proud of his role as midwife because the Special was not "a big stupid house as a monument to someone's big stupid life." Retired planner Jon Ellis recalled a plan services business at Broadway and Yukon, just down the street from city hall, where "you could buy a set of drawings for $100."[†]

The back yards were reduced even further by the erection of attached carports with decks above creating, on many lots, an almost completely paved space instead of garden or, at least, permeable soil. Sometimes the front yard was used for children's swingsets because of the proliferation of "stuff" out back.

It was inside where the Special really showed its value: the downstairs floor could be easily modified into extra bedrooms or an indoor play area, or closed off as a

---

[*] My analysis of the evolution of the Special leans heavily on Ken Terriss's research and experience.

[†] Both quotes from "The Residential Landscape" by Shelagh Lindsey and Helen Spiegelman in Schofield, p. 172.

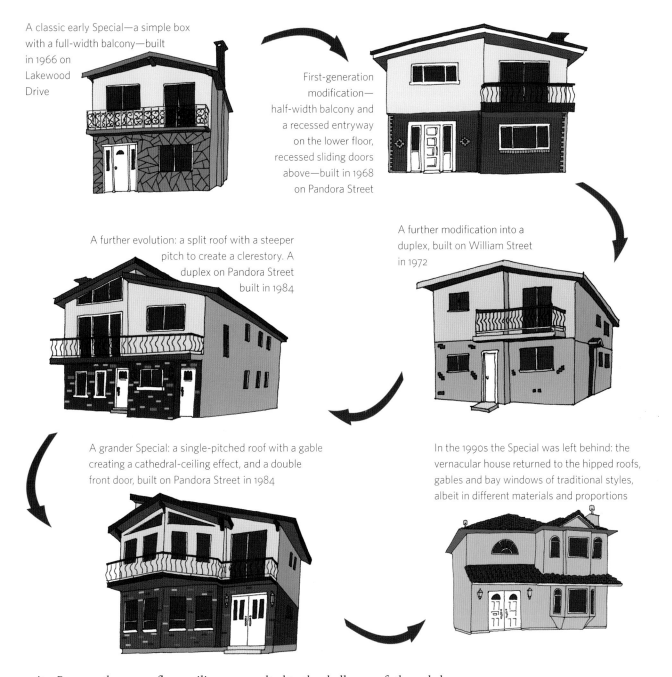

A classic early Special—a simple box with a full-width balcony—built in 1966 on Lakewood Drive

First-generation modification—half-width balcony and a recessed entryway on the lower floor, recessed sliding doors above—built in 1968 on Pandora Street

A further modification into a duplex, built on William Street in 1972

A further evolution: a split roof with a steeper pitch to create a clerestory. A duplex on Pandora Street built in 1984

In the 1990s the Special was left behind: the vernacular house returned to the hipped roofs, gables and bay windows of traditional styles, albeit in different materials and proportions

A grander Special: a single-pitched roof with a gable creating a cathedral-ceiling effect, and a double front door, built on Pandora Street in 1984

suite. Because the upper-floor ceiling was vaulted to the shallow roof, the only bearing wall was the one along the middle of the downstairs floor. They anticipated or perhaps responded to the change, for cultural or economic reasons, from the typical nuclear family of the mid-20th century to more complex arrangements involving grandparents, other relatives, boomerang children and other creative mixtures of consenting adults.

A zoning change at the end of 1974 began the modification of the original Special when it eliminated the "free" ground-floor basement. Houses were henceforth built as slab on grade, which saved even more money because of the simpler foundations but reduced the floor space from about 1,500 to 1,200 square feet per floor. They retained the ground-level entry, of course, also one of the features of modernist houses and the popular ranchers on large lots.

It's been almost 30 years since "community concerns about the quality of new single-family houses," as a report described them, prompted the city to sponsor an architectural competition to come up with designs for affordable, maxed-out single-family houses. Stuart Howard's winning design, "the same density in a more attractive package," fits into the neighbourhood at 4360 West 11th in Point Grey.[*] It apparently is the only one ever built.

In "The New Vancouver Special," the booklet published in 1984 that followed the competition, the Vancouver League for Studies in Architecture tipped its hat to the original Special's economic success. Whereas a postwar starter-house bungalow, as described above, of 900 square feet could be had for $99,000, an extra $20,000 would get a Special, with three large bedrooms, extra bathrooms and a separate suite. "For the prospective home buyer, the house is an unparalleled bargain," it said.

THE NEW SPECIAL COMPETITION ACKNOWLEDGED A NUMBER OF entrants who had proposed interesting ideas for single-family housing including a few—Barry Griblin, Robert Grant, Sebastian Butler and Patricia Baldwin—who suggested back yard or lane houses. After a 25-year hiatus, that idea re-emerged recently in a city policy to spur the "gentle densification," as commentator and developer Michael Geller described it, of the city's single-family neighbourhoods.

Lane houses were never common in Vancouver. In old areas like Strathcona and Grandview, a number of builders erected multiple houses on single lots through a combination of greed and authorities' lack of oversight (undersight?). An interesting assemblage is the two houses and an apartment building on a single 50-by-120-foot Kitsilano lot, at the northeast corner of 6th and Arbutus, built by carpenter Roland Scarlett between 1901 and 1910.

The lane house behind Umberto's restaurant, the "little yellow house," built when the city was two years old, on Hornby Street at Pacific, moved in 2004 to the lane end of a thin lot on Pendrell Street's Mole Hill block and was restored by the Vancouver Heritage Foundation. There were also a few infill coach houses built in the '80s and '90s in Mount Pleasant and Kerrisdale as part of heritage restoration agreements.

A lane house with its parent house, seen in the watercolour on the next page, is the last of its era in the West End. It sits at 1754 Pendrell, about six blocks west of Mole Hill, within sight of English Bay. A clerk for the CPR steamship department named Adorinam J. Paterson had the two houses built in 1904. By the time of the 1930s depression the 33-foot lot was home to two families and five roomers, density that the city's new lane-house policy will never achieve.

I was surprised to see the lane house still there when I returned to the city in 2010, as was a man named Floyd Gillis who had written to me a couple of years earlier: "I lived in that house from the time I was born in December 1955 until I was about

* Kalman et al., *Exploring Vancouver 3*, 1993, p. 172

seven years old. Our family—my parents and, at the time, three kids—lived on the top floor. A Mrs. O'Kane lived downstairs with her son, Michael. I believe the Henderson family owned both that little house and the larger one facing Pendrell Street. After 1756 Pendrell our family moved to a house at 1725 Pendrell (now a concrete high-rise) and later a house at 1032 Pacific (now a low-rise apartment complex). We moved out of the West End around 1970 or 1971."

The first group of new rental lane houses was completed at the end of 2010. On a 33-foot lot an owner could build a one-and-a-half-storey building totalling 750 square feet, of which about 200 square feet had to be garage space. A few of the putative garages had polished, heated concrete floors and large windows—either cars really have it good these days or the space will be rolled into the human habitation as soon as the city inspector disappears over the hill. At about a quarter of a million dollars the houses certainly aren't affordable to build—even at current, low interest rates they would take about 15 to 20 years to pay off. Perhaps the designs will improve to the point that they become as efficient as the small apartments described in the next chapter.

The last of the lane houses—in the West End at least—1754 Pendrell. This view of it was exposed a few years ago when a fire in the rooming house next door resulted in the demolition of its garage. At this writing, the planning department is considering a rezoning application for the site, a 21-storey tower atop a 5-storey podium. This would increase the building's floor space from 2.2 times the site area (allowed in the current zoning) to 6.17! If lane houses are supposed to be a gentle version of densification, this proposal is a brutal one.

The house at 4th and Scotia in SOMA (South Main, hopefully a temporary rebranding), surrounded by "artists' lofts," tarped in a half-hearted sort of a way after a fire and ready to surrender, in the summer of 2010. It was demolished later that year.

Lᴌ IKE PIECES OF SLOW-MOTION PERFORMANCE ART, THE CITY'S HAND-ful of derelict houses deteriorate little by little over the years. Because so many of them were so well built, they hardly rot, even in the West Coast climate. Some of them were left behind on odd lots when zoning in an area changed—the house at 4th and Scotia in Mount Pleasant (above) was one such example.

Lower Mount Pleasant was the city's first suburb—the first area of homes and businesses away from the downtown peninsula. A handful of buildings survive from the city's infancy: the 1888 Lindsay house at 144 East 6th (page 97) and two buildings from about 1892: the Nirvana restaurant at 2313 Main (page 79) and the house, recently used for a café, at 151 East 8th.* The neighbourhood developed so early due to the Westminster Road connecting Burrard Inlet to New Westminster, already well travelled by the time the railway arrived on infant Vancouver's doorstep in 1887. The 4th and Scotia house was connected to the city's water system in 1907 (the permit signed with a mark by its illiterate owner and witnessed by F.W. Boultbee, the city clerk), but doesn't appear in any earlier building permit registers. For most of the years since it was

---

*   Illustrated in *Vancouver Remembered*, p. 166.

TOP > The Galbraith House, at 8th and Queens in New Westminster, built in 1894, an extraordinarily ragged mess when I painted it in 1989. Defying all odds, it rose from the dead and, after a careful restoration, now operates as an inn and conference centre.

MIDDLE > After a similar near-death experience, standing derelict, unheated and abandoned on 7th Avenue for more than a decade, the Shaw house made a 90-degree turn onto Ash Street and underwent a 180-degree rehabilitation as part of a heritage-bonused development on the surrounding properties. It now operates as Caffè Cittadella, a chic little piece of elegant diversity amid the increasingly bulky architecture of Fairview Slopes. James Shaw built the house in 1894, three years after the CPR cleared the forest from Fairview Slopes. Like the houses on p. 96, it is an example of the Queen Anne style.

BOTTOM > The house of a hoarder: 5992 Trafalgar in 1989. Like most of the houses left from the 1920s on the West Side, it was smaller than what could be built under the zoning schedule. Typically, in those days (as today), change happened almost by stealth. A for sale sign would go up and as quickly disappear; survey stakes would appear; "Midnight Building Supply" would arrive and make off with anything—windows, doors, porch railings, shrubs—that wasn't nailed down; then, one morning at 5:00 a.m., neighbours would be awakened by the arrival of a big truck and the squeaking of caterpillar treads as a high hoe backed slowly off a low bed and took its position on the edge of the lot, awaiting first light and the start of the working day. By lunchtime, it would all be over, as in the illustration on p. 17.

ABOVE > Protestors campaigned to save the quirky old Stuart Building at Georgia and Chilco, on the edge of Lost Lagoon, until the bulldozers got it in July 1982. The next occupant of the site was equally strange—the multi-storey, three-unit condominium built by Stanley Ho, the Macau casino owner, with a fantastical landscape-sunset mural painted on its blank, east-facing wall. The view of the mural was finally obscured by a condominium development called Laguna, which now occupies the rest of the block, 45 years after the destruction, in a spectacular fire in 1960, of the Horse Show Building a.k.a. Stanley Park Armoury.

NEXT PAGE > My 2010 watercolour of the house that W.W. Stuart built in 1908, at 1829 Parker in Grandview, failed to show its extreme dilapidation. The porch roof was rotted through, the main roof was tarped and there was scarcely an unbroken pane of glass on the second floor. A sad state of affairs, both for its occupant and the neighbourhood.

occupied by workers: a helper at a nearby foundry in the 1950s, an inventory clerk at a wholesale firm in the 1960s.

Other derelicts had unsympathetic owners, or indifferent ones holding the property for speculation, or ones awaiting approval of complex developments that would require the restoration of the relic. The Shaw house at 7th and Ash, which I painted more than 20 years ago and which has since been restored, comes to mind.

The magnificently "gothick" Galbraith house at 8th and Queens in New Westminster was derelict for years. It is the type of house you occasionally see perched on hilltops near abandoned Nevada and California mining towns. It had a varied life: family home in the years after its erection in 1892, rooming house, wartime relaxation centre where servicemen could get a cup of tea and a chat.[*] After I painted it, I wrote in 1990 that it appeared to exist as a kind of working laboratory established to determine how long a landlord can avoid performing cosmetic maintenance and how long a wooden house can remain standing in the West Coast climate without falling down. It looked like a goner.

Yet in 2000 the Galbraith house was restored by Ron and Marie Jang, owners of Tanex Industries, a New Westminster–based manufacturer of wood products. The Jang's current shop is across the street from the original Galbraith company woodworking plant on 10th Street. Today, the Galbraith house "offers executive office suite rental and a unique setting for weddings and other functions including conferences, corporate seminars, meetings and office parties," according to its website.

Another type of derelict house is owned or tenanted by people without the means to maintain it or, perhaps, the perception to acknowledge its need for maintenance. The Trafalgar Street house I painted in 1989 was one such, an anomaly in stable Kerrisdale. It had become decidedly run down during its occupation by an eccentric man named Andy who evidently was a packrat. He could often be seen walking around the neighbourhood, wearing shorts and sneakers on even the coldest days, hunched and talking to himself. The house was demolished soon after I painted it.

The house at 1829 Parker Street (next page), built in 1909 by lumberman W.W. Stuart and converted into suites in 1939, is a well-known example of a derelict building in Grandview, eliciting shakes of the head from neighbours and passersby. Dan Mills, who has lived in it for 58 years, told me he hopes to get the money together one day to fix it up. The house has an exact twin at 364 West 10th Avenue in Mount Pleasant; known as the Grauer House, it was recently converted into suites and is now a designated heritage building.

The irony of Stuart's legacy is that the two buildings in the city attributed to him ended up in such a mess. His apartment house at Georgia and Chilco across the street from Lost Lagoon was a glorious wreck until it was torn down in the early 1980s.

---

[*]   Interview with Philip Henderson, 1991.

BY THE TIME THEY REACH THEIR 50TH BIRTHDAY, THE VAST MAJORITY of Vancouver houses will have endured a renovation or two. Because there is little consensus about "pure architecture" on the West Coast, houses get altered to suit the whims of their owners. And, because most early Vancouver houses have wooden exteriors that require maintenance, they have changed a lot compared to brick houses in towns like Toronto or Sydney. Although perhaps not by the owners of 500-year-old half-timbered houses in England, northern France or Scandinavia (or of 200-year-old houses in Nova Scotia or Newfoundland), wood is seen by many in Canada as a temporary material—not durable like brick or stucco or stone.

But it is extraordinary how adaptable—how forgiving—old wooden houses are. Windows can be removed, replaced, shifted. Siding can be altered, as it often has been in Vancouver, from the original wood to stucco, asbestos shingles or aluminum or vinyl siding. *Altered* is not really the correct word, though—in most cases the original siding has been simply covered over.

For the myriad houses completed in the great boom that ended in 1913, the scenario probably went something like this: by 1930 or so, when the houses needed to be repainted, the Depression was on and nobody had any money. Prosperity returned somewhat by the late '30s so some houses got a coat of paint. "By 1941, when almost three-quarters of Vancouver's dwellings had wooden exteriors, the housing stock was generally in good shape. Only 18.2 percent of all dwellings needed external repairs, and the homes of renters compared very well to those of owners."* People had money

---

*   Wade, p. 57.

Classic Vancouver stuccoes. One East Vancouver house had three of these applied to it in the 1950s.

TOP LEFT > A pebble-dashed stucco covered the basement level.

TOP RIGHT > A beer-bottle or glass-dashed stucco (a mixture of brown and green glass from smashed beer bottles and 7-Up bottles, combined with white pebbles), very common in new and renovated houses in the 1950s, covered the upper storey.

BOTTOM LEFT > A California stucco (smoother than the others, with a streaked pattern of red mineral) was used to highlight the porch.

BOTTOM RIGHT > Popcorn stucco was a common ceiling in 1970s Vancouver apartments.

during the war years but materials couldn't be had. Thus, by the end of the '40s, when building supplies were again plentiful, a lot of Vancouver houses were 40 or 50 years old and needed some maintenance. Then, one day, there was a knock on the door.

"You'll never paint again, lady!" the salesman said, or words to that effect.* The contract was signed and a few days later the crew arrived, first nailing chicken wire over the existing siding, then adding coats of stucco, often more than one kind on the same building. In the most radical examples even the soffits and posts would be stuccoed, and the old windows ditched and replaced by aluminum sliders, all part of the attempt to give the house a modern, up-to-date look. Our Kerrisdale neighbour in the early 1980s told us how she and her husband, newlyweds in the 1940s, were directed by the finance company to stucco their house as a condition of getting a mortgage. "Protects the investment," she was told.

A rough-cast white stucco had been used to fill the spaces between the vertical half timbers—the black (or brown) and white pattern common in medieval England and Normandy—on Tudor and Arts and Crafts houses in the early years of the 20th century. But the new stuccos were different, owing more to the Spanish tradition via California. Many period-style buildings, as described on pages 113–5, were stuccoed.

---

*   For "documentary" evidence, watch *Tin Men*, a Richard Dreyfus and Danny DeVito comedy about two aluminum siding salesmen in the early 1960s.

Beer-bottle stucco, so called, was the most common upgrade of old Vancouver houses in the '50s and '60s. Glass-dashed stucco is the more correct term and it certainly wasn't new to that era. As Nathaniel Hawthorne wrote in his 1850 classic *The Scarlet Letter*, with reference to the old colonial governors' hall:

This was a large wooden house, built in a fashion of which there are specimens still extant in the streets of our elder towns . . . It had, indeed, a very cheery aspect; the walls being overspread with a kind of stucco, in which fragments of broken glass were plentifully intermixed; so that, when the sunshine fell aslant-wise over the front of the edifice, it glittered and sparkled as if diamonds had been flung against it by the double handful.

Historian Jim Wolf[*] wrote to me about stucco, saying:

I have a couple of early references in New Westminster to bungalow houses designed by local architect J.B. Whitburn in the 1920s. They refer to California stucco and pebble-dashed stucco emphasized with broken glass. This term is confirmed in my International Reference Library intended for builders completing the International Correspondence Courses offered. The 1931 article on plastering by D. Knickerbaker Boyd outlines the various colour effects that could be obtained from the selection of the ingredients of the finishing coat of stucco and augmented by the application of surface coatings such as aggregates which would have included crushed glass.

Most Vancouver-area children have a personal stucco story. Here is Jim's:

As a kid I remember glass stucco covering nearly every 1920s and 1930s house that had not been clad in the cheap and plentiful cedar shingles. Playing

---

*   Jim found the reference to stucco in *The Scarlet Letter*. He is also the author of *Royal City: A photographic history of New Westminster, 1858–1960* (Heritage House, 2005).

hide and seek around these houses meant often getting scraped by the vicious shards of glass lining the walls. On a hot summer's day, hanging out beside my friend's glass stucco house, we often considered the origins of the various glass colours—root-beer brown was of course from the thousands of smashed-up beer bottles from the local beer parlour and the green in our minds was from Sprite or Seven-Up bottles. The really rare shards were the blue glass that could only have originated from mom's stinky Noxzema jars. Usually the stucco also included fancy-coloured rock particles that could be picked off pretty easily.

If the stucco was applied well, it preserved the wood siding underneath and could be pried off, falling in great sheets still attached to its chicken-wire netting. Tons of stucco hung from old houses; you can almost see them stand up straight and sigh when released from the weight. The nail holes have to be filled but after being scraped and primed the siding paints like new. And the quality of the wood is astonishing on even the most modest house of a century ago: boards 30 feet long without a knot, the kind of lumber that will never again appear on the planet—all the more reason to preserve what's there and resist the rules about rainscreening (described on page 27 in the Introduction).

Stucco also had its uses on interior walls, especially ceilings, where it could hide sagging plaster in the way a beard disguises the ravages of age. A spatter-coating of cellulose was a common fix. Textured "popcorn" ceilings also became very fashionable in new construction in the 1960s, making it easier to finish the drywall sheets that had replaced old-fashioned plaster; as the level of workmanship declined, new ideas and techniques came to the rescue!

Many renovations of old houses involve the almost complete gutting of the interior. Reusable lath and plaster are discarded, making it easier to rewire and possible to insulate the walls, but the resulting smooth drywall finish lacks the patina and character of the original. As mentioned on page 98, the sonic quality of the house's interior also changes. In the best renovations (in my opinion), the kitchens are improved and the bathrooms modernized, but as much of the house as possible is left alone. That's sustainability, in a word.

On the steep roofs of old Vancouver houses, crews typically rip off one or more layers of duroid shingles, plus the original cedar shingles, before starting fresh with new material. As with stucco or vinyl siding, almost always applied over the original, most replacement roofs were just nailed over whatever had begun to wear out. Reroofing a house properly can remove tons of load from the structure; fortunately, old houses were constructed of first-growth lumber and had no problem carrying the weight.

THE VANCOUVER APARTMENT

THE IDEA THAT APARTMENT LIVING COULD BE A LIFESTYLE CHOICE began to emerge about 60 years ago when Vancouver was half the age it is today. Before that, most people believed that apartment living was for one's carefree youth and that long-term tenancies smacked of hierarchical Europe or the crowded cities of the eastern seaboard of North America. The key to a successful life was owning a house on a piece of property "in fee simple"—the legal term for individual ownership. Another possibility—owning a strata-titled condominium, rather than renting an apartment—became an option in the 1960s.

A few buildings of the late 1920s, such as the Queen Charlotte Apartments (page 143), were exceptions, offering the "comforts of home" to long-term renters, but in those years there was a whiff of expediency to renting—a suggestion that people were downsizing from their overly large homes due to straitened circumstances—that is different from the exuberant embrace of city life that has been marketed so successfully to apartment renters and condominium buyers in the past 50 years.

Today, people might trade in a three-bedroom house on its own patch of dirt for a two-bedroom condo in the sky and find they don't have much money left over. Luxurious condominiums are expensive but people don't seem as concerned as before about trading apples for apples. Lifestyle is where it's at.

A half century ago apartment developers had to be careful not to compete directly with home builders. Thirty-four-year-old Tom Campbell, later the mayor but in 1962 an alderman and "one of Vancouver's most successful apartment landlords," described how a few garden-court apartments had been successfully built for families, but that the larger-size suites had begun to price themselves out of the market—renting these suites was becoming more costly than homeownership. "Luxury apartments with suites at $175 or more are in trouble because these tenants are under great pressure from home builders and mortgage companies to build or buy houses, Campbell said."[*]

Regardless of the types of available buildings, Vancouver had its share of renters from the beginning. The city in that respect wasn't much different from, say, Winnipeg. A century ago at the height of the boom, between a quarter and a third of wage earners rented accommodation—a six-room house with indoor plumbing that rented for $12 to $15 a month in 1900 went for $25 to $30 a dozen years later, this at a time when a labourer would earn $50 a month, a carpenter $80. Following the economic collapse and the dislocations of the war, two-thirds of Vancouver families were tenants.[†]

---

[*] "Apartments pop up despite vacancies" by Dick Dolman, *Province*, July 20, 1962. I wrote about Campbell's business and political careers in *Vancouver Remembered*, pp. 49–50 and 80–8.

[†] By comparison, in 2010, 52 percent of Vancouver households rent; the city has almost half of the rental

A rooming house at Robson and Gilford in 1982, one of the hundreds then left in the city from the Great Conversion that began more than a half century earlier. Family homes in areas like the West End were left behind when families migrated to newer suburbs; landlords found that rooms for rent and housekeeping suites were the answer to economic hard times.

Although apartment buildings had become fairly common in Vancouver a century ago, most tenants rented detached houses or roomed in the large converted homes left behind by the middle-class migration from downtown, Yaletown and the West End. According to historian Jill Wade in her study of housing conditions in the early days, more than 10 percent of the population lived crowded together in Chinatown and the East End—today's Strathcona and Downtown Eastside. Inspections by the medical health officer found many male immigrants, especially unmarried Italian labourers, living communally in Strathcona's small houses. That kind of overcrowding (defined as more than one person per room) had spread to the West End's rooming houses by the early 1920s.[*]

RUNNING A ROOMING OR LODGING HOUSE, LIKE RUNNING A CORNER grocery, was one of the few ways a woman could make an income. Some women were unmarried, some widows, some very entrepreneurial—renting an entire house and subletting its rooms. Some of the rooms quickly evolved into housekeeping suites with gas hotplates or small coal or gas ranges. Everybody shared the bathrooms— likely no more than two—in an old West End house that might have had 20 rooms. The pressure for that kind of accommodation eased as the 1920s continued, partly because some people left Vancouver in search of jobs elsewhere, partly because those with jobs migrated into homeownership as soon as they could.

By the Depression years of the 1930s, as people tried to survive economically, the rooming-house conversions of family homes pushed south of False Creek into Mount Pleasant, Fairview and Kitsilano. According to Wade, a large number of conversions in

housing in the region and more than a quarter of the province's supply. See vancouver.ca/commsvcs/housing/RentalHousing.htm.

[*] Wade, pp. 9–16.

The last rooming house in Fairview Slopes, at 1253 West 8th, in 1903 the home of a *Province* newspaper employee. It has lasted for a generation longer than most of its kin. Forty years ago, when the redevelopment of the south shore of False Creek was just getting going, the blocks of 7th and 8th between Granville and Cambie were dotted with houses like this, interspersed with small factories and a few well-maintained family homes. I've done it a favour in the watercolour—it carries an air of musty exhaustion that somehow, on that bright sunny day, eluded my paintbrush.

the 1930s were helped by a contradiction in the bylaws. The zoning bylaw attempted to outlaw individuals or families living in a single room with a gas plate and a sink and sharing toilet and bathing facilities with others, yet the building bylaw allowed remodelling of buildings into lodging houses with sleeping rooms and no cooking facilities. Landlords would supply illegal gas or electric plates or stoves because they were unwilling to cook for the tenants and restaurants were too expensive. With city staff cutbacks in the 1930s, "lodging houses were effectively unregulated." People did the conversions themselves "on the quiet" as they were unwilling to go to the expense and aggravation of applying for lodging licenses and enduring inspections. By 1940 there were 1,816 *licensed* lodging houses in the city, a fact that hints at the total number that actually existed then.[*]

The rental housing shortage increased greatly during the Second World War. On November 5, 1942, a ruling by the Canadian Wartime Prices and Trade Board lifted restrictions on subletting. Locally, one effect was to break the grip of the Shaughnessy Heights Property Owners Association on that area's single-family status. Regardless, the following July, lawyer Cecil Killam filed suit to stop conversion work on a house at 4350 Connaught Drive. The newspapers published photographs of homeless war widows and factory workers and their families alongside pictures of crumbling, vacant Shaughnessy homes and editorialized about the grim housing situation throughout the city.

Jacquie Hooper, a contributing writer for the *Vancouver Courier*, wrote recently of her sunny girlhood memories in a series of West End rooming houses with her widowed mother and older sister. Water was only available in the shared bathroom, although they had a hot plate in their room. The children shared a bed; occasionally a husband in uniform on leave would visit and put even more strain on the facilities. People moved their belongings from one rooming house to another with wheelbarrows.[†]

The wartime Order in Council 200 was in effect until 1951, allowing property owners to take in as many tenants as they could accommodate. That year the federal government ended rent controls, after 11 years, along with remaining wartime price controls. Until the mid-1970s rent regulation was largely absent from Canadian cities.[‡] Later in 1951, in response to a city threat to crack down on illegal suites, a group called the Kitsilano Improvement Association tried to get their areas rezoned to "two family," which would have legalized most of these suites. A survey in 1952 found that 84 of 281 houses in the dozen blocks bounded by 4th, Broadway, Trafalgar and Bayswater had been illegally converted to multiple use; in the northwest corner of the district, north of 4th and west of Bayswater, the number was 179 of 525.[§]

---

[*] Wade, pp. 48–50.

[†] "The rooming house life," *Vancouver Courier*, September 1, 2010.

[‡] Miron, p. 71. Rent controls came back into Vancouver with the Rentalsman program of the Barrett government years of 1972–5, and then carried on when Pierre Trudeau's federal government imposed wage and price controls in October 1975.

[§] "4 out of 5 suites in Kitsilano illegal," *Province*, July 8, 1952.

The wartime housing shortages seem like a lifetime away except that the situation was much the same in the 1960s and 1970s, the working families by then replaced with students, beatniks and hippies in large rooming houses and illegal basement suites, the wheelbarrows replaced by Volkswagen buses belonging to a friend of a friend. The old neighbourhoods have since been gentrified or redeveloped. Many old houses are now divided into suites that are comparatively spacious and luxurious and, usually, strata-titled. The illegal-suite game continues in East and South Vancouver neighbourhoods.

In Fairview Slopes, which has almost completely redeveloped in the past 40 years, there is one remaining rooming house—a tired-out old building between Birch and Laurel on West 8th Avenue—that has "the look." Now covered in duroid-shingle siding, with mature trees practically pushing its front porch over, it's a substantial house but a bit of a sad sack on its 100 feet of prime property.

Gustave Pierrot, a compositor (typesetter) at the *Province*, had it built in 1903. Evidently he was one of the upwardly mobile working-class people of that era who dabbled in real estate during the first decade of the 20th century. Land purchases were especially popular among "nurses, stenographers and clerks, industrial workers and labourers" and "when the boom collapsed, the multitude of 'clerks and artisans' had 'lost their all.'"[*] Pierrot moved on quickly; the location of the rooming house, in smoky Fairview Slopes above False Creek's mills, meant that subsequent occupants lived close enough to work to walk there. The Van Dyke family of boat builders lived in the building around 1911; Arthur Woolley, a teamster with False Creek Lumber, was there in 1920. In the 1940s, a widow named Ivy Johnson owned it and was renting out the rooms. This is confirmed by a 1953 upgrade to the water system, where city records for the building show "over two families" in residence.

I spent part of an afternoon in the summer of 2010 sitting in front of it painting and struck up a conversation with a couple in their 30s who had come by to look at it. He was German and had been a student at UBC in the 1990s; after graduation he had moved to the States. On this first trip back to Vancouver he brought his wife to see the place where he'd lived for some of his student days. Cockroaches, mice, endless waits for the bathroom . . . he shook his head as he remembered. Any positive memories? I asked him. One roomer was okay, but otherwise it was a "gong show."

A half century and a sea change in individual behaviour separates his recollections from Jacquie Hooper's wartime ones. Hard times created the earlier generation of genteel rooming houses, in an era when public decorum was still important. I wonder sometimes how the collective "we" would cope with a return to them.

T HE APARTMENT BUILDINGS OF A CENTURY AGO WERE, IN THE MAIN, solid brick structures. A few of them—the Banff and the Stadacona on Bute near Georgia and the Banffshire a block away on Jervis—have borne witness to the change from the Blueblood Alley mansions of the 1880s to today's office towers on the western edge of downtown. Their designs share fine entrance foyers, checks in their

---

[*]   McDonald, p. 139.

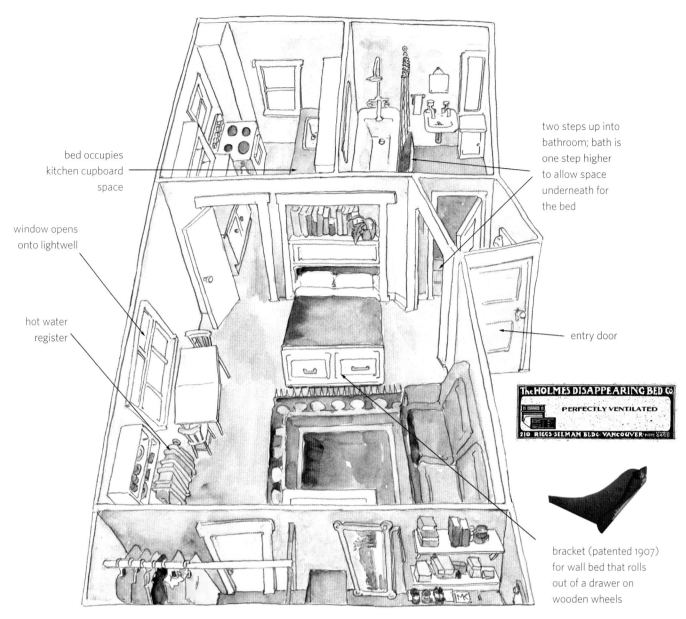

bed occupies kitchen cupboard space

window opens onto lightwell

hot water register

two steps up into bathroom; bath is one step higher to allow space underneath for the bed

entry door

The HOLMES DISAPPEARING BED Co
PERFECTLY VENTILATED
210 RIGGS·SELMAN BLDG· VANCOUVER· PHONE 6486

bracket (patented 1907) for wall bed that rolls out of a drawer on wooden wheels

Strathmore Lodge, originally known as the Royal Alexandra Apartments, at the corner of Comox and Bute in the West End. (PHOTO BY W.J. MOORE, 1927, COLLECTION OF JOHN ATKIN)

STRATHMORE LODGE

West End • 1909
bachelor suite, 375 square feet

NEXT PAGE > Although it's now more than a century old, the 17-suite English Bay Mansions at 1306 Bidwell, designed by architects Townsend & Townsend for two brothers named Stevenson, is actually the second building on the site. A bricklayer named James Jeffrey built three cottages on that block in 1899, the year streetcar service began along Denman between Davie and the Robson line; two of them (in the watercolour they would have been just past the apartment building) lasted until a few years ago. The rapid change between 1899 and 1910 reflected the popularity of English Bay beach, not just as a summertime attraction but as a place to live.

BOTTOM > English Bay about 1920, seen from a front window of the English Bay Mansions. The Alexandra Park bandstand and the promenading pier are visible, as is the Sylvia Hotel (then an apartment building) on the right and the Englesea Apartments in the distance. (HAND-COLOURED POSTCARD PHOTOGRAPH BY J. FRED SPALDING)

façades to allow a little light to penetrate into all the rooms, and flat roofs. They could be refugees from Toronto or New York City. The Irwinton at Robson and Burrard, the Manhattan at Robson and Thurlow, and the Beaconsfield nearby on Bute are similar.

There were other landmark buildings scattered about the city and completed before the First World War: for example, the Sylvia Court Apartments (now the Sylvia Hotel) at English Bay Beach, Caroline Court at 1058 Nelson, and Quebec Manor at Quebec and 7th. The last is a building credited to the itinerant architects Townsend & Townsend, but it shared with the Simpson Apartments (Davie and Denman, demolished), Shaughnessy Mansions (Granville and 15th, now incorporated into a new development) and the little Quebec Grocery on Broadway near Spruce a zigzag pattern of buff and red brick that caused architect Ross Lort to exclaim: "While they put up many buildings they only came up with one elevation; you see it today all over town and recognize it at once." It wasn't a compliment.

In Fairview within the old city boundary there is Shaughnessy Lodge at 10th and Birch and Douglas Lodge at 12th and Granville. The Ashnola Apartments at 6th and Main is one of the masonry apartment buildings erected near the strategic Mount Pleasant crossroads. Further south, well into the Municipality of South Vancouver, Quebec Mansions dominates the narrow corner of two side streets, 27th and Quebec. Some others were located in declining areas: Ferrera Court at Hastings and Jackson was intended by its Italian restaurateur owner to capitalize on the eastward expansion of the city along the Hastings streetcar line. More modest, wood-framed buildings include the Panama Apartments at 5th and Trafalgar, plunked just outside the CPR's boundary on what was cheaper land with no building restrictions.

Who lived in these buildings in the early years? At the Irwinton at 777 Burrard, in 1914, tenants included a real-estate salesman and the co-owner of a funeral parlour. Three tenants were women: a stenographer, a clerk at the Hudson's Bay Company

* Luxton, p. 362. English Bay Mansions (next page) is also a Townsend & Townsend design, but didn't have the patterned brick. See VPL 22251 for a 1926 photograph.

and the proprietor of the Luke Hat Shop a block away at Robson and Hornby, Isabel Luke. As the war progressed, many of the women living alone in downtown and West End apartments were widows. In the 1920s, directories noted an increasing number of female stenographers.

One of the biggest early apartments is the Strathmore at Pendrell and Bute, known as the Royal Alexandra, after Edward VII's queen, when it opened in 1909. It is a six-storey building with the kind of density typical of Haussman's Paris. Its studio and one-bedroom apartments are still much as they always were, a triumph of compact design that could well be emulated by architects and builders a century later.

The studio apartment illustrated on page 139 occupies about 375 square feet and yet has all of the elements of a much bigger space. It faces east and is on a check in the rear façade, with windows on two walls (one of the criteria of livability from the design bible *A Pattern Language*).[*] The floor space is ample for the double bed that emerges from a drawer, rolling on wheels milled from blocks of wood. It is not a Murphy bed—the type that folds upward flat against the wall. This model, its hardware patented in 1907, slides back into the wall. One side of it disappears into a space below one end of the kitchen counter; the other side occupies the space beneath the bathtub. (Shaughnessy Lodge has similar beds.)

To accommodate the bed, the bathroom floor is two steps higher than the suite's floor, the tub a step higher still. The kitchen is compact and functional, still with its tiled sink and wall taps. The small stove runs on natural gas but its predecessor would have burned manufactured (coal) gas a century ago. The space for the refrigerator probably held an icebox until the 1930s or 1940s. Another feature of the suite is the large closet, three feet deep and running the width of the living room, more storage

A modest apartment building—the Brisbane Rooms, at 727 Richards Street, in 1936. In the background, the Vancouver Block's clock (on the left) and the Hudson's Bay Company store (on the right) indicate the edge of the commercial downtown. (PHOTO BY LEONARD FRANK, VPL 7858)

* Alexander et al., p. 746.

space than many larger new apartments offer; at the end of the closet there is a shelf with a small door, which at one time would have been used for milk or ice deliveries from the corridor.

M ORE LUXURIOUS apartments than the Strathmore emerged in the prosperous 1920s. Charles Bentall found an excellent site to build one in the old Gabriola mansion at Davie and Nicola. He approached its owner, the widowed Mrs. B.T. Rogers, who had been living there with her three youngest children for several years following the sudden death of her husband (page 59). The Rogerses' grand project, called Shannon, at Granville and 57th (page 170), had languished due to shortages of materials when the war was on, but in January 1925 Mrs. Rogers decided to finish it, and she moved there in August of that year. She signed an agreement with Bentall to convert Gabriola into apartments and build a brick apartment building on its grounds to the west; she was the project's major financier. Those apartments were demolished in the 1980s after Gabriola was turned into The Mansion restaurant by steakmeister Hy Aisenstat.

Two years later, Bentall found another site to develop, a block north, and his Dominion Construction Company began work on the Queen Charlotte, "a new, high-class apartment building of reinforced concrete construction, fireproof to a maximum degree, the most representative structure of its kind erected in recent years in Vancouver," according to a brochure intended to attract tenants. It was built in the Mission Revival style, mainly seen in earlier, lavish homes such as John West's (page 112), perhaps to give it the flavour of fashionable Los Angeles.

The Queen Charlotte offered furnished and unfurnished apartments, all with hardwood floors of the best quality. Resident Daryl Nelson had his refinished in 1985 by B.C. Hardwood Floors, a firm established in 1904; Ray Crompton, the son of the firm's founder, told him that the quarter-inch oak strips spanning almost the whole living room were as good as any he had seen in Vancouver. Each suite had a tiled bath and kitchen sink, electric range and refrigeration—a cooling pipe from a basement unit, supplementing the block of ice in each suite's icebox. Like most buildings of that period, heat and hot water were supplied to all suites by a central boiler. The one-bedroom apartments had an In-A-Dor bed in the living room.

The settled West End—the sidewalk in front of the 1928 Queen Charlotte Apartments, at 1101 Nicola Street, on a summer day.

The central section of a 1913 panorama by W. J. Moore, from the roof of the Lee Building at Broadway and Main. Quebec Manor, then known as the Mount Stephen Block, rises above the rooftops (just left of centre). A few other apartment buildings dot Main Street and 7th Avenue. In the smoky distance, the Main Street bridge crossed False Creek; the tidal flats on the east side of the bridge (on the right) were, even then, being filled with excavation spoil from the Grandview Cut, dug by the Great Northern Railway as part of the plan to create railyards and a passenger terminus east of Main Street. (CVA PAN.N.161A)

A "manageress" lived in and only families could be tenants, with "the first-class character of the building being maintained at all times." According to the advertising brochure, tenants could rent garages for $5 a month and a valet would bring a car to the front of the building on request. Everything was up to date: "outside aerials are provided for radios . . . Hoover vacuum cleaners and Johnson's floor waxer and polisher are available for tenants' use . . . a resident maid and laundry service is maintained in the building for tenants' use, at a cost of 30 cents per hour, payable the following month." The Queen Charlotte was near enough to downtown's attractions to be within the 40-cent taxi-fare zone and met "the requirements of people who desire the same class of accommodation available in apartment hotels in the large cities of Eastern Canada and in the United States." All this starting at $65 a month, probably slightly more than the maid earned. The Queen Charlotte was converted to condominiums in the 1970s.

Another version of the apartment hotel was Quebec Manor, originally known as the Mount Stephen Block and finished in 1912, soon after 9th became Broadway, Westminster Avenue became Main and promoters touted Mount Pleasant as a major commercial centre. It had patterned brickwork on its four-storey façades as well as curved, wrought-iron balconies, and numerous arched checks cut deep into the building's façades. There are 32 suites; a typical two-bedroom is spacious, with more than 1,000 square feet of floorspace.

In the early 1980s the tenants of Quebec Manor formed themselves into a cooperative and were able to secure government assistance with the mortgage. Non-profit housing co-ops were and are popular with people who are willing to exchange the amassing of equity and the profit potential of normal real-estate ownership for security of tenure and a community of like-minded people. Residents pay a housing charge, like rent; for a two-bedroom apartment there the charge is currently about $900 a month, which covers everything except electricity.

THE MAINSTREAM RENTAL MARKET HAS BEEN A ROLLERCOASTER IN Vancouver ever since wartime housing controls were removed. In 1953 landlords petitioned the government for rent increases of 15 to 20 percent. The main concern of the Apartment and Rooming House Operators' Association was "to get control of our own houses. The regulation in regard to obnoxious tenants is bad. Some people, especially in rooms with gas plates, are a menace, yet they cannot be turned out."

In the 1940s and 1950s many builders and small developers bought double lots—typically two 33-footers—and put up wood-framed 10-suite walk-ups, very modest little buildings that nevertheless have provided a lot of people with affordable accommodation for half the city's life. Tom Campbell's father built 15 or 20 of them in the West End; Campbell himself took over and built several more in the early 1950s before deciding to develop more ambitious types of buildings.

The "10-suiter" was easy to build: four suites each on the upper two floors with a central corridor, staircases at both ends, two "basement" suites facing the front a half floor below grade, with the boiler, laundry and storage lockers occupying two suites' worth of space at the back (some managed to squeeze a small manager's unit into a back corner). Each suite had windows on two sides and shared a single common wall—typically the bedroom wall. Depending on the tenants, the buildings were comfortably quiet or horrid, as you could hear *everything* through the thin walls and ceilings, especially the clack-clack of high heels.

The South Granville area has the best collection of them in the city today. Like the West End a half century ago, the area has been a bastion of reasonably priced rental housing—just the sort of thing young people with low- to moderate-paying downtown jobs need. It's a very urban little pocket, slowly being eaten away by more luxurious condos, some of which are 10-storey-or-higher concrete buildings more aloof from the street.*

There was a glut of 10-suiters in the 1950s. The cost of a double-lot apartment site in the West End rose from $22,000 in 1954 to $45,000 in 1958. "Last winter you

---

* The city's strategy to preserve rental housing requires one-for-one replacement of demolished units in any redevelopment of more than six units.

Two apartment buildings from the interwar years.

LEFT > The Miramar, at 1465 West 15th, designed in 1929 by William Dodd—like his Alma Theatre (p. 85), an example of the Mission Revival style.

RIGHT > The Sussex, at 1556 West 13th, a Tudor-style nine-suiter built in 1930 for Kerrisdale investor R.C. Singleton.

couldn't find an apartment for love or money, but now we may have several vacancies on our books," said a real-estate company representative. Rents were even lowered by $5 a month in one West End building.[*]

Vacancy rates continued to be high as newer buildings came on the market. A particularly bad year for landlords was 1962, when depressed house prices helped keep rents low and the vacancy rate went to five percent (two percent is usually considered ideal). "Many of Vancouver's small-apartment landlords are being shaken out of the money tree by a few big operators," said one news story. New high-rises were "like magnets" pulling tenants from the smaller, older blocks that had been a gold mine for the small investor a few years earlier. Landlords had both to modernize and reduce rents to compete for tenants.[†] The only advantage the older places had over the new high-rise apartments was their larger size.

The 10-suite walk-ups were particularly challenged. Bought for about $10,000 per suite, heavily financed with two mortgages, taxes and maintenance, they experienced declining rental revenues that put some investors to the wall. One case study involved a building near Granville and 12th, built in 1951 and bought eight years later for a $46,000 down payment on a price of $102,000. High vacancies in 1960 forced the owner to move into the building with his family. Two years later, repairs and maintenance had created a deficit of about $1,000 a year, which the owner had to pay out of his salary. He was forced to consider dropping rents back to $85 a month, the same rate as those in a 40-year-old building.

Apartments had become a business for the bigger, more daring players, of whom two, Tom Campbell and Ben Wosk (page 190), stood out. As Wosk once said to lawyer Jonathan Baker, "Buy top land, pay top price and never sell."

---

* "Suite surplus softens rents" by Pat Carney, *Province*, September 4, 1958.
† "Small, older apartment blocks hit," *Province*, July 25, 1962.

THREE-STOREY WALKUP A.K.A TEN SUITER

West End, Kitsilano, Fairview, Mount Pleasant, Grandview, Kerrisdale, Marpole • 1940s–1950s
one–bedroom apartment, about 750 square feet

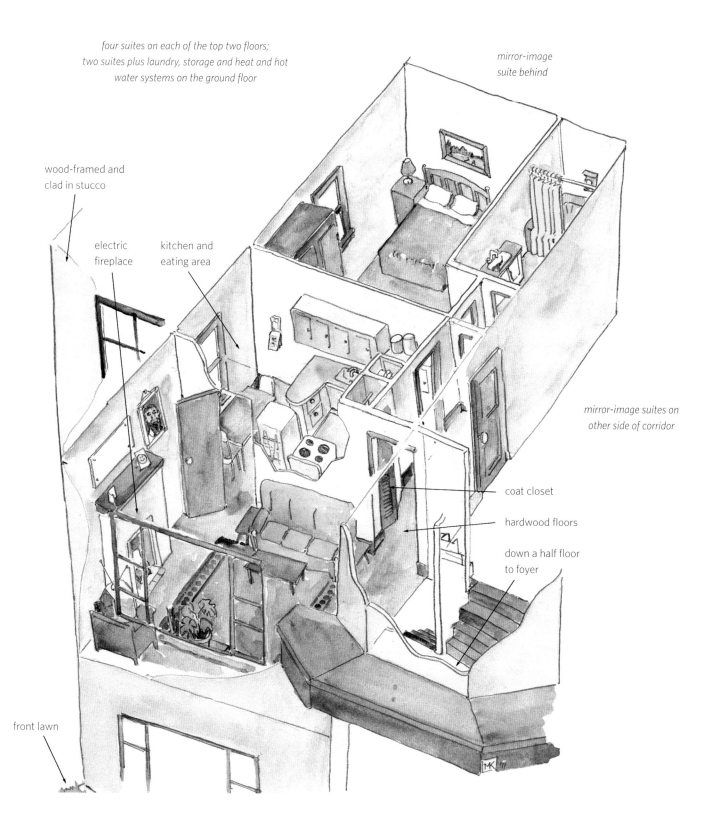

*four suites on each of the top two floors;
two suites plus laundry, storage and heat and hot
water systems on the ground floor*

*mirror-image
suite behind*

wood-framed and
clad in stucco

electric
fireplace

kitchen and
eating area

*mirror-image suites on
other side of corridor*

coat closet

hardwood floors

down a half floor
to foyer

front lawn

THE EVOLUTION OF THE VANCOUVER APARTMENT

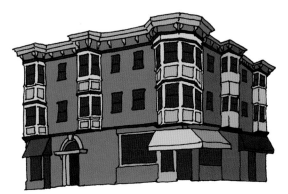

WEST END

Apartment buildings a century ago, around 1910, often had the bay windows and corner turrets typical of San Francisco buildings a generation earlier. Many were built above shops, a style that returned to Vancouver in the 1990s.

During the 1920s and 1930s, as illustrated on page 146, apartment buildings reflected the fashion for period or eclectic styles, as was the case with houses (page 113).

FAIRVIEW

FAIRVIEW

After the Second World War, apartment styles simplified, reflecting the influence of the modern movement. Small walk-up apartment buildings, typically of about 10 suites, could be utilitarian (right) or elegant (left). See page 147 for a typical floor plan.

GRANDVIEW

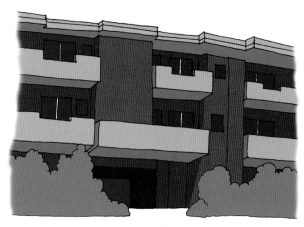

ALL NEIGHBOURHOODS

In the 1960s and 1970s, in all neighbourhoods in Greater Vancouver, a new style of low-rise "strip" apartment building—three storeys high, wood-framed, with a central elevator core above a basement garage—began to be built in multi-family areas. They were the first generation of apartment buildings to offer every tenant a balcony. Some were finished with wood and brick, others with wrought iron and stucco. See page 154 for a typical floor plan.

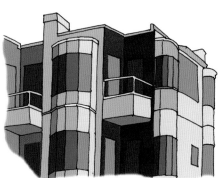

KITSILANO

Since the late 1970s, architects and builders have collaborated on increasingly complex floor plans, with angled roofs, bay windows and solariums, and tiny inset balconies. With scarcely a right angle in some of them, the problems of keeping out the rain increased, leading to the "leaky condo" crisis of the 1980s and 1990s. See page 157.

KITSILANO

Campbell had the same modus operandi.

He owns some 700 suites in seven blocks built since 1958, worth an estimated $7 million. His vacancy rate is . . . less than one percent. He keeps construction costs and rents down to cater to the market for single-bedroom suites. Rents at his 234-suite Parkview Towers [at the south end of Burrard Bridge] range from $80 to $115. He builds by the package method, acting as lawyer, owner, planner, developer, builder, agent and manager. "I do everything except the janitor's work, and I'm not above doing that," he said. His tenants are 25 percent recently married, 25 percent single business-people and 50 percent retired people. *

A STRING OF DIAMONDS—ENGLISH BAY APARTMENTS AT DUSK, a mid-1960s photo by Clyde Herrington of the view from an apartment near the edge of Stanley Park, looking back toward English Bay and the city. The dark building near the right-hand edge is the Sylvia Hotel, dwarfed even then by surrounding buildings, and an interesting contrast with the picture on p. 140.

Creeping into the market in the mid-1960s was a demand for "hotel-level" lavishness in the new high-rises:

Most of Vancouver's children will probably be cliff-dwellers and elevator commuters when they grow up . . . but their steel and concrete "caves" will have hardwood floors or wall-to-wall carpets, picture windows with a fabulous marine view, air-conditioning, coloured plumbing, dishwashers, and balconies in the sky . . . The city's growth trend now is upward, and closer in to the centre." †

New costs entered the equation: city zoning required off-street parking, estimated to cost a builder $1,000 per suite.

Some owners tried different strategies to keep competitive. The beautiful Beaconsfield at 884 Bute Street was run in the early '60s by Pat Lusk and her husband as a women-only apartment. According to a newspaper story, the 140 "girls" shared the suites, three to four in each, with everything supplied. "Furniture, linen, dishes, television, telephone, and even a free newspaper. They're bachelor girls aged 18 to 30 and they come from all over the world." Pat allowed no pets except birds, but the "girls are always sneaking in cats," and she complained gently about all the broken hearts she had to mend. Men would be easier, less demanding tenants, she claimed. ‡

---

* "Apartments pop up despite vacancies" by Dick Dolman, *Province*, July 20, 1962.

† Ibid.

‡ "She prefers men to 140 girls" by Tom Ardies, *Province*, February 16, 1963.

April 22, 1966

"... when I first came to Vancouver the mountains gave me a feeling of being cut off from everywhere, but I got over it ..."

Len Norris's observation of the West End's changing face, in 1966.
(USED WITH PERMISSION)

Some landlords—representing about 10 percent of the city's apartments, in Tom Campbell's estimation—tried to introduce leases to replace the month-to-month tenancies that were part of the local culture, and the term "lease-breaking party," to spur an eviction notice, went into the language in about 1964. Another innovation was the demand that tenants pay the last month's rent as well as the first month's when they moved in. And there were social changes as well: in a 1967 series of newspaper articles, Nikki Moir introduced the public to the "swinging social set" that was based in West End and Kitsilano apartments.

The 100,000 Vancouver renters, divided equally between apartment-dwellers and tenants of large old houses converted into suites, faced a tightening market and rising rents by the mid-Sixties. In 1966 Montreal Trust reported zero vacancies in the 1,400 rental units it administered. The Kerrisdale apartment zone was completely built out and the city began to consider new apartments in Point Grey and Dunbar. Attempts by Pemberton Realty and others to expand the Kerrisdale zone west to Larch and south to 45th were turned down by the planning commission.

ABOVE > Architect Warnett Kennedy (1911–2000) was an unusual combination of the conservative and the radical. The son of a seaman, he studied at the Glasgow School of Art and apprenticed to a firm of Scottish architects. A wartime article, "The Prefabricated House: A Plea for Action," (in *The Builder*, September 25, 1942, pages 268–9) hinted at his political and modernist leanings. He immigrated to Vancouver after the war, working on the Annacis Island development, and serving as an alderman in the 1970s, where he clashed colourfully with Harry Rankin, the left wing's venerable gadfly. Rankin referred to him as "Wornout Kennedy"; he shot back with "Comrade Rankin." He publicized his futuristic theories in a 1974 book, *Vancouver Tomorrow: A Search for Greatness*, and followed that up with *Vancouver: Fight for It or Lose It!*, in 1982.

LEFT > The Ambleside waterfront in the mid-1960s, with high-rise apartments popping up among the homes and beach cottages of 40 years earlier. The curved building on the right, Crescent Apartments at 2135 Argyle, was the harbinger of this new West Vancouver forest, designed by Kenneth Gardner and Warnett Kennedy in 1961. (PHOTO BY HERBERT L. McDONALD)

T HERE WERE OTHER APARTMENT TYPES IN THE '50S AND '60S THAT were different from the walk-ups and high-rises. Local modernist architects who had been designing innovative houses on the city's untrammelled edges (page 118) had lots of opportunities to rebuild the West End in the postwar years. William K. Noppe's 1948 Beach Town House Apartments at 1949 Beach Avenue, seven storeys high, pointed the way.* It advertised "smart modern and beautiful living," a new version of the "respectability" that had been the selling point of the Queen Charlotte apartments a generation earlier.

The suites are very spacious—a two-bedroom apartment recently advertised for sale is 1,255 square feet, enormous compared to most modern units. The building was also a harbinger as it became an apartment corporation, commonly known as a cooperative (see page 155), like its down-the-street neighbour Ocean Towers. The lifestyle of that period seems in retrospect so unfettered: the retired father of a friend of mine who lived there restored a vintage Cord automobile in one of its private garages in the 1970s.

Hycroft Towers at 16th and Granville is another notable modernist building, by Semmens Simpson, from 1950–1. Originally rental apartments but now strata-titled, Hycroft also has large suites: some of the one-bedrooms, for example, are about 900 square feet. Its ample rooms and wide corridors harken back to a more gracious era; with its views and easy walking access to transit and the shops of Granville Street, it has long been a classic.

Inevitably there were imitators and poor copies, modernism requiring a deft hand and excellent workmanship to get right. But some Vancouver modernist architects themselves got into trouble with their public-housing message, almost messianic in tone, about improving the lives of people, which dovetailed with social planners' missions to clean up slums and create a rational new world. The "public" in the significant Vancouver example, in Strathcona, were owners and tenants who were forced from their homes and relocated into austere new towers in two superblocks east of Chinatown. The resulting battle to save the rest of the neighbourhood and stop the downtown freeway changed the city's course forever.†

The problem was that "a large number of people disliked the authoritarian, albeit benevolent or paternalistic, and centralized redevelopment process that . . . [UBC professor Leonard] Marsh and most modernists regarded as essential to the effective solution of social disparities in housing."‡ The provincial Social Credit government refused to give this urban renewal process enough support and when the federal Liberal government decided to change tack in 1972 and support incremental community change the wheels fell off the modernist juggernaut.

Modernist market-housing buildings similarly fell out of favour before promoter-architects such as C.B.K. Van Norman could construct utopian schemes like Park

---

*   Noppe's other enduring landmark is Pacific Coliseum at the Pacific National Exhibition, home to the Vancouver Canucks at the time they ascended to the National Hockey League in 1970.

†   See *Vancouver Remembered*, pp. 112–3. A more recent, detailed history with a lot of very interesting insider anecdotes is chapter 2 of Mike Harcourt et al.'s *City Making in Paradise*.

‡   Windsor-Liscombe, p. 59.

Harbour. Norman was a notable proponent of linking shopping malls (such as Park Royal, which he designed) to superblocks of high-rises using freeways, believing them to be a solution to urban congestion.* His Beach Towers, which Block Brothers Realty developed in the 1960s on Beach Avenue between Bidwell and Cardero, was as close as he got to emulating the idealized Radiant City of French architect Le Corbusier.

MUCH MORE MODEST THAN THE MODERNIST HIGH-RISES WERE THE three-storey "strip" apartments that proliferated across the city in the 1960s and 1970s. As with the Vancouver Special (page 121), it has not yet been possible to pin down who did the first one and how the style evolved. Most of these apartments are wood-framed constructions above a single-level concrete garage (in itself a modification from the old walk-ups) and feature a central entranceway, elevator core, three storeys of apartments (in some cases topped with a penthouse) and a windowless central hallway running the length of the building.

There is a rhythm to a typical strip-apartment façade, with some balconies projecting forward, others being recessed, some open to the sky, others covered. These apartment buildings were constructed with a myriad of finishes: some are very woodsy, with cedar boards, others are faced with ashlar and skinny wrought-iron. Unlike the Specials, which are very consistent in finish, they have great variety within an almost identical basic form.

The 1960s and 1970s were the era of apartments with an L-shaped kitchen-dining-living room, cablevision in every suite and an intercom at the front door that connected to each suite's telephone (everyone learned to dial 6 to let a visitor into

The Little Mountain Housing Project of the early 1950s, at 33rd between Ontario and Main, was a more gentle kind of charity than the tsunami that hit Strathcona in the 1960s. Its 224 units rented, on average, for $69.40 per month, of which $24 was a subsidy split between the three levels of government. Dubbed "Parasite Park" by local property owners and real-estate dealers, it was said to have an institutional atmosphere due to the plethora of rules, and spawned the Riley Park gang in the 1960s and 1970s. The watercolour shows the last, four-unit building remaining on the site in the summer of 2010; the rest had been cleared away, leaving a park-like landscape of grass and trees, while the neighbourhood suspiciously awaited the start of a new, mixed-use development.

*   Windsor-Liscombe, p. 158.

THREE-STOREY APARTMENT BUILDING 1960S–1970S

all city neighbourhoods • 1960s–1970s

one-bedroom apartment, about 650 square feet

wood-framed building above concrete garage with elevator in the middle

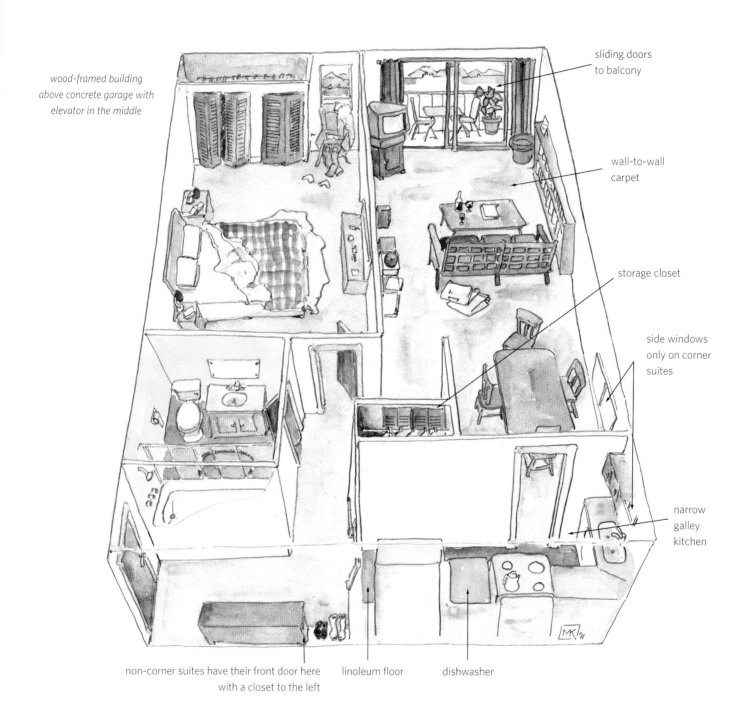

sliding doors to balcony

wall-to-wall carpet

storage closet

side windows only on corner suites

narrow galley kitchen

non-corner suites have their front door here with a closet to the left

linoleum floor

dishwasher

the building). As in the illustration on page 154, the standard one-bedroom apartment filled an even rectangle and could be repeated down a long corridor. The bedroom had its own window but no balcony, while the living area culminated in a glass wall with sliding doors that opened onto a narrow balcony. The big problem with the design was that most of the suites were *not* exactly like the one in the illustration (a corner suite with windows on the side wall); most were cave-like, with windows at one end only and no natural light entering the kitchen.

By the early 1970s the rental market was as tight as it had ever been, with vacancies at a small fraction of a percent (in 2010 the vacancy rate was 1.2 percent, according to city statistics). To try to get the jump on the competition, people looking for apartments would congregate at the 6th Avenue loading dock of the Pacific Press building, just east of Granville where the distribution trucks were marshalled, at about 10:15 each morning. The *Vancouver Sun*, then an afternoon paper, had the biggest classified ad section. Within a few minutes of 10:30, an employee carrying a bundle of papers would emerge and instantly be mobbed, taking quarters and handing papers to people who would sprint to their cars. The most successful had a driver/accomplice who would tear off for Kitsilano or wherever while the targets were being identified. Often places were rented by a resident manager to the first person who rang the bell. Others responded to phone calls, so a pocketful of dimes and a knowledge of local phone booth locations was necessary.

The view from an apartment at 2nd and Arbutus in Kitsilano: 1950s and 1960s apartments in the foreground, peaked-roof condos in the middle and the 1960s high-rises of the West End in the distance.

I N THE POSTWAR YEARS THERE WERE ONLY TWO OPTIONS FOR PEOPLE who wanted to own their residence: the detached home, of course, and the cooperative purchase of a multi-family building. In the former case an owner had fee-simple title to a piece of land, something of almost religious symbolism; in the latter, an owner had shares in a corporation and a lease on a suite.

The Law Reform Commission preferred "apartment corporation" to "cooperative," because the latter might be confused with cooperatives (such as Quebec Manor, referenced above) in the non-profit housing sector. In cooperatives, units might be subsidized and members do not profit from any increase in the value of the land or building. In apartment corporations, a variety of techniques are used that share the creation, by private agreement, of a web of rights and obligations between the "owners" of the various individual apartments. Typically, a corporation is created to hold the legal title of the building; each "owner" is a shareholder and the right to occupy a particular dwelling arises under a long-term lease between the owner and the corporation.

In 1991 there were about 5,500 dwelling units in BC that were parts of apartment corporations, "a distinct and highly desirable alternative to condominium living."[*] The major advantage to the members of a corporation is their right to admit only those people they feel are simpatico. In that respect, a corporation functions like a private club, ensuring a building of relatively like-minded people, as in the fabled co-ops of wealthy New York City. Of course, this advantage can be a disadvantage, for example, when an owner wants to sell or sublet, as it reduces the number of potential buyers.

The need for a different system that would make apartment ownership more like home ownership jibed with most developers' desire to get their money out of a project quickly. Canadian legislators in the 1960s found a suitable model in a statute from New South Wales. Alberta introduced legislation first, in 1966, followed a few weeks later by BC with the Strata Titles Act. Updated in 1974, the latter was replaced by the Condominium Act of 1979 which was further modified following the Barrett Commission's first report on "leaky condos" in the late 1990s.

In a law lecture in 1968, J.C. Cowan described the condominium or strata-title concept as permitting people to "legally build and own 'castles in the air.'" It provided a framework of rules for group living, most importantly that no one person could have exclusive control and, generally speaking, that the majority ruled.[†] Unlike shareholders of apartment corporations, condominium owners could sell their homes to anyone.

The boom in condominium sales in the 1980s and 1990s prompted innovative designs when developers tried to get more natural light into their suites and create more interesting balconies and decks. Not surprisingly, these designs were harder to build, with more corners and edges on their "dry country" flat roofs where water could pool and penetrate. Architects, perhaps, did not receive enough practical training and contractors used materials such as chipboard, which attracts moisture like a sponge. When combined with the building code's mandate to make buildings effectively airtight, the result was like a tomato sandwich in a baggie.[‡] Buyers and tenants wanted in-suite, humidity-producing appliances like dishwashers and clothes washers and dryers and, because buildings no longer breathed the way they once did, it should have been no surprise that the ones that didn't leak rotted from within.[§]

[*] Law Reform Commission of British Columbia, "Apartment Corporations," May 1991.

[†] Jonathan Baker uncovered this in a case involving easements, *Shaw Cablesystems Ltd. vs. Concord Pacific Group*, 2008.

[‡] Interview with Jonathan Baker, 2010.

[§] Interview with Robert Lemon, 2010.

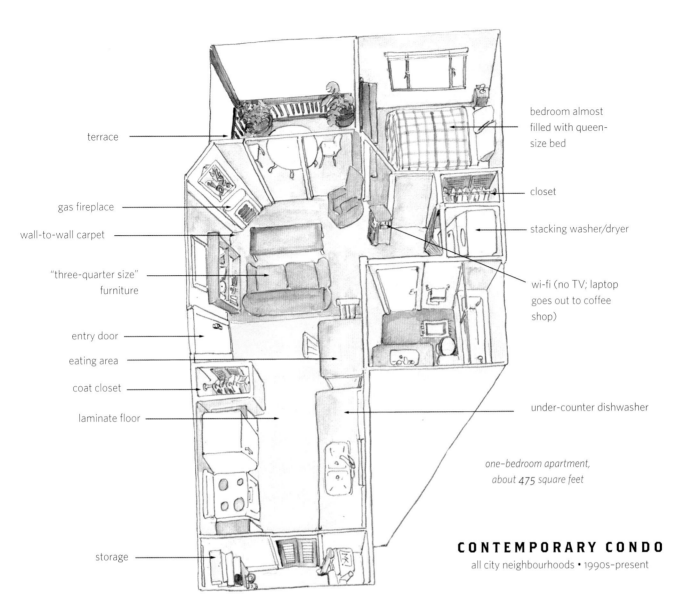

terrace

gas fireplace

wall-to-wall carpet

"three-quarter size" furniture

entry door

eating area

coat closet

laminate floor

storage

bedroom almost filled with queen-size bed

closet

stacking washer/dryer

wi-fi (no TV; laptop goes out to coffee shop)

under-counter dishwasher

one–bedroom apartment, about 475 square feet

CONTEMPORARY CONDO
all city neighbourhoods • 1990s–present

The upshot was the leaky-condo crisis, which wrecked more lives in Vancouver than anything other than the drug trade. Many condominium owners were hit with huge assessments to repair rotting buildings and effectively lost their life savings. One of the more high-profile victims was *Vancouver Sun* columnist Elizabeth Aird, who "herself experienced the agony of owning a leaky condo . . . which gave her deep insights and empathy for others in similar situations."[*]

A 2007 study indicated that developers could obtain a 40 percent rate of return on an investment in condominiums, but only a 2 percent return for purpose-built rental housing.[†] Fortunately for the supply of rental housing, about 17,000 investor-owned condos were being rented in recent years.[‡]

---

[*]   Charlie Smith, writing Aird's obituary in the *Georgia Straight* in 2006 following her sudden death at age 50.

[†]   vancouver.ca/commsvcs/housing/RentalHousing.htm

[‡]   *Vancouver Condominium Rental Study*, by CitySpaces Consulting with Urban Futures Inc., prepared for the City of Vancouver, December 2009, p. 3.

The missing tile in the city's multi-family building mosaic is fee-simple row housing. The "fee-simpletons" are a dogged group, unwilling to forsake their almost mystic attachment to individual responsibility and ownership versus what they see as the collective potential nightmare of strata life. Fee-simple row housing's great proselytizer was the politician, landscape architect and gadfly Art Cowie, who died in 2009 at age 75, just before his set of row houses was completed at 33rd and Cambie.

Technically, Cowie's are "zero-lot-line houses." Built very close together, they do not share the party wall of a classic row house due to a peculiarity of the province's Land Titles Act. The city's legal department believes that repair of the party wall will not "run with the land" and be enforceable on future owners, potentially rendering the city liable.[*] It obviously is a "rule thing" that will be sorted out at some point. Like some other rules, such as the city's requirement for a minimum number of parking spaces, which held up residential conversion of the upper floors of Gastown's buildings 20 years ago, it will be solved eventually.

I HAVE FOUND IT VERY INTERESTING, WHILE SNOOPING IN THE FURnished apartments we have sublet in recent years and in other places, to compare what young condonauts and renters own now compared with what those a generation or two ago owned. The older units have substantial unbroken walls where a bookshelf can live or a piece of artwork hang. On our modest incomes of 40 years ago we would have had cable television (probably black and white), an FM radio and stereo with a pile of LPs, a landline, and a reasonable collection of pots and pans, plants, wall-hangings and furniture. People didn't eat out much. Cars were cheap and simple; if you wanted one you also might keep it running with the help of a friend and a handful of tools.

The new condos are much smaller and the spaces more broken up, with few places where even a TV or couch can fit. Often a flat-screen TV will hang on the wall like a black minimalist painting but it might not be connected to anything other than a DVD player or laptop. There are few books, fewer pictures and little clutter in the units I've seen. Furniture, except for the sumptuous beds that all but overflow the tiny bedrooms, is doll-like, usually referred to as three-quarter size. Often there is no stereo and no collection of CDs, although there might be speakers for an iPod or computer.

The key device is the wireless router. The laptop accompanies the occupant, often to the local café where comfortable chairs are staked out for hours. Some people avoid the expense of an Internet connection and instead use a smart phone and a café's wi-fi or do all their web browsing at work. Landlines went the way of the passenger pigeon years ago. Cars are an expensive nuisance for people who live close in; Zipcars and car co-ops give many people all the freedom they need. A transit pass worth $80 to $150 is a monthly item on the budget. People eat out a lot.

It is a very different city, but it's mainly the toys that have changed.

---

[*] A good review of the project is "Finally a row house of one's own" by Adele Weder, *Globe and Mail*, August 6, 2010.

NEIGHBOURS

THE PLANTED CITY

Vancouver was founded in the 1880s just at the point when new technology—refrigeration and fast long-distance transport—increased the options for feeding urban populations.[*] Like most cities, Vancouver supported a farming hinterland and was in return fed by it—indeed, as with all cities, its commercial and cultural life wouldn't have lasted a week without the labour of its humble farmers.

In the early 1860s, in the wake of the Cariboo gold rush and 25 years before the railway's arrival, a group of settlers including the McCleery brothers, Hugh Magee and Henry Mole began farming the Southlands flats and Sea Island near the mouth of the Fraser River. Their customers lived in New Westminster, a rowboat ride away, and at the salmon canneries and fish camps that dotted the riverbank and soon concentrated at Steveston.[†]

Once the railway arrived, ice harvesting became profitable. Texas Lake near Yale in the Fraser Canyon was the source of the first ice sold in Vancouver, delivered locally by horse-drawn dray. Soon, commercial ice making began, then gradually kerosene or electric refrigerators became affordable for the average family. But it was a slow process. In 1941, more than half the city's rental housing had no refrigeration of any type other than, perhaps, tin-lined meat safes vented to the outside or the traditional bush cooler of a tin tub with a wet burlap sack draped over it. Slightly more than one-quarter had mechanical refrigeration, while about 14 percent still used ice.[‡]

Chinese men no longer able to get railway-construction work began market gardening in the 1880s on the rich floodplain downstream from New Westminster. One later arrival was Hok Yat Louie, who used the time driving a vegetable wagon to Vancouver's Chinatown to learn English; he went on to build the H.Y. Louie wholesale produce company and his son, Tong, created the local IGA supermarket and London Drugs chains.[§] Other Chinese market gardens sprang up on patches of suitable soil, such as on 41st just east of Fraser. Another enclave was the south end of Crown Street along the edge of Musqueam Creek on the First Nations reserve; Chinese farmers worked leased patches of land there from the 1870s until 1969.[¶]

---

[*] Necessity being the mother of invention, a Scottish-born journalist and inventor named James Harrison designed the world's first ice-making plant at Geelong, Victoria, in Australia in the 1850s. His first client was a brewery in Bendigo, then in the midst of a gold rush. His efforts in the 1870s to develop refrigerated ship chambers spurred the development of the country's meat-export business. From the *Australian Dictionary of Biography* (adbonline.anu.edu.au/biogs/A010479b.htm).

[†] *The Story of Dunbar* (edited by Peggy Schofield) has complete information on the farms. The story of the McLeery and Mole families is told by writer Helen Spiegelman, who drew on the memories and photographs of Betty McQueen (1916–2009), a descendant of both families.

[‡] Wade, p. 58.

[§] See Perrault, *Tong: The Story of Tong Louie, Vancouver's Quiet Titan.*

[¶] Spiegelman in Schofield, pp. 30–2.

One agricultural curiosity a century ago was the CPR gardens (now Point Grey Secondary School's playing fields), located next to the Vancouver–Steveston interurban line, which grew fresh vegetables for the company's trains and hotels. Ten blocks south, the Royal Nursery Company, an investment of entrepreneur and land developer R.D. Rorison, established a nursery with greenhouses for indoor and outdoor plants and shrubs for homeowners in the prosperous years just before the First World War. As is the case today, exotic plants were popular; it's hard to find a studio photograph from that period that doesn't feature an aspidistra. Two other well-known sources of plants were Sherdahl's and M.J. Henry nurseries, along the Westminster Road, later renamed Kingsway, between 12th and 15th.

Because it was one of the few well-maintained roads in the city, Westminster Road also had its fair share of dairies, the cows in the early years roaming widely through the brush and scrub that somehow thrived on the rain-leached, acidic soil of the logged-off rainforest. The Garvin and Jones dairies stood on opposite sides of Jones Creek near Windsor Street which, once it flowed northward and was joined by Gibson Creek, became known as China Creek (page 196).

The Morrisette House on Blenheim at Mayfair is a relic of the rural Vancouver that developed on the city's south slope above the working farms of the Southlands flats. Standing on 10 acres in 1914, it evolved into a rooming house on a large lot and was threatened by redevelopment in the 1980s. Owner Victoria Zabolotny worked with architect Rick Balfour to subdivide the property using a heritage covenant. After a lengthy hiatus, it sold in 2010 and a restoration and infill project commenced. A photograph of the house soon after its construction appears in Schofield, p. 155.

Across the road from the M.J. Henry Nursery, with its barn sitting on the 16th Avenue city boundary at Fraser, was the McGeer Dairy; according to legend, future mayor and senator Gerry McGeer honed his oratorical skills talking to himself during his boyhood milk deliveries. Fraser Street was originally the North Arm Road—the first north-south connector that, with a bridge crossing the river and Mitchell Island to Richmond—became a vital connector for produce making its way by wagon toward Vancouver.

William Shannon ran a dairy herd on the south slope of the city near Granville Street—hence Shannon Road, now 57th Avenue, a name that survives on the old Rogers/Taylor estate (page 170). Out on Point Grey, the Stewart dairy farm occupied the bluff above Spanish Banks and, it is said, delivered its milk cans to trucks on Marine Drive using a funicular railway; the foundations of its house are still clearly visible in the bush next to the clearing known as the Plains of Abraham. The False Creek flats that were railyards for the Great Northern and Canadian National railways were also used as cow pasture during the 1920s and 1930s; a few Strathcona families kept cows in tiny back-lane barns.

As the city grew, milk from the Fraser Valley nourished the growing Vancouver population. The BC Electric Railway company's interurban to Chilliwack did not stay profitable for long on passenger volume, but its milk runs were an essential part of the region's economy until the service ended in 1950 and trucks became the mode of transport. The vanished industrial area south of Broadway near Arbutus was home to the Jersey, the Guernsey and the Associated dairies. Bottling plants obtained their milk from Richmond farmers via the Steveston–Vancouver interurban line. The last city bottling plant was Avalon Dairy, begun in 1906 with six cows on cleared bushland south of 41st Avenue on Wales Street in East Vancouver; it was put up for sale in 2011.

The old Palm Dairy site on Main Street at 18th was redeveloped in 2011 with condos and retail designed by architect Joost Bakker, who worked with partner Norman Hotson to refurbish Granville Island's abandoned factories. At the southwest corner of Commercial and 2nd, the Crystal Dairy (currently Wonderbucks) had a milk and ice cream bar—modified into a soda fountain in the 1930s—and was *the* place to hang out in its day.[*]

Many suburban families grew their own vegetables in their back yards and kept hens. A century ago, newspaper advertisements touted the independent lifestyle of the small-scale egg producer, and flocks of a hundred or so hens were common on vacant lots on the suburban outskirts of South Vancouver. During the Depression, especially, a bit of agriculture could be essential to survival. Historian Jill Wade describes a "76-year-old widow, 'a very fine type of old pioneer' according to a city

---

[*]   King, p. 65.

The daffodil field and orchard at 51st and Balaclava in Southlands, as it was in 1989. Email from Rick Maynard, 2009: "I am now the proud owner of the daffodil orchard in *Vanishing Vancouver*. I have lived in Southlands all my life and every spring have admired the King Alfred daffodils. Drs. Margaret and Lawrence Young, former owners, are in a retirement home and were very happy to have us buy the property because we guaranteed them we would preserve the orchard and flowers. We will continue farming the property as my son is graduating from UBC in Agriculture and it is his passion to put the property back into a market garden."

official, [who] owned a small cottage and several sheds 'all looking their age' on Victoria Drive. She had no electricity and no water supply . . . Receiving a $15 monthly old-age pension, she lived on one dollar and the product of ten hens and used the rest to pay off her debts."[*]

Subsistence agriculture continued in Southlands and on the city's southern and eastern outskirts even after the last of the big farms—the McCleerys', then run by their Logan descendants—had been taxed out of existence and turned into a golf course in the 1950s. One remnant from that rural past is a small orchard of ancient apple trees at the southwest corner of 51st and Balaclava; its underplanting of daffodils, started in the 1920s by Archie Urwin to provide an early cash crop, continues to bloom and brighten the pale Vancouver springtime.

Subsistence agriculture—the modern version of feeding oneself and one's family, or at least having a go at it—has had a tremendous resurgence in the past decade or so. Vegetables are in, flowers out. Vegetable gardens are practical things and the demand for allotments in the city's many community gardens is high. Added into the back yard mix are hens, nowadays heavily regulated compared with earlier times and promised a comfortable dotage in the city's care facility rather than a quick trip to the soup pot. For all the overkill, as it were, of the city's poultry policy, it is wonderful to hear chickens laying their eggs in the city. Who else could take the unwanted contents of a fridge and the scratchings of a patch of lawn and give them back as perfect protein?

---

[*]   Wade, p. 54.

A HOUSE THAT STRADDLED TWO LOTS AT THE CORNER OF 23RD AND Highbury in Dunbar provides a lesson on how much the city has changed in the past couple of generations. For more than 40 years, Audrey and Robert Ostrom lived there and raised their family on his income as a commercial fisher—not on a high-tech trawler but rather on a traditional longliner salmon boat—and with proceeds from her skill and diligence as an urban farmer and craftsperson. The garden produced for most of the year and its bounty was "put by," preserved for winter eating or given to friends. Vegetables, raspberry bushes and fruit trees grew on the land that, according to Vancouver's "Greenest City" philosophy, ought to be paved over for a lane house.

Due to advancing age, the Ostroms realized they had to move on. They could find no way to preserve their home, which was wider than a single lot. In 2010, after a spring and summer of tidying up, during which almost the entire contents of the garden were transferred to friends and acquaintances, they reluctantly moved to a condominium. Robert's health, which had been challenged by the extreme stress of moving, deteriorated quickly and he died that November. By that time their house was demolished and two buildings, each larger than the old place, immediately began to rise on the lots.

Dunbar in the 1960s was still an affordable place. Bus driver Angus McIntyre, who became well known for his 40 years behind the wheel and his tours in vintage trolleys for Heritage Vancouver, was able to buy a home there with his worker's income.[*] Nowadays a 33-foot lot in Dunbar is worth a million and a half, requiring many times the income a bus driver or commercial fisher earns.

The home of Robert and Audrey Ostrom on West 23rd Avenue, at the corner of Highbury in Dunbar, in the spring of 2010, shortly before its demolition. The side and back yards were intensively cultivated with vegetables, berry bushes and fruit trees while the front displayed flowers, shrubs and vines.

---

* The *Buzzer* blog, August 26, 2009.

GARDENS ARE THE MOST EPHEMERAL PART OF A CITY'S HISTORY. FASHions change and gardens get makeovers like aging kitchens. People move on and properties are redeveloped, invariably denser than they were, leaving less open space. People have less time now and many don't see the focused puttering of gardening as being sufficiently worthwhile.

The photo on the next page captures Vancouver's bungalow landscape of 1950 or so, before TV antennae sprouted from every rooftop. It was probably taken by Jessie Acorn, standing on her neighbour's front steps to look across the street at her own house (which still survives) at 2046 West 48th; today the dark bungalow (on the left) is gone and the shacky cottage (on the right) has been replaced by another vintage house moved from elsewhere. Everything was *tidy*: the roses, the curving path, the gentleman in his waistcoat, the bungalows that were then about 25 years old. Only the city had fallen down on the job, not having gotten around to curbing the street.

In most areas of the city at that time, lawns and their grooming were part of the imperative of neatness, a duty for everyone. As if by statute, every house had at least one shrub. Typically it was a mop-top hydrangea like the one in front of the dark bungalow; today it would be a rhododendron. Comparatively few properties were really worked by gardeners who passionately grew roses and honeysuckle and the plants of English cottage gardens: phlox and stocks and hollyhocks, pinks, lily of the valley and sweet william.

Compared to traditional Ontario or Maritimes residential areas, where one lawn merged seamlessly into another and the houses stood proudly in a park-like setting, most of Vancouver's narrow lots were delineated with picket or wire fences. Sometimes a shrub or two and a few strategic rocks edged the front yards along a lot's boundaries, defining the turf without the "keep off" connotation of a fence and a gate. Rockeries were another fenceless way to define boundaries, especially on properties where the lawn and house were on a terrace above the boulevard and sidewalk; heather that brightened the grey days of winter was a popular choice for them. Hedges were another fence substitute; a popular choice was bright green, waxy-leafed laurel, as tireless and evergreen in the mild climate as the grass.

The 1980s and 1990s will probably be seen by future garden historians—should there be any—as a high point. Since the war years there had developed a real culture of flower gardening, most notably in the West Side's comfortable homes on large lots. Many of the gardeners collected a vast range of plants from all over the world. Somehow people had a different balance in their lives. The time-expenders of social networking and email were still in the future. Books like *The Twelve-Month Gardener* became bestsellers.[*]

Around the millennium this generation of skilled gardeners began to move on, some due to age, toward smaller gardens or condos or to greener pastures on the Sunshine Coast and elsewhere. The Rogers, Turvey and Fancourt-Smith gardens in Kerrisdale were among those erased from the landscape when the properties were redeveloped. Denis Yeomans's superb collection of antique roses at the corner of

---

[*]   Elaine Stevens et al.

Dunbar and 51st was divvied up among friends when he moved away.

The watercolours on pages 168 and 169 capture the rustic quality of that part of Kerrisdale 20 years ago. There was an air of a rural estate about a number of the homes, which look like pages torn from the British *Country Life* magazine, especially on the long block that runs south from 45th to 49th between Macdonald and Elm, in a unique 1909 subdivision by a man named Christopher Foreman. The lots there are 315 feet deep, more than double the typical depth for that part of the city, because Trafalgar Street was not opened south of 45th Avenue. The first house on the block was 6238 Macdonald, owned by the Burgess family when I painted it in 1990. Twenty years later the area is much changed: the houses are bigger although mainly still in period styles, the landscaping more formal.

One garden that survived partially was the Crawford garden at 45th and Macdonald, where a 1920s Georgian house sitting at the front of three very deep lots was retained as part of a complex development that put infill houses on its expansive grounds and retained many of its mature trees. The development was controversial—the issue with neighbours, much as at Greencroft in Shaughnessy (page 112), was the change from single-family ownership to strata title—but council supported it nevertheless. The alternative would have been two or three great big houses facing Macdonald Street, as was happening further south.

The best gardens of the era were recorded and analyzed in the book *Gardens of Vancouver*,* which explores influences on the city's gardeners. Of the 26 gardens

The home of Jessie Acorn, at 2046 West 48th, seen along with a neighbour and his rose garden, probably in the 1940s.

* Christine Allen and Collin Varner.

The property of Arthur Ross, at the southeast corner of 45th and Macdonald, in 1992. Its expansive garden, set in an almost-rural park, was established mainly by the previous owner, John Crawford, in the 1930s and 1940s.

included in the book, 11 were in English and cottage styles, reflecting the city's dominant culture a half century ago and complementing the Tudor and Craftsman designs of the houses. Two showed very strong Japanese influences, while another two retained the West Coast woodland landscape and combined the gardens' design with modernist architecture. Three of the gardens were "tropical visions" using plants with exotic leaves and shapes to magically escape the confines of the rainforest and its dark blue and green palate. One of them, by design guru and nursery owner Thomas Hobbs, used a 1920's-vintage "Hollywood Spanish" house on the Point Grey heights as the stage set for a Mediterranean garden that was "all about faking it," as Hobbs said, describing how he had selected plants that would survive in a West Coast climate.

For a time recently the bloom seemed to have gone off the rose. Fewer people were joining city garden clubs, meeting attendance slumped, memberships declined and interest even in the master gardener program at VanDusen Botanical Gardens diminished a little. More people were having their gardens done by others, which perhaps indicates a combination of affluence and a lack of free time. These designed gardens typically had plants that were chosen for their ease of maintenance, structural quality and drought tolerance. It's rare now to see the old labour-intensive herbaceous border that varies with the season.

Any decline in flower gardening has been countered by an increase in vegetable gardening, part of the green fad that may be here to stay but harkens back to the vegetable patch and orchard that were once common on city lots. In newspaper "house for sale" ads a century ago, fruit trees were often mentioned as inducements. City council has done its part, following the lead of the residents along the old interurban line between 49th and 57th in Kerrisdale and on the former Heatley Avenue dump site

in Strathcona, and opened underused parts of parks and vacant land for community allotment gardens.

The property at 6238 Macdonald in 1990, 132 feet wide by 315 feet deep—more landscape than house.

THE BIGGEST OF THE OLD VANCOUVER ESTATES, SHANNON AT 57TH AND GRANVILLE, is the subject in 2012 of surgery so extensive that, like Woodward's (page 44), it will be a case of "the operation was a success but the patient died." Shannon was the dream of sugar-refinery owner B.T. Rogers (page 58), incomplete at the time of his death in 1918. It was completed by his widow, Mary Isabella Rogers, and occupied by her from 1925 to 1936 and then by industrialist Austin Taylor until his death in 1965.[*] A proposal to add rental apartments to it in early 1967 was controversial for the same reason alluded to above—that part of Kerrisdale was a single-family area.

The proponents then were Peter Wall and Peter Redekop, both aged about 30. Although their plan met with a lot of opposition, the city eventually rezoned the site and allowed the construction of six two-storey apartment buildings along the perimeter walls in return for the heritage designation of the mansion. Designed by Arthur Erickson, the new buildings blended in with the gardens and trees and didn't clash or compete with the red brick mansion or its outbuildings. Nearly 40 years on, the estate and its tenants were just another part of the area; according to neighbourhood lore, the apartments had become a port of call for estranged husbands in wrecked West Side marriages while divorces were finalized and properties divided. In recent years, tenants complained about lack of maintenance. The mansion's main-floor interior was left dusty, unrestored and unused.

---

[*]   Photos and more detail about Shannon appear in *Vancouver Remembered*, pp. 208–9.

In the weird world of 21st-century Vancouver development, the estate's long-abandoned Italian garden and rose garden became chips that could be traded for high-density infill. Parts of the mansion's interior, plus seismic upgrading of it, plus the old coachhouse and gatehouse on Granville Street, were tossed in for restoration and designation, too, in a 2009 proposal by Wall Financial that included a 23-storey residential tower on the corner of Granville and 57th. As seems to be the way, the developer had asked for the moon and stars and negotiated backward to settle for the moon: in 2010 it was down to 14 storeys, then in 2011 it was "mid-rise" 10-storey buildings. The final proposal, debated during three marathon public-hearing evenings in July 2011 was a further token reduction in building height.

In my opinion, the seven new buildings, including ones of seven, eight and nine storeys, will overwhelm the estate, leaving the graceful three-storey mansion as a diminutive relic. Although roses only grow well in full sun, the rose garden will be shaded by an eight-storey building on its south side. The Italianate garden will be similarly shaded in late afternoon and evening by six- and eight-storey buildings.

Consultants assessed the proposed heritage restoration work on the buildings and gardens at $9 million and made it part of the justification for the increased density, which will put 735 residential units on the site. Also justifying it was the city's EcoDensity policy, which aims to "fully consider and test higher-density options to achieve sustainability, complete-community and public-benefit goals."

Even a cursory examination, acknowledged by city staff in their nonetheless positive response, showed the development was clearly not a complete community. The only food shop within a reasonable walk was a boutique supermarket several blocks away. The Marpole shops are a dozen blocks to the south down a long hill. There is one bus on Granville Street, which travels at a glacial pace. Just like many developments in Fraser Valley communities (which smug Vancouver shakes its head at), the new Shannon Mews will be "car-captive," with more than a thousand people coming and going daily in private automobiles. The neighbourhood remained bitterly

opposed and fought it to the end, but council approved the rezoning by a narrow margin, the week after it had voted in its Greenest City 2020 initiative.

THE TWO PRIVATE GARDENS ON PAGES 172–175 ARE LONG GONE. A FEW trees and bits of stone wall from the Wilson estate are identifiable on King Edward Avenue but there is no trace of the Dick house and garden on South West Marine Drive at 64th Avenue. The Wilson property is dotted with anonymous Dunbar houses while the Dick property has a modest rancher quite different from its neighbours—those of the restless rich, who have demolished and rebuilt many homes on that "Millionaire's Row" in the past 30 years.

Charles Henry Wilson was a contractor and land speculator like so many in early Vancouver. He arrived in the infant city three weeks after the 1886 fire and went into business with Sanford Johnston Crowe, who became a city alderman from 1909 until 1915 and later an MP before his appointment as a Liberal-Unionist senator in 1921. Crowe served until his death at age 63 in 1931; a stub of road north of 2nd Avenue east of Cambie Street preserves his memory. Wilson Heights is the area on 41st Avenue east of Knight; a United Church near Argyle Street is the only building keeping alive Wilson's name.

About 1905, Wilson and Crowe bought adjoining five-acre properties between Balaclava and Blenheim on King Edward Avenue (Chaldecott, it was then called). The area was still forest but Blenheim Street (then known as Johnson after the builder of the von Alvensleben house, page 195) was cleared through to the south. Wilson had his crews clear 41st Avenue between Blenheim and Granville in 1905 and had it named for him; by 1910, Wilson Road had extended eastward toward the "heights." The name was changed to 41st Avenue following the amalgamation of Point Grey and South Vancouver with the city in 1929.

While Crowe never developed his patch of bushland, Wilson built a home and laid out extensive gardens about 1914. No historic pictures survive but its layout was remembered well by one of his granddaughters, Evelyn McKim, who walked me around it about 1992, pointing out the locations of trees and pathways so that I could draw a plan of it. I subsequently confected a watercolour of it in its splendour for her, adding a small plan copy that she pasted onto the back.[*]

During the Great Depression, retired and in straitened circumstances, Wilson and his wife, Eva, decided they needed to subdivide the estate and with great regret cut up the gardens. They continued to live in their house, reorienting its driveway so that the entrance would be at 4175 Balaclava Street, their address until Wilson's death at the age of 92 in 1947. The houses along King Edward west of Balaclava appear first in the 1935 city directory; they were designed by the Wilsons' son-in-law, a Danish-born architect-builder by the name of Holger Tang who had married Isabel Mary Wilson in 1930.

The back part of the property was also subdivided and Tang built the house at 3204 West 26th for himself and his family. His day job was as real-estate manager for Safeway until he died in 1942, only 42 years old. With the final subdivision of the property, the Wilsons' Craftsman-style house had an address of 3223 West 26th Avenue, presenting its front porch to its back yard, where it survived until a few years ago.

The photographs on the next two pages show the home and garden of clothier William Dick (page 67) and his wife, Clara, at 2000 South West Marine Drive, looking out over the Fraser River in the 1920s. The house, by an unknown architect and built probably in 1922, is in a kind of Italian Renaissance style; the garden, very formal and clipped, would have required a small army to maintain. The images by Leonard Frank capture the property as it was soon after the garden was planted, although the house had been in existence long enough to bristle with ivy. The family had a set of photographs taken later by the noted art photographer John Vanderpant, who died in 1937, but they are so soft focus (that is, blurry) that they were never framed or displayed.

William Dick died in 1939; caretakers named Alan and Edith Oddy lived there in 1940 but thereafter the house disappeared from the directory. Perhaps a fire destroyed it; there is no one left alive to explain. A man named C.J. Duncan put in a new water service for the rancher that now occupies the property, using the street number 2008, in 1950.

NEXT PAGE > A re-creation of the Wilson estate at King Edward and Balaclava, as it would have been about 1930.

BELOW > The modest home of Holger and Isabel Tang, son-in-law and daughter of Charles and Eva Wilson, at 3204 West 26th, on land that was part of the Wilson estate.

---

[*] Tom Grant helped me remember Evelyn McKim's name as I had no record of it. "I recall they had a framed watercolour on the wall," he wrote to me about visiting her in 1998 or so, "which I attempted to take a photo of—it didn't turn out." I've been unable to contact her or her descendants.

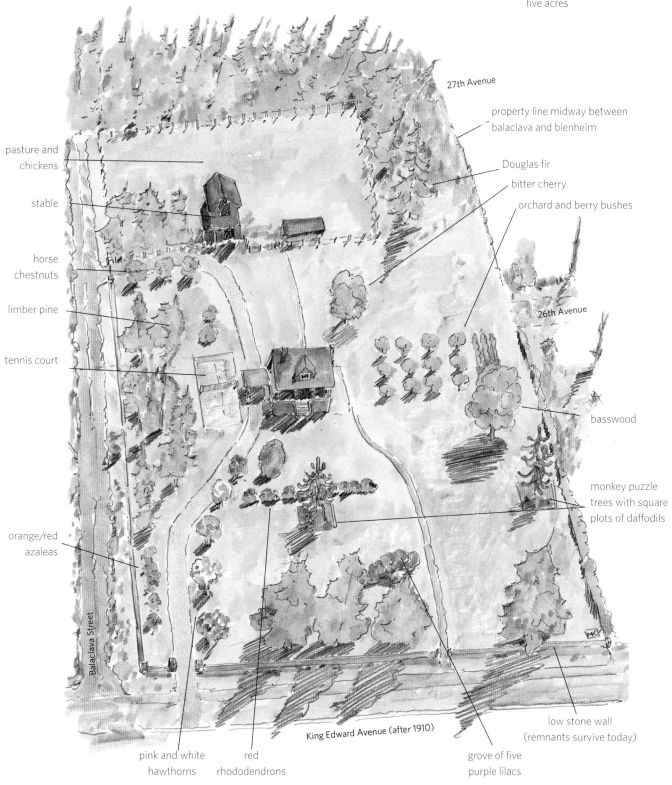

WILSON ESTATE
King Edward and Balaclava • 1905-35
five acres

27th Avenue

property line midway between
balaclava and blenheim

Douglas fir

bitter cherry

orchard and berry bushes

pasture and
chickens

stable

horse
chestnuts

26th Avenue

limber pine

tennis court

basswood

monkey puzzle
trees with square
plots of daffodils

orange/red
azaleas

Balaclava Street

low stone wall
(remnants survive today)

King Edward Avenue (after 1910)

pink and white
hawthorns

red
rhododendrons

grove of five
purple lilacs

The estate of clothier William Dick and his wife, Clara, at 2000 South West Marine Drive, photographed by Leonard Frank about 1930. Not a trace of it remains today. The photograph above shows the view from the garden edge down to the hayfields that then lined the bank of the Fraser River. (COLLECTION OF BILL AND JOANNE DICK)

A VIEWPOINT WITHOUT A VIEW —that might have represented the zenith of the city's lunacy. Obscured by trees, the view of the city and mountains from atop Queen Elizabeth Park became a major debate between the park board and local residents in 2008. Tree-hugging Vancouver was never more in evidence. Nevertheless, trees were chopped and trimmed, restoring a portion of the view that was the raison d'être for the park's development more than a half century ago. Vancouver has many trees but the park's old nickname, Little Mountain, attested to its uniqueness.

The panorama above is a collage of Kodachrome slides from three different viewpoints taken by Ruby Kluckner, my aunt, in the winter of 1965. Allowing for the distortion and flattening of her 35mm lens, it gives a good idea of what an average person would have seen, especially from the viewpoint above the sunken garden (on the left) that had been planted during the previous decade in the CPR's old basalt quarry. Today, that view of Fairview, the West End and Stanley Park, seen in the composite photo on the next page, is almost completely blocked in spite of the park board's

LEFT > A panoramic view of Vancouver from Little Mountain, formally known as Queen Elizabeth Park, in 1965.

PREVIOUS PAGE > From the viewpoint in the early 1950s, after the second Hotel Vancouver (p. 18) came down. The line of low apartment buildings along Cambie Street is clearly visible in the left centre. (PHOTOGRAPHER UNKNOWN, COAST PUBLISHING COMPANY)

BELOW > A composite photograph of the view today, from above the Quarry Gardens (the left-hand image from the panorama is the base). In spite of the park board's trimming efforts, the view across Fairview to the West End and English Bay is still blocked.

efforts. However, the right-hand portion of the scene, taking in the towers at Burrard and Georgia Street more or less, and everything east, can be seen now much as it was a half century ago.

The trees above the sunken garden are mainly western red cedar, shapeless and dull in their large clumps. However common, these trees were the attraction for some people. An extreme position was that of park board commissioner Loretta Woodcock, who had fought hard to save the 70 trees that were cut down. She believed that construction of new towers, miles away, would block the view from Queen Elizabeth Park! "If it turns out the view corridor is not going to be maintained, we wouldn't have had to worry about it and those trees could have been saved," she was quoted as saying.*

A view of what? How about a view of the new towers? Why are the only views worth saving the ones of distant mountains?

---

*   "Proposed tower threatens park's mountain view" by Sandra Thomas, *Vancouver Courier*, December 22, 2010.

SUBSISTENCE FARMS ON THE EDGES OF CITIES GET SWALLOWED UP BY growth and time. By the 1970s one such edge was Langley, only a part of which is good farmland and protected within the Agricultural Land Reserve. Out there amidst the subdivisions, woodlots, hobby farms and country estates, Jan and Dyna Tuytel created The 100 Aker Wood, named for the setting of Jan's favourite childhood book, *Winnie-the-Pooh*.

In its broad brushstrokes the couple's story is an immigrants' tale like many others. But in one way the Tuytels' home was different. Whereas many such places were "stump farms," theirs was a picturesque, crafted landscape with unique, handmade buildings. It was five acres that felt like infinity.

Born in 1926, Jan Tuytel grew up on a dairy farm in Alblasserdam, a town in the province of South Holland. His generation of Dutch people lived through the Great Depression and more than five years of Nazi occupation during the Second World War. Elder son Neo wrote,

> After the war, [Jan] enlisted in the army and sailed to Indonesia where
> he served for three years during the colonial rebellion. His forebears had

all been farmers in the lowest lying polder of the Netherlands. He was the first Tuytel, ever, to leave the Alblasserwaard. . . . When he returned home the apron strings had been cut. He bought a motorcycle, courted Dyna Hoogendijk and emigrated to Canada in 1952. He had $150 in his pocket, a couple of wheelbarrows and some shovels with him, and spoke very little English.

[Jan] would proudly tell you that a customs officer looked at the wheelbarrows and shovels and noted that he had obviously come to Canada to work. He would also tell you that, at the train station in Montreal, he tripped and fell in a mud puddle. Unbowed and independently minded as always, he ignored the immigration officer's suggestion that he head to Edmonton and carried on to the Fraser Valley where some friends had settled.

Jan and Dyna Tuytel's 100 Aker Wood, with its home spanning a small creek and its workshop and barn, in Langley, 2010.

There were many Dutch immigrants in the Fraser Valley in the late 1940s, a large number of whom started as labourers and went into dairying as opportunities arose. Some leased from older farmers, some saw the opportunities in poorly drained land—Pitt Polder being the prime example. One of Jan's aphorisms was "there are

Jan and Dyna Tuytel, 2008

more poor farmers than poor land," a variation on one I knew, that "a poor carpenter blames his tools."

But Jan had little interest in following other immigrants' footsteps, although he initially worked as a labourer and lived on a farm in Surrey. Another early job was shovelling manure in the legendary 10-sided Ewen barn in east Richmond.* Figuring this was little different from the grinding labour of his Dutch childhood, he struck out on his own as a landscape gardener on Vancouver's North Shore.

In 1953 Jan returned to the family farm during the catastrophic flooding of the Netherlands. On that trip, he proposed to Dyna and she followed him to Canada the next year. Their first home was a basement suite in West Vancouver. While she was pregnant with the first of their two children, in 1956, they bought a house in North Vancouver. As Neo described it, "Like in a scene out of *The Beverly Hillbillies* he promptly dug up the recently landscaped back yard and planted a vegetable garden."

Along the way Jan had taught himself stonemasonry. His first fireplace for a cottage on Bowyer Island fell down. He rebuilt it and over the next couple of decades built numerous other, often exquisite fireplaces, foundations and retaining walls, mostly for summer homes on the Gulf Islands and Sunshine Coast. He taught himself his next profession by completely renovating their home in North Vancouver as well as building granite retaining walls, re-landscaping the yard, and planting and tending their vegetable and flower gardens.

In 1965, Jan bought five wooded acres in rural Langley where, using all his talents, and with the weekend and summertime efforts of Dyna and their sons, he created his life's principal work—a rustic cottage home, workshop and barn, surrounded by gardens, fields and even (for a time) trout ponds. Everything was done by hand: the road into the property, the clearing of trees, putting up a cabin, digging the ponds, expanding the cabin into a house and home, building the fieldstone foundation and fireplace, hauling gravel (using his original wheelbarrows and shovels) for the septic field, even cutting and splitting cedar logs into shakes for the roofs. The family moved to Langley in the summer of 1972. Dyna cross-stitched an old Dutch saying and hung it by the fireplace: "Happiness is a fat wife and a barn full of hay."

The ponds, which doubled as skating rinks in the winter, were eventually filled in and the trout replaced with prize-winning Romney sheep. Jan added extensive flower beds to his productive vegetable garden, proving another of his favourite sayings, that the apple doesn't fall far from the tree. Like his father he raised livestock, and like his mother he grew roses. In 1993, shortly after my wife, Christine, and I moved to a farm in the Fraser Valley, I took the course Jan offered in Langley on raising sheep and bought the core of my flock from him; Christine collaborated with him on rose-growing projects and shared weird and exotic plants. We became close friends.

Jan became increasingly interested in the traditional skills he remembered from the "hungry years" of his boyhood on the farm in Holland. Weaving willows into sheep fencing and plant supports was one activity; when he found that the common

---

* The one so lacking in maintenance that it blew over in a windstorm in 1995 shortly after the Historic Sites and Monuments Board of Canada declared it a National Historic Site.

willows growing in that part of the Fraser Valley weren't suitable for his purposes, he explored further afield, eventually finding the type he wanted along a riverbank north of Squamish. He took cuttings, planted himself a row and soon had a plantation that he coppiced every spring for raw materials for his plant supports, bird nests and other creations.

When Jan's gardening associates told him how enchanting his creations were, he began to produce more, giving many of them away and eventually teaching workshops in the technique at VanDusen Gardens. He made traditional brooms and forged hand tools in his workshop, all of which provided gifts for friends and a small income when they were sold through gardening shops. By his mid-70s he had become an active member of the VanDusen Garden Society and a star attraction at their annual sale where he sold hundreds of the plants he raised in his greenhouse and gardens.

In 2006, a multiple bypass slowed Jan down a little. "Unbowed," Neo wrote, "he carried on with his gardening, the VanDusen sale and a newfound avocation of devouring classical literature, from Greek philosophers through Russian novelists; not bad for a guy with a grade eight education."

A fast-moving cancer carried Jan away in the spring of 2010. He always told me he wanted to be carried out feet first and to all intents and purposes got his wish. Following his death, Dyna lived on for a time at the farm as friends and relatives rallied around to tend the garden and care for the sheep. I could write endlessly about him, but suffice it to say I doubt I'll ever meet anyone like him.[*]

From the driveway, deep in forest trees, a view that opened suddenly into a sunlit glade, with the vegetable garden and berry bushes on the near side of the Tuytels' house, sheep pastures on the far side.

---

[*] Jan, who always pronounced his name "John," is the mentor character in the two books I wrote about our years on our small farm, *The Pullet Surprise* and *Wise Acres*. Thanks to his sons, Neo and Casey, for sharing the family stories.

LEGACIES AND MEMORIES

THERE ARE JUST A HANDFUL OF PLACES IN VANCOUVER WHERE THE street grid is broken up with short blocks, large properties or other curiosities. One is the neighbourhood around the old Franciscan monastery in Grandview. Like in an Italian village, the ringing bell of Saint Francis of Assisi church on Napier Street carries through the quiet parish streets at midday, answered by the distant "O Canada" four-note horn atop Canada Place.

Nearby Commercial Drive was first identified in the newspapers as Little Italy about 1967, 20 years after Italian migrants from Strathcona and new immigrants began to flavour the old Anglo working-class Grandview area. Described as a city within a city, the area bounded by Campbell, Nanaimo, Hastings and Kingsway was home to about 30,000 Italians.

The pull to Grandview was probably the church, which began in the mid-1930s to hold services at the Franciscan monastery established in 1924 in the old William Miller mansion, Wilga, at Semlin and Napier.* In earlier years, the Catholic parish ministering to the Italian population was Sacred Heart Church at 525 Campbell Avenue in Strathcona. The push from Strathcona was increased prosperity throughout society, which gave Italian-Canadians more opportunities than they had had when, mainly as labourers, they had crowded into the tenements and small houses along Union Street around the turn of the 20th century. The changing ethnic mix of Strathcona, especially the wave of Chinese immigrants settling there around 1950, undoubtedly helped.

One of the early arrivals in the Saint Francis area was Guiseppe Pennimpede, known as Joseph Penneway, who built the first house on Venables, at the corner of Lakewood, in 1908, the year after the area was subdivided and city water service arrived. His family later added a grocery store to the front of the house, which survived until about a decade ago. He also built the houses at 2034 and 2062 Venables as investments.

The impetus for a Franciscan parish came in June 1930 from a number of people living near the monastery. The group included the Italian consul, Mr. Masi, and the vice-president of Metropolitan Life Insurance Company, Frank Rita. Eventually 200 people signed a petition and in September 1936 a new parish bounded by Hastings Street, 1st Avenue, Templeton Street and Commercial Drive was carved from three earlier ones. The church's first rector, Reverend Father Boniface, noted in his 1959 history of the parish that even in the beginning there were a lot of immigrants in the area, a great diversity of nationalities and challenges in weaning families away from

---

* See *Vancouver Remembered*, pp. 218–21 for the story of William and J.J. Miller and their two Grandview mansions, Wilga and Kurrajong.

the downtown church.* Only one of the 14 presidents of the altar society in the '40s and '50s had an Italian name; one had a Chinese name.

"For one year the parishioners had crowded into the small Monastery chapel for the three Masses on Sunday, but this could not keep on for any length of time," Boniface wrote. "A church had to be built."

Late in the fall of 1937 he submitted a sketch of a plan to George Aspell, "known as one of British Columbia's best draftsmen," to be worked out "in a Roman-Mission style with no pillars, a large sanctuary, a sacristy to the east of the main Altar, a choir for the religious community to the west with a corridor connecting it with the monastery, concealed or recessed confessionals, a baptistry [and] a glazed-off vestibule supporting the organ loft to the south."

The Franciscan monastery, its front porch closed in, at the corner of Semlin and Napier in the late 1950s. (PHOTO FROM *THE HISTORY OF SAINT FRANCIS PARISH, VANCOUVER*)

The plans were ready by the beginning of 1938 and contractor S.J. Grant of North Vancouver won over five other bidders; he began construction on February 20 and worked so quickly that the church was ready by the end of June. The pipe organ was installed in 1942 and the pulpit of fumed oak in 1953. A number of articles in the church had been used by priests in hiding at Berington Hall in England during the Penal Laws. The baptismal font of beaten brass "formerly served as a flower stand in the Czar's garden, Petersburg." Boniface noted that the alms box had been stolen from the church a number of times "but always found its way back intact" as it weighed 65 pounds and the thieves found it hard to carry very far.

During those years of church building the Italian community was coming to terms with the reality of Mussolini's Italy. On May 22, 1936, according to a news report, "150 loyal Italian wives of Vancouver" exchanged their gold wedding rings for steel ones at a ceremony on board the Italian ship MS *Rialto* in the harbour. The rings were donated to the Italian Red Cross, part of a fundraising campaign to support the Italian adventuring in Ethiopia.

That October, on Columbus Day, "cheers for Mussolini rang out through the Silver Slipper Hall . . . Glasses were raised and drained to the conqueror of Ethiopia." Reports of subsequent events make no mention of him and the tone changed totally in June 1940. CITY ITALIAN COLONY WORRIED, THINKS IL DUCE WON'T FIGHT, one newspaper headline reported. Those who spoke for the community believed that the Catholic Church and lingering anti-German sentiment left over from the First World War would stay Mussolini's hand.[†]

Events changed suddenly when Mussolini allied Italy with Hitler's Germany. An announcement on June 11 from Ottawa stated that no Italian funds could leave Canada

---

*   Reverend Father Boniface, *The History of Saint Francis Parish, Vancouver.*

†   Quotes from Matthews newsclippings, "Italians," City of Vancouver Archives. The Silver Slipper is an unusual Spanish Revival building on East Hastings near Hawks, now the home of the Vancouver Table Tennis Club.

A CORNER OF GRANDVIEW

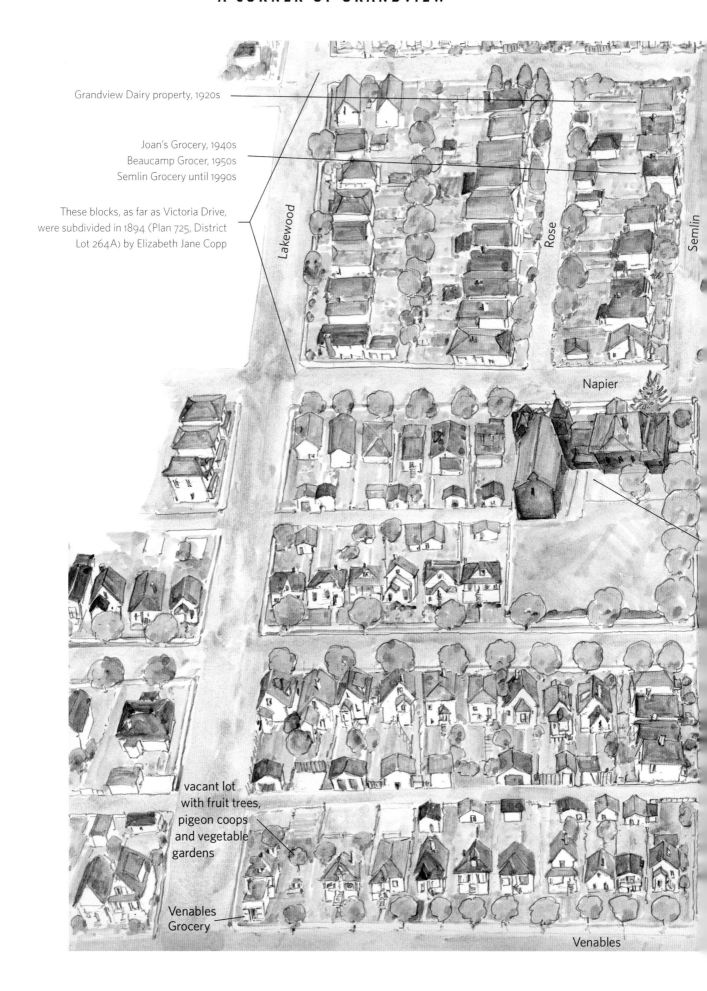

Grandview Dairy property, 1920s

Joan's Grocery, 1940s
Beaucamp Grocer, 1950s
Semlin Grocery until 1990s

These blocks, as far as Victoria Drive,
were subdivided in 1894 (Plan 725, District
Lot 264A) by Elizabeth Jane Copp

Lakewood

Rose

Semlin

Napier

vacant lot
with fruit trees,
pigeon coops
and vegetable
gardens

Venables
Grocery

Venables

William

Lily

Victoria

St. Clare's convent

Parker

MK

Victoria Drive Grocery, built 1922 (see page 76); next door (1188 Victoria) was Betty's Chinese Kitchen and Bovalen Cafe at various times

Six speculative houses by carpenters MacLellan & McLennan, built in 1909, 1115 to 1149 Lily Street

The Copp house, built 1910–1, operated for many years as a rooming house by M. Montiuk, now the Aberdeen Mansion Bed & Breakfast (PHOTO BY STUART THOMSON, 1932, CVA 99-4159)

1090 Victoria Drive, built in 1906 for John Hawkins and converted into a private hospital several years later

1020 Victoria Drive, built for John Hawkins in 1910 (designed by A.E. Beswick); both houses are now Britannia Lodge, a special needs and assisted-living mental-health facility.

St. Francis of Assisi church, built in 1938, adjoining the 1908 home (Wilga) of William Miller, which became the Franciscan monastery in 1924. I painted the watercolour in 1993 for the church when it began its fundraising campaign to restore the old house.

St. Clare's Convent on Napier Street, across Semlin from the monastery, in the 1950s. (FROM *THE HISTORY OF SAINT FRANCIS PARISH, VANCOUVER*)

and the following day the community started a self-registration process coordinated by the Canadian-Italian War Vigilance Committee. By that time, Angelo Branca had emerged as the community's leader and chaired the committee.[*]

As of June 20, all Italian nationals and anyone naturalized since September 1929 had to register with the RCMP. In addition, all such persons had to surrender firearms, dynamite, gunpowder and other potentially hostile materials. Branca predicted that, as most Italian immigrants had arrived between 1900 and 1914—the years before the start of the First World War, in which Italy was on the Allied side—there would be little disruption (he was proved right). Newspapers estimated 3,000 to 4,000 ethnic Italians in Vancouver at the time and another 15,000 in the rest of BC.

The postwar influx of new immigrants made an impact on Saint Francis of Assisi church in the late 1940s. Of about 1,250 baptisms at the church in the '40s and '50s, 270 were children with Italian names. The church responded quickly—its parish school at Venables and Victoria across the street from the Grandview United Church[†] turned sod on July 2, 1947.

In the 12 blocks around the church, examined in detail in the map on pages 184–5, the numbers of households with Italian surnames in the city directory grew rapidly, from 5 in 1949 to 42 in 1958 and to 79 in 1968, before falling back to 59 in 1978. Asian migration also increased. In the past 20 years, the notable change has been the arrival of young families who are restoring the century-old houses and gentrifying the area.

Commercial Drive was at its most Italian in the late 1960s and 1970s, the successor to European/German Robsonstrasse and Chinatown as an exotic destination for shopping and dining in what was, still, a very British-Canadian city (Greek Kitsilano flourished during the same years). In the popular imagination, Italians were a kind of happy, picturesque folk, eager for a street party, a sea change from the restraint of traditional Vancouver, and of traditional Commercial Drive, too.[‡] Also arising at that time was an edgy counterculture, politically hard left, adding to The Drive's burgeoning reputation as the centre for the city's lesbian population.

As for the church and monastery, they settled comfortably into the changing neighbourhood. In 1947, the old house across Semlin from the monastery that had been run for many years as the Norman Apartments became a convent for the Order of Poor Ladies, usually known as the Poor Clares (for Clare of Assisi, their founder). Saint Francis of Assisi (1182–1226) lived a life of poverty and service to the sick and founded the Order of Friars Minor—the Franciscans. After hearing him preach, Clare

[*]   Branca (1903-84), later a BC supreme court and court of appeal judge, was a noted criminal lawyer and once a Canadian amateur middleweight boxing champion. His biography is *Gladiator of the Courts: Angelo Branca*, by Vincent Moore (Douglas & McIntyre, 1981).

[†]   Since 1973 the building has been the Vancouver East Cultural Centre, also known as The Cultch; before that it had a brief career as the Vancouver Free University. See Aronsen.

[‡]   See King, *The Drive: A Retail, Social and Political History of Commercial Drive, Vancouver, to 1956.*

of Assisi established her order. He is the patron saint of animals and the environment and one of the favourite saints in Italy. She is the patron saint of television, so named in 1958—"one Christmas when she was too ill to leave her bed she saw and heard Christmas Mass, even though it was taking place miles away."[*] Appropriately, she is also the patron saint of sore eyes. The convent building is now used as a church and monastery by St. John of Shanghai Orthodox Church.

Saint Francis was in the news once for a bizarre murder that seems more in character with contemporary Vancouver than the quiet town of the early 1960s. As *Vancouver Sun* reporter Moira Farrow wrote:

> *Father Cuthbert Seward, 51, rector of St Francis church, was shot and killed as he opened the door of the adjacent monastery Friday night. Two hours after the shooting, police arrested a 29-year-old unemployed mechanic in his apartment six blocks away from the monastery. Police said the man has a history of mental illnesses and is believed to have threatened several times to shoot a priest . . . Two children playing a game of tag outside the monastery said they saw a man drive up to the door about 7 pm. They told police they saw the man leave the engine running and walk calmly up to the door carrying a rifle over his shoulder. A moment later they heard a shot then saw the man walk back to his car.*[†]

The parish raised the funds in the early 1990s to restore the monastery to its original glory, as it was when completed for William Miller in 1908. The project, by Rhone & Iredale architect Charlotte Murray, won a Vancouver Heritage Award.

L IKE THE WILLIAM MILLER MANSION THAT BECAME A MONASTERY, A handful of other houses in Vancouver recall an era in which governments provided few health and social services and individuals went into business or acted through their churches to fill the gaps. The mansion of Miller's brother J.J. at the corner of Salsbury and Napier was a private hospital for many years. The John Hawkins home at 1020 Victoria Drive has just been renovated into an extension of the care home next door, itself a converted house. The Glen Brae Private Hospital in Shaughnessy Heights became the Canuck Place children's hospice in 1995 (page 23).

The McCallan House at 67th and Hudson in Marpole was rented in 1927 to the newly formed Crippled Children's Hospital Society and converted into a 16-bed hospital—the forerunner of a building that opened at 250 West 59th Avenue in 1933 and was superseded by the current Children's Hospital on Oak Street in 1982. Marketed to builders as a tear-down in 1989, the

The city's first children's hospital, at 8264 Hudson in Marpole, was the former home of farmer J.M. McCallan, built in 1912, when the area was still known as Eburne Station and Hudson Street was called Bridge Road because of the low swingspan that crossed the Fraser River to Eburne on Sea Island. Hudson Street near the bridge was the community's commercial centre. Other shops clustered around Townsend Road (70th) and Granville, including the store illustrated on p. 72. I painted the watercolour in 1989 when the house was marketed as a tear-down.

---

*   catholic.org/saints

†   "Priest Without an Enemy Shot Dead in Monastery," *Vancouver Sun*, April 20, 1963.

old house was instead renovated as "family-style living for independent seniors" by the Abbeyfield Housing Society. Architect Charlotte Murray of Rhone & Iredale won another Vancouver Heritage Award for the conversion.

The Anglican Women's Auxiliary Memorial House at 334 West 14th in Mount Pleasant also was first a family home. A turreted Queen Anne, like many built in the city just before the First World War, it was the 1910 home of William Lawrence, a baker, and subsequently his widow and daughter. In 1950, the Women's Auxiliary of the Church of England in Canada (known since 1966 as the Anglican Church Women of the Diocese of New Westminster) decided to purchase it from Miss B. Lawrence with funds left them "in memory of those departed."* It cost $8,000.

The house served multiple functions. Its main-floor rooms became a central meeting place while the upstairs rooms provided accommodation for missionaries visiting the city, speaking at local churches to raise funds and recouping their strength before returning to Asia, India or Africa. The basement was used for an outreach program, where donated clothes were sorted and baled for shipment to remote churches in the Yukon. "The thrift stores support the churches in the North," said Sheila Puls of the Women's Auxiliary, "and provide an opportunity for counselling with the priest over a cup of coffee in the corner of the shop." Hand-knitted sweaters were prized in the North, "but hated in the city because you can't throw them in the washer and dryer," her husband, Bob, added. Any clothing that was too light for the North went to the Downtown Eastside.

The house has been kept in as good repair as finances allowed. Maz Atri, the caretaker, has lived on the upper floor for many years. But, according to Sheila Puls, the house "doesn't in fact fulfill the mandate anymore." She noted the high costs of impending maintenance, the general decline in traditional churches like the Anglican and the United (while evangelical churches, especially in the Fraser Valley, are growing like wildfire), and the reality that "old ladies who stuff the bales for outreach can't afford to live in Vancouver anymore."

According to current plans, at some point in the near future the house will be sold. Then someone will likely convert it into condos, with a lane house stuck out the back for good measure. Another piece of the city's diversity will fade away. But from the house's point of view—should it have one—this will be a reasonable outcome, as it has survived long enough under the care of the Anglicans to be valued as a home again and supported by the sympathetic zoning structure the city put in place for that part of Mount Pleasant. This zoning was prompted by the efforts of John and Pat Davis and their sons on the 100 block of West 10th Avenue in the 1970s. The Davises' well-restored, brightly painted Victorian and Edwardian houses, some with well-designed infill cottages, have inspired other renovators to work with the existing houses rather than tear them down and replace them with generic apartment buildings.

---

*   In "Through the Years Centennial Edition," a booklet published by the New Westminster Diocesan Board in 2004.

ANGLICAN WOMEN'S AUXILIARY MEMORIAL HOUSE

334 West 14th Avenue • 1950–2011

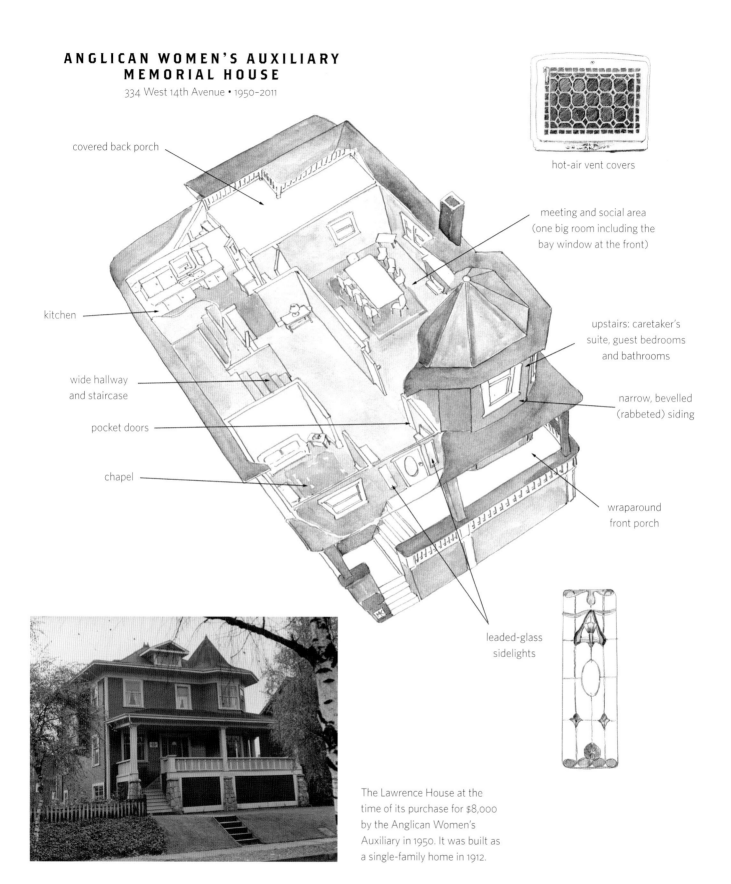

hot-air vent covers

covered back porch

meeting and social area
(one big room including the
bay window at the front)

kitchen

upstairs: caretaker's
suite, guest bedrooms
and bathrooms

wide hallway
and staircase

narrow, bevelled
(rabbeted) siding

pocket doors

chapel

wraparound
front porch

leaded-glass
sidelights

The Lawrence House at the
time of its purchase for $8,000
by the Anglican Women's
Auxiliary in 1950. It was built as
a single-family home in 1912.

THE OLD ALEXANDER SABA PROPERTY, A CRUMBLING MINI-ESTATE OF just over an acre, hidden behind hedges of tall trees, with a tennis court and a flower-lined driveway that curved in from a gate on Granville Street, is slated to be redeveloped with 62 seniors' units. Built in 1929, the house at 6511 Granville was Saba's home for 20 years, then Ben Wosk's for the next 40. For the last 20 years it has been tenanted, deteriorating gradually as the frantic Granville Street traffic increases year by year. Other large properties on that stretch of Granville south of 41st have recently been converted into townhouses, including some aimed at seniors.

Michael Saba arrived in Nanaimo in 1900 from Beirut, where his family had worked in the silk business for generations, and quickly sent a ticket to his brother Alexander to join him. They began as door-to-door peddlars and within a few years had $2,500 in capital to open a store at 137 West Hastings. Quickly gaining a reputation as the city's silk specialists, they moved west to 564 Granville with other high-end businesses and by 1913 were advertising "new season Pongee silks" and using the slogan "The Oriental Store." In 1922, the year after Michael retired and moved to Los Angeles, Saba's settled at 622 Granville where sons Edgar, Clarence and Arnold gradually took over the business. Alexander Saba died at age 87 in 1970; the firm itself closed its doors quite recently. [*]

The second owner of the house was businessman Ben Wosk who, with his brother Morris, left a distinctive imprint on the Vancouver skyline. Unmistakable pale-blue tile—supposedly an unwanted shipment they obtained at a bargain price—clad nearly all their buildings, including the Wosk's Furniture stores that dotted the Lower Mainland. "A wizard he is / That's why it is / Nobody undersells Wosk's" went the jingle in countless radio ads over the years.

The Wosks came to Canada from Odessa in 1928, landing in Halifax. With aid from the Hebrew Immigrant Aid Society, they made their way west by train to Vancouver, where their cousin Abrasha, one of the founders of the Jewish community's home for the aged, had sponsored them. [†] With their father, Joseph, the Wosk brothers started a

The Saba/Wosk house at the southwest corner of Granville and 49th, in the summer of 2011. Built in 1929, it was a grander Georgian than most in that neighbourhood. The glimpse of the house along the driveway that curved in from Granville Street was all most people ever saw of the property.

[*]   Matthews newsclippings 8301, City of Vancouver Archives.

[†]   www.jewishvirtuallibrary.org

Stanley Park's Hollow Tree was probably the city's first world-famous image, in postcards sent by the thousands around the globe beginning 120 years ago. Much reduced by age, disease and storm damage, the tree was a rumpled column a few years ago when the park board announced it ought to be removed due to safety concerns. Following a spirited campaign led by the Stanley Park Hollow Tree Conservation Society, it was stabilized "with a non-intrusive micropile system, designed and implemented by a team of local engineers, constructors and volunteers," privately funded. Propping up a dead tree would be a dubious activity in a natural landscape but is understandable in a cultural one like Stanley Park, where every place tells a story.

business collecting second-hand goods, fixing them up and reselling them—a classic Jewish immigrant's tale—opening the storefront at 1263 Granville in 1932 that grew into the 12-store furniture chain.*

Like developer-mayor Tom Campbell, the Wosks acted as their own contractor and quickly saw the possibilities in rental housing. "Vancouver shouldn't be a hick town," Morris said. "It should show off its skyline. There's nothing like a high-rise building to do this . . . People take pride in showing them off to visitors. Nobody wants to brag about a two- or three-storey building."† "We develop to retain, not sell," Ben said of Stan-Ken Investments, the company named for two of their sons.‡

In another interview in 1971, by which time he owned about 35 high-rises, Ben Wosk said, "Blue is a lucky colour for Jews. It's the colour of water, of the sky, the colour of life."§ By that time, the brothers had gone their separate ways, following an action brought by Morris and an out-of-court settlement in 1968, leaving him with the Blue Boy and Blue Horizon hotels and Ben with Stan-Ken and the seven retail stores in Greater Vancouver.

Two projects in the early 1970s brought Ben unwelcome publicity and indicated how closely developers and city hall were once allied. He had served for many years as one of the provincial appointees to the Board of Variance—at one point, he voted for the variance that Tom Campbell needed to build Parkview Towers at Cornwall and Chestnut.¶ In the fall of 1970, when Campbell was mayor, Wosk managed to add a beer parlour (the Jolly Alderman) to his Plaza 500 hotel as a variance to his approved plans. Then, the Board of Variance voted to tweak the zoning regulations to allow him to build the tallest building in Vancouver, the Landmark Hotel at Robson and Nicola. Although Wosk didn't attend that meeting, the other provincial nominee—a director of Wosk's until the previous day—did, and voted for it. Both men promptly had their "appointments rescinded" by municipal affairs minister Dan Campbell.** Two years later, Wosk demonstrated another side of his personality when he voluntarily reduced the height of a high-rise at Kitsilano Beach, which been approved and was under construction, from 10 storeys to 3 (see page 204).

Ben Wosk served the community on the Vancouver General Hospital board of directors, in Big Brothers, as chair of the building committee for the Schara Tzedeck auditorium and school and in numerous other organizations. He died in 1995. Morris Wosk's philanthropic works were mentioned earlier in connection with the Morris Wosk Centre for Dialogue (page 11) and it is said he gave $50 million to charity during his lifetime; his son Yosef has continued the family tradition. Morris died in Las Vegas in 2002.

* "Morris Wosk's extended family," by Kyle Berger, *Jewish Independent*, April 19, 2002.

† *Vancouver Sun*, February 22, 1962.

‡ *Province*, May 25, 1966.

§ *Province*, January 12, 1971.

¶ Interview with Tom Campbell, 2001.

** *Vancouver Sun*, December 26, 1970, and Allan Fotheringham's column, *Vancouver Sun*, January 21, 1971.

T HE NAMING OF A CITY'S places gives a shot at immortality to people and corporations. It took the years of labour of Elizabeth Walker, city archives staff and the Vancouver Historical Society to deliver the definitive goods on the city's street names.* New parks sport the names of outstanding citizens, especially in the redeveloping Downtown South and Yaletown areas, but there are few monuments to individuals.

Vancouver isn't a great city for heroic sculpture, perhaps due to a combination of Canadian reticence and a general skepticism about the achieve-

Sixth D. C. O. R. on Review Cambie Street Grounds, Vancouver, B. C.

ments of now-dead rich people. David Oppenheimer, mayor 120 years ago, has a small bust at the entrance to Stanley Park; the legendary lifeguard Joe Fortes is honoured by a discreet fountain at Alexandra Park on English Bay. Queen Victoria, Robbie Burns and Pauline Johnson have monuments in Stanley Park from a century ago; Lord Stanley's is more recent, and Terry Fox has had two. There are few others due to citizens' preference for public art that is more abstract and conceptual, as perhaps it ought to be.

The city attempts to keep the public domain public, but potential issues arising from fundraising and the subsequent naming and renaming of public facilities (and rooms within them) were complex enough to generate a 41-page staff report in 2005. The policy that emerged showed an interesting split between sports and cultural facilities on the one hand and the park board and community centres on the other. In the former, people were positive toward corporate naming of new facilities; in the latter, people were negative toward corporate naming at all. Renaming any existing facilities to favour corporate benefactors was given the thumbs-down.

Private facilities are the new frontier for naming rights. Capilano Stadium at Little Mountain (that is, Queen Elizabeth Park, named for George VI's consort rather than his daughter Elizabeth II) was named for the Sicks' Capilano Brewery. Its baseball team, the Capilanos, was killed by television in the 1950s along with the rest of the league. A team re-emerged—the Mounties—owned by Nat Bailey (founder of the White Spot restaurant chain), who posthumously became the namesake of the stadium. After a hiatus, baseball restarted in the late '70s at "The Nat" under the sponsorship of Molson's, whose beer—Canadian—became the team's name. In a deal announced in

The Cambie Street Grounds became Larwill Park, named for Albert Larwill, the founder of the Vancouver Athletic Club, more than a century ago; for a half century beginning in the 1940s it was Vancouver's intercity bus depot for Greyhound and other lines. In this postcard from the martial years before the First World War, agile men who climbed the telephone poles had the best views! In the right distance, the two buildings are Central School and the domed provincial courthouse, now Victory Square. The soldiers are the Duke of Connaught's Own Rifles, now usually called the British Columbia Regiment, still headquartered at the Beatty Street Armoury; the row of houses and the church face Cambie Street. (THOMPSON STATIONERY COMPANY, VANCOUVER)

---

*   Elizabeth Walker, *Street Names of Vancouver.*

Malkin Bowl in Stanley Park, a scene of summertime entertainments since 1934. (COAST PUBLISHING COMPANY)

W.H. Malkin, wholesale grocer, mayor and civic benefactor. (PHOTO FROM *WHO'S WHO IN BRITISH COLUMBIA*, 1958 EDITION)

2010, the stadium was renamed Scotiabank Field at Nat Bailey Stadium!

When the old Carling O'Keefe Brewery site at 12th and Yew was redeveloped in the 1990s, any suggestion for a name that directly commemorated beer, brewing or the brewery's founder, Henry Reifel, was dismissed, but for two of the buildings on the site, the name "O'Keefe" had the right ring, as did "Carling." Brewer Otto Marstrand got a street named after him there, even though *his* plant stood on the edge of Brewery Creek east of Main Street—the other side of town.

Corporate immortality is a real long shot. Witness General Motors Place, the successor to the Coliseum at the Pacific National Exhibition. Just as everyone became used to the name, it was changed to Rogers Arena, after the Toronto-based telecom provider, "blasting the company's message into a market in which Telus retains the largest share of wireless customers."* A rumour in 2011 suggested that Telus would one-up its rival by purchasing naming rights for the former BC Place Stadium.

As the last vacant block in the downtown, Larwill Park is immensely valuable and coveted by the Vancouver Art Gallery, which wants to expand from its current home in the former courthouse at Georgia and Howe in order to store and exhibit its growing collection, including the ever-larger works of many contemporary artists. Apropos of the city's need to maintain its layers of history, the park had an interim use as a bus depot from 1946 until the 1990s, when Greyhound moved to the former CNR station on Main Street. At the entry to the depot, there was an art deco–style winged Pegasus cast onto a concrete slab. It was taken away for safekeeping when the depot was demolished and ought to be reinstalled. It's art!

THERE IS A CHECKERED RECORD OF FAMILIES' LEGACIES IN VANCOUver. Although it took the park board 13 years to complete the namesake park for which Jonathan Rogers left $100,000 in his 1945 will, it is still there (at 7th and Columbia in Mount Pleasant), awaiting the rejuvenation and repopulation of that light-industrial area.

Another part of the Rogers family bequest, that of wife Elisabeth in 1960, was the family mansion at 2050 Nelson Street. Following a lifetime of charitable gifts and arts patronage, Elisabeth left the house "to the governing council of the Salvation Army to be used as a home for aged women and women convalescents and to be named the Elisa-

---

*   "Rogers nabs naming rights on Telus's turf," by Iain Marlow and Rebecca Lindell, *Globe and Mail*, July 6, 2010.

beth Rogers Home for Women." Later that year the beneficiary announced it was selling the house, claiming it could accommodate more women in a purpose-built facility elsewhere. Although the house was demolished in 1962, no "Elisabeth Rogers Home for Women" has ever been established.

Malkin Bowl in Stanley Park was a gift from wholesale grocer and mayor William Harold Malkin, to commemorate his wife, Marion, who died of cancer in 1934. Malkin himself died in 1959, the year before Elisabeth Rogers, and was more successful than her in tying up his public bequests.

In 1947, he gave the city six vacant acres for parkland, south of 43rd Avenue between Balaclava and Blenheim, a part of his old Southlands estate, which fronted onto South West Marine Drive. On its northern side, it abutted the old von Alvensleben estate—Crofton House School since 1948—that occupies the blocks between 43rd and 41st. As I wrote 20 years ago in the original *Vanishing Vancouver*:

> [A] *fight began in 1964 between the park board and the school board for the northern half of the park, which the latter wanted as the site of an annex to Kerrisdale elementary school. When Malkin gave the land to the city he had insisted that the land be used for park, and the wording of the gift was such that the city could not find a convenient loophole. The issue was resolved in an extraordinary way: the city bought a 14-foot-wide strip at the extreme southern end of the Crofton House School property north of 43rd Avenue, and closed 43rd between Balaclava and Blenheim; on the resulting piece of land it managed to insert the new Kerrisdale school annex, whose southern wall sits right on the boundary of Malkin Park.*

The original lease between the park board and the school board ran from 1965 to 1985. It has been renewed twice, most recently in April 2009. It permits the use of 1.215 hectares (the northern half) of Malkin Park during the day from 8:00 am to 5:00 pm, "when the Kerrisdale Primary Annex School is in operation for various school programs and unstructured play." Although an acknowledgement of Malkin and a description of the park are included on the park board website, there is nothing on the parksite itself, not even a sign. South of the playing field the "park" is bushland overrun with blackberries, home to a pack of coyotes according to a disgruntled local dogwalker.

W.H. Malkin, who served a term as mayor in 1929–30, was the most publicly active

The house of Alvo von Alvensleben, Malkin's neighbour to the north. (POINT GREY GAZETTE, JUNE 4, 1913)

Von Alvensleben was a flamboyant German count and real-estate speculator. A supposed conduit for investments from the Kaiser's inner circle, he was mysteriously alluded to as a spy "from Vancouver" in this Chicago photograph, stamped with a 1915 date. After the war, he never came back to live in the city. (COLLECTION OF JIM WOLF)

of three brothers who arrived in Vancouver from England in 1895. Within 15 years he had prospered sufficiently to erect the large brick warehouse on Water Street that has been home to the Old Spaghetti Factory since the Gastown revival of 40 years ago. The three brothers had 13 children between them, the longest-surviving of whom, James Marshall Malkin, died in 2010 a month before his 95th birthday. With his business partner Alan Pinton and long-term employees, Jamie Malkin built an industrial supplies business, Malkin & Pinton, that served BC industry for many years.*

As for Malkin Bowl, the park board's intention to demolish it, so evident several years ago, has evaporated, and a new 10-year lease with Theatre Under the Stars was signed in 2010.

N OW KNOWN AS NORTH CHINA CREEK PARK, THE SWATH OF GRASS ON Great Northern Way below the King Edward campus of Vancouver Community College was going to commemorate settler Charles Maddams and his family, who established themselves there in the 1880s and whose farm was a minor landmark in the city's early years. Maddams first saw the area, it is said, on a hunting party organized for the lieutenant governor, and bought five acres of sloping land above the False Creek tidal flats.

Until a century ago, when the Great Northern and Canadian Northern Pacific railways established their stations side by side facing Main Street and spread their railyards across reclaimed land east toward Clark Drive, False Creek east of Main was a shallow lagoon at high tide (photo, page 145). From a dock at the foot of Carolina Street, the Maddams family rowed to the city for supplies and tied their skiff to the wharf of the Royal City Planing Mills at the south foot of Carrall Street. Later, they established another small wharf at the foot of the aptly named Dock Street, now Windsor.

They planted fruit trees and berry bushes as cash crops, raised chickens, hunted ducks and fished along the False Creek shore, all in an attempt to earn a living. Their major income source was rhubarb, of all things, sold by the ton to W.H. Malkin & Co. Their fine, cross-gabled farmhouse had a wraparound verandah, cherry trees in the front yard and climbing roses on trellises. As the city expanded toward them the house gained a street address: 941 East 7th Avenue, near the southwest corner of the park. City directories listed it as the home of "Charles Maddams horticulturist."

Maddams's early neighbours were Chinese pig farmers along "China Creek," which had carved a ravine on its descent from higher ground and emptied into False Creek near the foot of Glen Drive, just east of the Maddams property. The ravine became a garbage dump in the interwar years before being covered up—following protests about the stench—after 1946, when the city established a new landfill in the bush of southeast Vancouver at 63rd and Kerr.

---

*   Ethel Wilson, the British Columbia novelist, wrote about the Malkin family and cast them as characters in *The Innocent Traveller*, begun in 1930 and published in 1949. Annie Malkin, W.H.'s mother, was Ethel's maternal grandmother and brought her to Canada at the age of 10, in 1898, after both her parents died. See David Stouck, *Ethel Wilson: A Critical Biography*. Thanks to Stephanie Gould for pointing out the connection.

Bicycle racing on the China Creek cycle track during the British Empire and Commonwealth Games in 1954. (*PROVINCE* NEWSPAPER PHOTO, VPL 43579)

On the dump site, organizers of the 1954 British Empire & Commonwealth Games erected a splendid, high-sided bicycle track, reputedly entirely made of (now rare) yellow cedar. It was the era of Lorne "Ace" Atkinson, whose bicycle shop is still a fixture on West Broadway in Kitsilano. Atkinson rode for Canada in the 1948 Olympics in London and finished fifth in the 10-mile track championship at the 1950 BE&C Games while managing and coaching the Canadian team. He served on the committee that established the China Creek Cycling Track and placed fourth in the 10-mile track event, Canada's best showing ever. He died in April 2010, at the age of 88.

Even during the era of the cycle track 60 years ago the Maddams family were long gone from their idyllic farmhouse. As happened to so many Vancouverites in the boom of a century ago, they lived beyond their means, finding themselves gradually bankrupted by loan payments on their overvalued property and city taxes they couldn't afford. Their final year there was 1924, after which a series of tenants occupied it until salesman William Bingham and his wife, Mabel, moved out in 1951. The house was then demolished.

The city purchased or repossessed the land and intended, according to news stories in the late 1940s, to name it for the pioneer family. "Park, Once Farm, Proud Memorial" wrote reporter Ed Moyer in December 1948. A handsome bronze plaque was commissioned and unveiled on the city's birthday in 1955.* At some point in the subsequent years, work crews dug into the gentle hillside along 7th and Windsor to create a flat playing field below. An unintended consequence was the creation of one of the city's best toboggan runs on the steep slopes along the south and west sides.

As for the cycle track, it deteriorated in the 1960s and was patched up in the 1970s but became derelict soon thereafter. By the early 1980s, when the King Edward Campus of Vancouver Community College needed to move from 12th and Oak due to

---

* A photo of the plaque is in the City of Vancouver Archives, Matthews collection, MON p. 72.

Family photo albums are the last frontier for people trying to unravel the city's history. These images from a 1920s album capture 1185 Harwood Street in the West End, the home of Alexander Morrison, a partner in Armstrong, Morrison and Company, the greatest bridge builders in western Canada. (The company's workshop turned out the second automobile to be seen on city streets, a modification of a Stanley Steamer imported by W.H. Armstrong, in 1899.) Alexander Morrison was an elderly man when these photos were taken, and died in 1928 at the age of 76. His home had fantastic leaded glass, visible in the photos. According to family memories, the interior was decorated with murals painted by a Scottish artist and the library held

a complete set of encyclopedias in Gaelic. After the death of Morrison's wife, Margaret, the property went to American relatives who had no interest in Vancouver, and was subsequently sold. Eventually, it became the Margaret Private Hospital (photo in *Vancouver Remembered*, p. 118), but was demolished for an apartment building about 1960. The Morrisons' nephew, Murdoch Birnie, was raised by the Morrison family after his mother died; with his wife, Annie, he looked after the home during winters that the Morrisons passed in the United States. Their daughter Bernice, born in 1919, is the only person left alive who remembers the house in its prime. (INFORMATION AND PHOTOS FROM PAT SHORE, NÉE BERNICE PATRICIA BIRNIE)

Vancouver General Hospital's expansion and was seeking a new location, the site was a plum ripe for the picking.

There is no record in current park board material of the Maddams family, the park naming or the plaque. The link with the early city is the evocation of China Creek, recalling the nameless farmers of more than a century ago. However, the family is commemorated by a one-block street running from 14th to 15th just east of Knight Street—one of their investment properties of a century ago.[*]

THE WHARF AT JERICHO BEACH, DEMOLISHED IN 2011, MANAGED TO dodge for decades the pasture-izing tendencies of the park board and recalled Jericho's past as a seaplane and flying-boat base, a role it held for 30 years from 1920. Until the early 1980s when the park board cleared the last of them away, Jericho's three flying-boat hangars were a reminder of the city's strategic location during the Second World War and how the coastline was once guarded against smuggling and illegal immigration. Today, just three buildings remain from Jericho's military days: the sailing centre, youth hostel and Jericho Arts Centre.

The wharf was also the last relic of Habitat Forum, the "people's sideshow" of Habitat: the United Nations Conference on Human Settlements, held in downtown Vancouver in June 1976. Skeptics such as *Province* columnist Lorne Parton saw the forum as the "last hurrah of Hippiedom." Supporters felt it cemented Vancouver's fledgling reputation as a city concerned with the issues of livability, innovative urbanism and environmental protection that had arisen a few years earlier with the founding of Greenpeace, the elections of the NDP provincial government and the TEAM city council and the redevelopment of the south shore of False Creek.

The hangars and the wharf provided Habitat Forum with its "Douglas Fir and batik setting," in *Province* reporter Harvey Southam's words. The idea for the forum had been promoted for more than a year by Al Clapp, a former television producer whose imaginative, hands-on role as project manager created a marvel of ingenious recycling. He personified the muscular, can-do hippie, a more ambitious version of the sort of person who was then building superbly crafted "hobbit houses" on the Gulf Islands or in the Kootenays. Clapp supervised a workforce of young unemployed people, ex-convicts and pensioners making $150 a week on a Local Initiatives Program grant, including a 68-year-old retired woodworker known as Claude who ran the makeshift sawmill that used salvaged beach logs and other old timbers as the raw materials for the refit.

The three hangars were linked by a boardwalk made from recycled fir and cedar, covered by sheet metal from an abandoned farm. Hand-carved benches, tables and planters dotted the site. Inside one hangar was an ethnic village and audio-visual theatre; another was the social centre with a 205-foot bar reputed to be the longest in North America. The centrepiece was the auditorium occupying one of the hangars, "based on a set I designed for a CTV pilot show," Clapp said. "It's designed to get

---

[*] See "Historical Walking Tour of Gibson Creek Through Kensington–Cedar Cottage" by Dan Fass, www.vcn.bc.ca/gibbys.

away from that boring row upon row of people."* The wharf also benefitted, getting the original railings from the Lions Gate Bridge that had been removed the previous year in a refit; during the conference, Harbour Ferries ran a service every two hours between the Jericho wharf and its own wharf at the foot of Denman.

Another feature of the site was the Appropriate Technology Village, coordinated by Jim Bohlen (1926–2010), one of the founders of Greenpeace, who said his intention was "to shock visitors into realizing their homes and energy-use patterns are grossly wasteful." Domes and log cabins were displayed, all shunning expensive, sophisticated technology. A 30-foot wind turbine towered over the site and a bicycle generator showed how electricity could be produced anywhere. One small house used solar energy and a composting toilet. Another project demonstrated how to build bricks from sulphur and sand. Throughout the forum, in contrast with today's strategies, the focus was on simple, inexpensive technologies—Stewart Brand's *Whole Earth Catalogue* and E.F. Schumacher's 1973 book *Small is Beautiful* provided the meta-narrative.

The forum had several themes: the man-made and natural environments, social justice and the question of differing values and cultures, sharing and managing the world's resources, national settlement policies, people's participation in planning and implementation, land use and ownership, community action for a better habitat, rural economy and appropriate technology. Speakers included Mother Theresa, who made headlines for suggesting that Prime Minister Trudeau "should buy cheaper clothes, eat less and translate his words of love into action." Anthropologist Margaret Mead spoke at an Interfaith service. Innovator Buckminster Fuller spoke about the recycling of resources and, a few days later to 2,000 people, about "spaceship earth" and how problems could be solved with technology, receiving kudos even in the mainstream press for being so positive about the future.

Free spirit Margaret Trudeau was in Fuller's audience. At a reception her husband said to Al Clapp, "I don't know what you've done to Margaret. As far as she's concerned there isn't even an official conference."[†] She spoke to about 1,500 people at the forum on the need for a commitment to clean water and led a "water walk" from Spanish Banks to Jericho to imitate the daily task performed by millions around the world who lacked running water. The throng carried pails of water and were accompanied by a school band and a group beating drums and gongs.

Even Dave Barrett, whose NDP government had been crushed the previous autumn, held a forum attended by more than 2,000 people on the importance of politics and people power. Other issues such as land speculation, First Nations land claims, women's property-ownership rights in the Third World and prison rehabilitation briefly took centre stage, but the debate over nuclear power, coordinated by Greenpeace, came to dominate the forum.

There was comic relief, too: on June 10, the founder and spiritual director of the Institute of Applied Metaphysics, Winnifred Barton, forecast the end of the world, complete with the arrival of extraterrestrial beings, for 6 pm on June 13. However, she

---

*   "Recycle City is Magic in the Making" by Harvey Southam, *Province*, March 1, 1976.

†   "Dignitaries dodge showers, tour aquarium" by Harvey Southam, *Province*, June 1, 1976.

The old Jericho pier in 2011, shortly before its demolition.

didn't show up that day for a seminar at the QE Playhouse which was slated to end at 6:00 pm along with the world; instead, participants had to vacate as another group had booked the hall.

As for Al Clapp, he held a meeting to discuss the future of the site but soon resigned, complaining of indecision on the part of the forum's board members. The newspapers editorialized about how wonderful it all had been but, they sighed, echoing the stance of city officials, it would take too much money to upgrade the site and make the facilities permanent.

A farewell to that utopian spring was a concert held to finance the voyage of the *Greenpeace VII* anti-whaling ship. Clapp tried to organize a first-anniversary festival but couldn't get park board support. Alderman Mike Harcourt, an early skeptic of the Habitat Forum, accused the park board of being interested only in tearing down the buildings to "get on with their grassed-over parking lot vision."* Over the next five years the three hangars were demolished, the diminishing voices of protest ignored.

Thirty-five years later the voices protesting the demolition of the deteriorating wharf were also ignored. The economic argument once again trumped the historical and sentimental one. Just for good measure, an environmental one was slipped in: the ancient pilings were leaking creosote into English Bay, according to a government report, and "the shade created by the wharf is a deterrent to fish, who are forced further out in the water where there are more predators"†—a statement that would be baffling to any child who has successfully caught fish while dangling a hook from a pier into the sheltered waters below.

DESPITE THE ATTENTION NOW PAID TO ENVIRONMENTALISM AND SUStainability by the city and many citizens, the kind of simple houses promoted by Habitat Forum many years ago are very hard to find, especially on the west side of the city. No surprise there. But a keen eye can still spot a few such places, even near Kitsilano Beach, relics of an era when there were fewer people competing for the views and proximity to the seaside.

By about 1967 the secret was out and the beach area around the foot of Yew Street began to redevelop with upscale apartments and condominiums, pushing out the hippies and retired people who had created its rather faded ambience. Along the lane between Cornwall and York were a handful of cottages, just the sort of thing now fashionable in the city's "EcoDensity" mindset. Today, as shown on the next page, there is just one remaining.

The park and beach, an informal campground in the first decade of the 20th century, took a while to assemble. In 1909, the 43 acres bounded by Yew, Balsam, Cornwall and the streetcar tracks were purchased by the city for $63,600. Four years later, at the height of the property boom, the CPR sold the rough triangle north of the tracks as far as McNicoll, with Arbutus on its eastern edge, to the city for $207,800. The provincial government formally deeded the foreshore rights to the city in 1928, and in 1930–1 the city picked up the remaining area north of Cornwall from Yew to Arbutus from a handful of private owners for $51,300. Included was a building on the southeast corner of Yew and the tracks assessed at $8,725, for which the city was prepared to offer $12,000. The owner wanted $50,000; the city eventually expropriated the property.

Work began immediately to complete the park, and in August 1931, to the cheers of a crowd of 5,000, the tide-filled pool opened. Another attraction was a dance hall; it and local booster Bert Emery's summer concert schedule drew the ire of three apartment-house owners and the manager of 4th Avenue's Kitsilano Theatre (page 85). In an early version of "no fun Vancouver," the protesters described the beach as having a honky-tonk or Coney Island atmosphere.

Most of the small houses then extant on the blocks east of the beach toward

---

*　*Province*, March 30, 1977.

†　*Vancouver Sun*, September 12, 2010.

KITSILANO BEACH

1940s–1950s

Postcard photo
by Rolly Ford, circa 1960

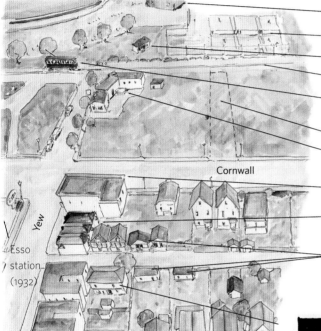

bathhouse

tennis courts

caretaker's cottage

location of Engine 374, 1947–83 (now at the Roundhouse Community Centre)

streetcar (until 1947)

Thistle Street (incorporated into Kitsilano Park in the 1930s)

fish 'n' chips shop and dining room

Cornwall

Blenheim Apartments

Yew

five BCMT&T Model J prefab cottages

Esso
station
(1932)

back-lane cottages (demolished by the mid-1970s)

The last of the back-lane houses, 2011

Oh Kitsilano, Queen of Summer, thou
Hast shared with us long hours of calm content.
To sombre Fall's impending hand we bow,
Yet grateful for another season spent
Within thy sovereign influence benign.
Beneficence unbounded, beauteous Queen,
Thy sceptre shall 'mid mem'ry's treasures shine,
Symbol of sunshine, sea and skies serene.

—First verse of "Kitsilano," by A. Gordon Rooke,
"Kitsilano's Blind Poet," *Kitsilano Times,*
September 26, 1940

Burrard, which had been a working-class area with the city's only Sikh temple, at 1866 West 2nd Avenue, gradually disappeared. The blocks to the west of the beach retain only a handful of curiosities, including two cottages, with the look of summer shacks on the Gulf Islands, on Stephens Street just south of York Avenue, built in 1900 or 1901, soon after a group of influential Vancouverites filed a subdivision plan in 1897 for the land from Macdonald to Trafalgar, the waterfront to Broadway. The subdividers included C.J. Major, the executor for former premier John Robson's estate, merchant and former mayor David Oppenheimer, and lawyer Gordon Edward Corbould, one of the largest landowners in the city.[*]

The "ugly jungle of concrete structures rising high into the sky,"[†] also known as the West End, was a concern to Kitsilano residents throughout the late 1960s. As an issue, it came to a head in 1972 when developer Ben Wosk began work on a 10-storey apartment building at 2280 Cornwall, directly south of the pool. A handful of high-rises had been built several years earlier higher up on the slope: the *St. Roch* at 2323 and Century House at 2370 West 2nd in 1966; Las Salinas at 2310 West 2nd and Seaside Plaza at 2324 West 1st in 1968. However, most people, including several NPA aldermen, presumed the height limit was 3 storeys at the beach, not the 120 feet or 12 storeys actually permitted by the zoning. Following furious protests led by Bruce Yorke, then the Vancouver Tenants Council secretary and later a Vancouver alderman, Wosk agreed to build just three storeys "on condition the area is rezoned so that no other high-rises can be built."[‡] One more high-rise was completed in 1974, higher up on the slope at 3rd and Balsam, before the height reduction went into effect.

[*]   Historian Bruce Macdonald found the subdivision plan in the Land Title Office.

[†]   Margaret Chunn, *Vancouver Sun*, February 23, 1972.

[‡]   *Vancouver Sun*, February 16, 1972.

An example from 1982 of sustainability (a term not then known) or, perhaps, of the simple life. Renters intensively planted the back yard of this house on 8th, just east of Arbutus, with vegetables, and obtained a load of mill ends (the offcut bits of two-by-fours and other scraps that could be had by the truckload, cheap) for its wood stove. This was a city-owned house, part of the land assembly created along the interurban tracks (now called the Arbutus Corridor) for the Burrard-Arbutus Connector, an arterial roadway recommended by Harland Bartholomew's Plan for Vancouver in 1928. Although houses were bought for roads and parkland (the Delamont Park blocks between 5th and 7th), the city never acted on the plan. Nevertheless, it demolished this house about 20 years ago.

PEOPLE LIKE ME WITH A SORT OF SPATIAL MEMORY RAPIDLY DEVELOP elaborate webs linking buildings, pathways and places—an internal GPS. Other people's memories seem to be triggered by smells or perhaps by music: a certain perfume conjures up a lost love, violins stir—that sort of thing.

One memory-trigger for me is the one-block street called Cameron Avenue at the foot of Alma across from the Hastings Mill Store—the oldest building in the city, floated in the 1930s to Kitsilano at the time of the demolition of the historic sawmill east of Gastown. A flight of stairs descends from Cameron's Dunbar Street end to the natural beach below, a favourite walk many years ago at low tide back in the days when Greeks cast smelt nets into the water at twilight on summer evenings.

Long before my time there was a row of four-room cottages like a summer resort on the water side of Cameron Avenue, built in 1919-20 by the Canadian Pacific Railway and leased out to tenants by E.W. Bateman, the company's right-of-way agent. Evidently the property was not considered valuable or the company would have built more substantial houses as it had on Kitsilano Point a decade earlier. The Cameron of Cameron Avenue was Ward Six alderman a century ago; according to S.J. Montgomery, the retired secretary of the board of works, "he had something to do with the property along the shoreline there; the Canadian Pacific Railway owned it; they had a lot of property out there; back of it is nice flat land; it might have been useful for railway purposes if their English Bay branch had been extended."[*]

The CPR also owned the land east of Trafalgar Street. Between Trafalgar and Cameron Avenue, however, the waterfront lots along Point Grey Road were owned by private residents and speculators. But one can imagine the CPR using its

---

*   Quoted by J.S. Matthews, "Notes on Street Names and Places," City of Vancouver Archives.

political clout to run a trestle along the shoreline, or building an embankment or filling part of English Bay to create railyards. It's not so far-fetched an idea, as the foreshore there almost became the route of an Ocean Boulevard with a groomed beach in the 1960s.[*] Regardless, Cameron Avenue was somewhat out in the sticks; according to a newspaper report on January 11, 1945, "the land in front of the nine houses has become so saturated with sewerage water overflowing from the septic tanks that the bank is gradually slipping into Jericho Beach . . . in one case there appears danger of a house itself sliding onto the beach."

3697 Cameron Avenue, at Alma, in 1940, one of the set of cottages facing the water built by the Canadian Pacific Railway. (PHOTO BY LEONARD FRANK, VPL 16105)

Although all those cottages are gone, replaced by much larger houses looking out onto the bay and looming above the beach, a cottage almost identical to them survives across the street at the corner of Alma and Cameron. It was built in 1926 for Arthur H. Beakes and his wife, Elsie. "Three rooms one tap one bath," notes the water-connection permit in the city archives. In the 1920s, Beakes was a salesman for Stonehouse Motors; in directories in the late 1950s, shortly before his death at the age of 70 in 1963, he is listed as an attendant for Hudson Parking. His widow and then his daughter lived on in the cottage until the mid-1990s, by which time wealthier people had created a "Golden Mile" on Point Grey Road and demolished, rebuilt or consolidated most of the early houses and properties above the beach.

The Beakes cottage is, after all, *at the beach,* within a minute's walk of the Royal Vancouver Yacht Club, the Jericho Lawn Tennis Club and the multi-million dollar homes of Point Grey Road. Seven of the top 25 most expensive houses in the city—including 4 in the top 10 of the website GreatEstates.ca—have addresses on Point Grey Road. The most expensive of them, and number two on the list, valued in 2010 at about $20 million, belongs to Jacqui Cohen, owner of the Army & Navy stores and one of the city's prominent socialites and charity benefactors.

Across the street from the Beakes cottage, hidden by trees, is the site of the house where Jacqui Cohen's brother Jeffrey lived. In the 1970s, as they do today, the gossip columns breathlessly reported the activities of Vancouver's young elite, including Jacqui and Jeffrey, their sister, Karen, and Gordon MacMillan Southam, a grandson of lumber tycoon H.R. MacMillan and scion of the newspaper family that owned the *Province,* who lived a couple of blocks away at 3479 Point Grey Road. They were my age, more or less, but lived in rather different circumstances.

---

[*] See *Vancouver Remembered,* p. 170.

Newspaper clippings from 1976, 1978 and 1982, recording the fates of some of Vancouver's young elite of the day.

Southam, then age 25, was a friend of a friend in that "few degrees of separation" way that Vancouver has always had. Heading home from a party the night after his famous grandfather's funeral in February 1976, he crashed his Mercedes convertible into a stone wall on Point Grey Road just west of Trafalgar, killing himself. By happenstance due to a dinged car door, I went to the ICBC claim centre on West Broadway and saw the Mercedes, a crumpled wreck, pushed off to one side awaiting the coroner's verdict.

Two years later, 26-year-old Jeffrey Cohen, having ascended to the presidency of Army & Navy Stores, died of a heroin overdose following numerous attempts at rehab and run-ins with the police, many involving his Lamborghini sports car. His sister Karen was similarly ill-fated—she was engaged to a nightclub owner named Marvin Goldhar, whose Shaughnessy house was firebombed on the night of July 17, 1982. When he went to an apartment at 2264 Cornwall to confront the man he thought was responsible, he was stabbed to death. Two weeks later, Karen lost control of her Ferrari on the Stanley Park causeway and crashed at high speed, killing herself. She was 28.

My memory connects a set of dots: a cottage near Point Grey Road, stone walls and mansions, an apartment building on Cornwall across from Kitsilano Beach, and Vanier Park, where the Gordon MacMillan Southam Observatory stands near the H.R. MacMillan Space Centre—the building most Vancouverites still refer to as the Planetarium.

A MORE FAMOUS COTTAGE THAN THAT OF ARTHUR AND ELSIE BEAKES sits at the back of two 33-foot lots on a very suburban part of 14th Avenue in West Point Grey. Bought in 1959 by architect Arthur Erickson, the property is at the crest of one of the little hills rising to the Point Grey headland and was never developed with a normal house as the original owners likely intended. Focusing on the void of vacant property rather than the building, Erickson reversed the normal relationship of house to yard and transformed most of the property into a tranquil garden.

As he did with private home commissions such as the Denis Lloyd house on West 35th Avenue near Blenheim,[*] Erickson dug a pond and used the spoil to create a berm on the cottage's far side, eventually enclosing the entire space with a high, solid fence. He joined the garage to the cottage and subtly modified them to add to the Japanese flavour of the pond and its plantings, creating a surprisingly modest home for one whose career had such a dramatic arc.

The foot of Alma Street with, on the right, the Beakes cottage, which the family gave up in the 1990s when the Beakeses' daughter couldn't raise the money to pay her share of the underground wiring her Cameron Avenue neighbours wanted. The cottage has survived because its new owner has apparently been unable to buy the house next door in order to consolidate enough property to build a substantial home. The Beakeses' grandchildren, Ian, Ken and Keith Wallace, are influential members of the arts community.

---

[*]   Built with the help of Erickson's architecture students, according to Richard Keate.

Hints of Japan at the Erickson house and garden in West Point Grey, in the autumn of 2010.

By the time of Erickson's death in 2009, a campaign of hagiography had dulled the memory of the bankruptcy that followed his years of lavish living while conducting an international practice. He had had a creative late career in partnership with Nick Milkovich Architects. His major works of the 1960s and 1970s, including SFU (with then-partner Geoffrey Massey) and the Museum of Anthropology at the University of British Columbia, were universally regarded as classics; the Evergreen Building on West Pender received a heritage designation and the public gathering space at Robson Square came into its own during the 2010 Olympics. With his "cosmopolitan and socially engaged cultural inquiry" he had become one of Canada's handful of "philosopher kings" in company with Pierre Trudeau, Marshall McLuhan and Northrop Frye.[*] You could tell Erickson had achieved iconic status by the number of people, none of whom knew him, who referred to him simply as Arthur.

It was during the low point in his career, in 1992, that landscape architect Elizabeth Watts founded a group of "friends" who worked tirelessly to free his house and garden from the lawsuits that had attached to it during his $10 million bankruptcy proceeding. The Arthur Erickson House and Garden Foundation emerged, saving the estate from almost certain erasure. Like all such groups, the foundation has an ongoing program of events and fundraising to ensure the property's long-term survival.[†]

---

[*]   Edward Dimendberg, "The Man Who Wasn't There," in Olsberg and Castro, *Arthur Erickson: Critical Works*, p. 172.

[†]   The reality in the wake of Erickson's death is much more complex, as described on p. 15.

DRAWING A LINE IN THE MUD

NEXT PAGE > Yin and yang—fairly low density in the neighbourhoods (in the watercolour, Fairview Slopes), high density on the downtown peninsula a 20-minute walk away. Each works for different sorts of people at different phases of their lives. The cluster of well-maintained 1908 houses at 8th and Birch have been divided into apartments for generations.

BELOW > It's not easy being green. Busy schedules, strata bylaw restrictions and changeable weather make laundry lines a rarity, especially when compared with the city of a couple of generations ago.

AT THE RISK OF APPEARING IMPRACTICAL OR NOSTALGIC, I FIND myself reflecting on relatively trivial matters, like laundry lines and unpaved back lanes, when I try to analyze why the poetry is seeping away from my Vancouver. People are too busy to hang out laundry, perhaps, or they're gone from home too long to trust their sheets and towels to the city's fickle weather. But laundry is so *interesting* to look at, as are potholed, unpaved lanes with their mix of fences, views into back yards, weeds and ditches. I am a very visual person, and visual people should never be put in charge of anything.

Yet a city of laundry lines would get a tick-mark from the environmental arbiters, and a lane . . . well, once it's paved it becomes a bit of a speedway, not just because harried local people coming and going in their cars are no longer slowed by potholes and dust. In districts that have been traffic-calmed, the lanes have proven ideal throughways for commuters dodging the congestion on arterial routes. So the city establishes a speed-hump program to slow drivers down and a hump-placement policy to be arbitrated among the neighbours. The lane no longer absorbs water, so drains have to be installed and edges bermed. Signs are posted to try to make some of them one-way only. Regardless, motorists jackrabbit through them in both directions; to anyone who challenges them, they might quote novelist Saul Bellow: "I wish to obey better laws."

Who does the city make laws for? When you look at a place like Vancouver, you could argue that zoning rules—especially those that aim to increase density—are meant to benefit people who don't live there yet (and developers) rather than established residents. Yet cities have to change and options need to be available in all districts for people at different phases of their lives. Owners benefit from increased property values, don't they? Yes, as long as they're willing to leave town.

"Too much change too fast." Those five words pretty well sum up the cry for help Vancouverites made 20 years ago as they

attempted to digest the post-Expo real-estate boom and its impact on city neighbourhoods. The changes since have been even more dramatic, but very different, as the city has urbanized and densified in a way unimaginable a generation ago. The downtown condo-dwelling Vancouverite of every age and income level dominates the city's self-image, yet has had little impact on the habits and environment of the house dwellers. Although there are lots of arguments still about the architectural merit of the high-rises on podiums that have made the city's skyline like a hedgehog on steroids, few dispute the value of those new neighbourhoods.[*]

That "too much change" kind of pressure on the neighbourhoods resumed in the past few years, spurred by speculators and immigrants (wealthier people than existing residents), as well as migrants within the city, who have bought and demolished or renovated—shuffling the deck, as it were. For every modest home demolished on the West Side and replaced with a McMansion, there's a former rooming house converted and gentrified on the East Side. Poor people, needless to say, are left with few options. There ought to be a debate about giving the city the power to impose super-taxes on vacant houses, vacant condos and flipped properties—anything that would hinder speculators messing around with the neighbourhoods of ordinary citizens.

Everything about the tax assessment system shouts that property is valuable, buildings disposable. An older house that has just had a $40,000 kitchen renovation and that is well maintained, with a tight roof, hardwood floors, deluxe carpets, fine leaded windows, several bedrooms and updated bathrooms, is assessed as an "improvement" worth a paltry sum: for example, the house on Connaught Drive illustrated on page 217 is "worth" about $140,000, the property nearly $3 million. Is this reflecting reality or creating it? If it costs a quarter of a million dollars just to build a 700-square-foot lane house, how can a six-bedroom mansion be assessed at half that much? That's faster depreciation than a new car!

It's exactly a half century since Mr. Justice J.G.A. Hutcheson of the BC Supreme Court, ruling on a case involving the Dundarave property of Wallis and Effie Lefeaux, agreed that property should be assessed on its potential value and suggested that homeowners such as Lefeaux were standing in the way of the community's development.[†] Lefeaux had challenged the property assessment system when his taxes shot up from $800 to $2,300 following an apartment rezoning, arguing

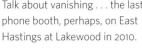

Talk about vanishing . . . the last phone booth, perhaps, on East Hastings at Lakewood in 2010.

* "Why did you want to make your city look like Singapore?" author and critic Witold Rybczynski asked his audience at a lecture in Vancouver on October, 17, 2011.

† *Vancouver Sun*, November 2, 1962. The "Establishment" may have been getting back at a "class enemy." Lefeaux (1881–1972) was a lawyer who defended military objectors during the First World War and advocated for the leaders of the Winnipeg General Strike. Shortly thereafter, he travelled to Russia, returning again in the mid-1930s. He worked as an organizer of the Cooperative Commonwealth Federation in the early 1930s and ran three times for provincial and federal office, all the time having to deny that the CCF was allied with the Soviets, before finally succeeding provincially in Vancouver Centre in 1941.

that he was using his property for single-family purposes only.

There's an echo today of the 1960s and 1970s, when poor people and tenants became radicalized as they were turfed out to "make way for progress." The enemy then was the development industry, according to books such as James Lorimer's 1972 *A Citizen's Guide to City Politics* and Donald Gutstein's 1975 *Vancouver Ltd.* Today, it's the shrinking middle class who are feeling threatened as speculators and mooted rezonings challenge their security in the city's home-owning neighbourhoods and even in the long-established, high-density West End. *Vancouver Sun* real-estate columnist and developer Bob Ransford, for example, argues that planners should "try to build better capacity [for density] at the neighbourhood level by educating people on planning principles, terminology and on big trends."[*]

The Lefeaux house at 2258 Bellevue in West Vancouver in 1989, shortly before it floated away to a new life on Bowen Island. Its tax assessment as an apartment-development property in 1962 prompted owner W. W. Lefeaux to challenge, unsuccessfully, the system that forced owners to pay for a property's potential use rather than its existing one.

The current push, well expressed in the Shannon Mews rezoning (page 170), comes from an odd alliance between environmentally minded urbanists and free-market extremists, the kind of people who see the city's areas of single-family housing as "underdeveloped" and argue that it would be worth increasing density to increase supply on the off chance that the price of a dwelling might fall.[†] Mike Harcourt, the former mayor and sustainability guru, even suggested that the region ought to get rid of single-family zoning altogether.[‡] A counter-argument, by lawyer and former city councillor Jonathan Baker, expressed Vancouver's dilemma: "We cannot continually increase densities in neighbourhoods without fundamentally altering the city's character."[§] People want to live in Vancouver, he wrote, because the city's planning policy, as expressed through its zoning, has produced a livable city. Long-time Victoria councillor Pamela Madoff expressed a similar opinion to me: "You cannot create a city that will meet the demand for it."

"Building affordable housing" is an oxymoron. Every new condo or house is more expensive to buy than what it replaced and if it's cheaper it's only because it's smaller. However, "affordable housing" too often means a building that isn't getting regular maintenance. Somehow, the connection between retaining buildings and the "green city" juggernaut has to be made.

---

[*]   "Charrette system may be just what city needs for planning," *Vancouver Sun*, August 6, 2011.

[†]   For example, "Vancouver's high housing prices threaten growth" by Michael Goldberg, *Vancouver Sun*, August 31, 2010.

[‡]   "I'd get rid of single-family zoning because housing is too unaffordable," he said. CBC News, July 15, 2011.

[§]   "The argument against increasing density," *Vancouver Sun* letters, September 11, 2010.

"... Simple law of supply and demand ... the rarer a thing gets, the more it costs ..."

But in the new environmental reality, Vancouver's ability to retain its old, moderate-density neighbourhoods will depend only partly on retaining and upgrading buildings. The next frontier has to be to get the middle classes back on city buses. About a third of the people in older neighbourhoods like Kitsilano, Mount Pleasant and Grandview are transit users, a number that drops to 12 percent or less for Kerrisdale.[*] There have been a few tentative improvements: transit lanes help the new express buses move along at a clip that makes them an option for busy people. The old city buses, which stop every block or two, have not improved at all in the 55 years since they replaced the streetcar fleet. In fact, they're worse, because they get stuck in the dense traffic that was once a rarity in the city.

I referred in the Preface to the yin and yang nature of Vancouver, the low-rise, leafy "streetcar suburbs" near the dense, glass-and-steel downtown. There's another aspect to it: the fee-simpletons in their wooden houses next to the strata-titlers clustered along the transit routes and on the downtown peninsula. Each represents a different type of stability and stewardship for people at different phases of their lives. We ignore either one at our peril.

Vancouver craves international recognition of itself as a mature city and has managed, mainly through individual initiative (supported inconsistently by city policy), to retain some of the historic layers on its landscape. Every significant, desirable city on the planet is just such a mix of the old and the new. Vancouver will continue to mature, and to be desirable, as long as it keeps that goal in mind, even while trying to be the greenest city on the planet.

---

[*] "Metrotown the most transit-friendly neighbourhood in the region," by Chad Skelton, *Vancouver Sun*, August 11, 2011.

BIBLIOGRAPHY

Alexander, Christopher, Sara Ishikawa, and Murray Silverstein. *A Pattern Language.* New York: Oxford University Press, 1977.

Allen, Christine, and Collin Varner. *Gardens of Vancouver.* Vancouver: Raincoast Books, 2000.

Aronsen, Lawrence. *City of Love and Revolution: Vancouver in the Sixties.* Vancouver: New Star Books, 2010.

Bentall, Shirley. *The Charles Bentall Story: A Man of Industry and Integrity.* Vancouver: Bentall Group, 1986.

Boniface, Reverend Father. *The History of Saint Francis Parish, Vancouver.* Vancouver, 1959.

Carlson, Keith Thor, ed. *A Stó:lō-Coast Salish Historical Atlas.* Vancouver: Douglas & McIntyre, 2001.

Davis, Chuck, ed. *The Greater Vancouver Book.* Surrey: Linkman Press, 1997.

Harcourt, Michael, Ken Cameron, and Sean Rossiter. *City Making in Paradise: Nine Decisions that Saved Vancouver.* Vancouver: Douglas & McIntyre, 2007.

Kalman, Harold. *Exploring Vancouver 2.* Vancouver: UBC Press, 1978.

Kalman, Harold, Ron Phillips, and Robin Ward. *Exploring Vancouver 3.* Vancouver: UBC Press, 1993.

King, Jak. *The Drive: A Retail, Social and Political History of Commercial Drive, Vancouver, to 1956.* Vancouver: The Drive Press, 2011.

Kluckner, Michael, ed. *M.I. Rogers 1869–1965.* Privately published, 1987.

Kluckner, Michael. *Vancouver Remembered.* North Vancouver: Whitecap Books, 2006.

Kluckner, Michael. *Vanishing Vancouver.* North Vancouver: Whitecap Books, 1990.

Luxton, Donald, ed. *Building the West: The Early Architects of British Columbia.* Vancouver: Talonbooks, 2003.

MacDonald, Norbert. "CPR Town: The City-Building Process in Vancouver, 1860–1914." In *Shaping the Urban Landscape: Aspects of the Canadian City-Building Process*, edited by Gilbert A. Stelter and Alan F. J. Artibise. Montreal: McGill-Queen's University Press, 1982.

McAlester, Virginia, and Lee McAlester. *A Field Guide to American Houses.* New York: Alfred A. Knopf, 1988.

McDonald, Robert A.J. *Making Vancouver: Class, Status, and Social Boundaries, 1863–1913.* Vancouver: UBC Press, 1996.

Min, Christa, ed. *Vancouver Matters.* Vancouver: Blueimprint, 2008.

Miron, John R., and Canada Mortgage and Housing Corporation. *House, Home and Community: Progress in Housing Canadians, 1945–1986.* Montreal: McGill-Queen's University Press, 1993.

Mitchell, David. *W.A.C. Bennett and the Rise of British Columbia.* Vancouver: Douglas & McIntyre, 1983.

Olsberg, Nicholas, and Ricardo L. Castro. *Arthur Erickson: Critical Works.* Vancouver: Douglas & McIntyre, 2006.

Perrault, Ernest. *Tong: The Story of Tong Louie, Vancouver's Quiet Titan.* Madeira Park: Harbour Publishing, 2003.

Schofield, Peggy, ed. *The Story of Dunbar: Voices of a Vancouver Neighbourhood.* Vancouver: Ronsdale Press, 2007.

Schreiner, John. *The Refiners.* Vancouver: Douglas & McIntyre, 1989.

Shadbolt, Douglas. "Postwar Architecture in Vancouver," in Vancouver Art Gallery, *Vancouver Art & Artists, 1931–83.* Vancouver: Vancouver Art Gallery, 1983.

Stevens, Elaine, Dagmar Hungerford, Doris Fancourt Smith, Jane Mitchell and Ann Buffam. *The Twelve-Month Gardener.* Vancouver: Whitecap Books, 1991.

Stouck, David. *Ethel Wilson: A Critical Biography.* Toronto: University of Toronto Press, 2003.

Wade, Jill. *Houses for All: The Struggle for Social Housing in Vancouver 1919–50.* Vancouver: UBC Press, 1994.

Walker, Elizabeth. *Street Names of Vancouver.* Vancouver: Vancouver Historical Society, 1999.

Walker, Lester. *American Shelter.* Woodstock, New York: The Overlook Press, 1981.

Windsor-Liscombe, Rhodri. *The New Spirit: Modern Architecture in Vancouver, 1938-1963.* Vancouver: Canadian Centre for Architecture, Douglas & McIntyre, 1997.

Yesaki, Mitsuo. *Sutebusuton: A Japanese Village on the British Columbia Coast.* Vancouver: Peninsula Publishing Company, 2003.

ACKNOWLEDGEMENTS

A GREAT NUMBER OF PEOPLE HELPED ME WITH THE RESEARCH ON AND interpretation of the modern city: Jim Wolf, James Johnstone, Bruce Macdonald, Michael Geller, Robert Lemon, Donald Luxton, Ken Terriss, Richard Keate, John Atkin, Taryn Boyd, Viola Funk, Daryl Nelson, Allen Price, Jonathan Baker, Marco D'Agostini, Sheila and Bob Puls, Ross Hill, the Arthur Erickson House and Garden Foundation, Tom Grant, the staff of the City of Vancouver Archives, Eric Swanick of Simon Fraser University Special Collections, Leanne Penco, Audrey Ostrom, Neo and Casey Tuytel, Diane Switzer, Anne Wyness, Bill and Joanne Dick, Erik Phillips, Patrick Gunn and Sandra Buckingham. Michael Burch at Whitecap Books deserves a medal for sticking with me for more than 25 years.

I owe special thanks to Stephen L. Norris, son and estate executor for *Vancouver Sun* cartoonist Len Norris, for granting me permission to use four of his father's cartoons. He was equally generous five years ago with my book *Vancouver Remembered*.

All uncredited artwork and photographs are by the author.

Photographs credited as CVA are from the City of Vancouver Archives; those marked VPL are from Vancouver Public Library Special Collections.

As I did with *Vancouver Remembered* in 2006, I have attempted to track the photographers whose work was reproduced as postcards, to no avail, with the exception of Dan Propp (www.danpropp.com), who gave me permission to use his photos on pages 41 and 63.

Clyde Herrington

A number of images are by Clyde Herrington, the entrepreneurial photographer who "in 1958 . . . sold the then Minister of Recreation and Conservation, Earl Westwood, and Highways Minister, Phil Gaglardi, on the idea for *Beautiful BC* magazine," according to the flyleaf of *Industrial British Columbia* magazine, which Herrington founded with businessman Bill Mainwaring after leaving *Beautiful BC*. *Industrial British Columbia* was to appear yearly but disappeared, as did Herrington to the best of my knowledge; his photographs in this book are from the 1966 edition of the magazine, the only issue I've been able to locate.

The photographs of the swimmers (page 119) and of West Vancouver (page 151) are from a pictorial book similar to *Industrial British Columbia*, Herbert L. McDonald's *British Columbia: Challenge in Abundance*, the province's centennial publication in 1966. Simon Fraser University Archives has a number of McDonald's photographs but has been unable to trace him or his descendants.

INDEX